THE LAST KINGS OF NORSE AMERICA

THE LAST KINGS OF NORSE AMERICA

RUNESTONE KEYS TO A LOST EMPIRE

ROBERT G. JOHNSON & JANEY WESTIN

BEAVER'S
POND
PRESS

Cover photo by Janey Westin

ISBN 13: 978-1-59298-419-0

Library of Congress Catalog Number: 2012902818

Printed in the United States of America

Second Printing: 2014

18 17 16 15 14   6 5 4 3 2

Cover and interior design by James Monroe Design, LLC.

Beaver's Pond Press, Inc.
7108 Ohms Lane
Edina, MN 55439–2129
(952) 829-8818
www.BeaversPondPress.com

BEAVER'S
POND
PRESS

To order, visit www.BeaversPondBooks.com
or call (800) 901-3480. Reseller discounts available.

To Elizabeth Guliver Johnson,
for her enduring support
over the many years of our investigations.

And to Charlie,
for his interest and support.

CONTENTS

PART B: DISCOVERIES ON THE GRAENAVELDI

APPENDICES

FOREWORD

Who discovered America? Columbus? Leif Erickson? The Chinese, Africans,[1] or Muslim Arabs[2]? Some other explorers? There are prevailing claims and theories that credit each of the above. Mainstream history acknowledges the early voyages to North America by Leif Erikson (or Erikisson, ca. 970–1020) and his contemporaries in the eleventh century, but because no permanent settlement was established, and because knowledge of the exact location of the "land to the west" was lost to later generations, Christopher Columbus continues to receive full credit for the discovery of America. Notwithstanding, of course, that the new lands were named for Amerigo Vespucci, who was not even a seaman, much less an explorer of any note or substance prior to his first voyage.[3]

The possibility of a Chinese discovery of America has captured the media's attention in recent years. In 1973, Dr. Hendon Harris, a Christian missionary to China, published *The Asiatic Fathers of America*, a

---

1. Ivan van Sertima, *They Came Before Columbus: The African Presence in Ancient America* (New York, 1976).

2. The most complete summary can be found in: Fuat Sezgin, "The Pre-Columbian Discovery of the American Continent by Muslim Seafarers," in *Geschicte des arabischen Schrifttums*, vol. 13 (Frankfurt am Main, 2006); a reprint of this article can be found at: http://www.laits.utexas.edu/gma/mappamundi/docs/precolumbamerica.pdf.

3. For the naming of America, see Martin Waldseemüller, *Cosmographiae Introductio* (St. Dié, 1507). For the most recent work on Vespucci, see Filipe Fernández-Armesto, *Amerigo: The Man Who Gave His Name to America* (London, 2006; rprt. New York and London, 2008).

single volume containing two books: *The Chinese Discovery and Coloniza-tion of Ancient America–2640 B.C. to 2200 B.C.* and *The Asiatic Kingdoms of America–458 A.D. to 1000 A.D.*[4] His work relied heavily on a series of maps he had found in Asia, which depicted a land far to the east named Fu Sang, "discovered" and colonized by early Chinese explorers. In 2002, British submariner Gavin Menzies promoted the idea that the Chinese discovered America by sailing west, around the horn of Africa into the Atlantic. His book, *1421: The Year China Discovered America*, sparked a controversy in both scholarly and popular circles that spanned the globe.[5] Although scholars generally discredit Menzies' theories, the question asked by both authors are valid: Could the Chinese have discovered America? So far, there is no evidence to support Menzies' case, and Harris' arguments have been forgotten by all but a few.[6]

The case of the Norse discovery of America is less complicated and less fraught with controversy, at least since the discovery and excava-tion of L'Anse aux Meadows on the northern tip of Newfoundland in the 1960s. Here, incontrovertible archaeological evidence supported the stories told in the Icelandic sagas. In 1964, the U.S. Congress declared October 9 Leif Erickson Day in acknowledgment of Norway's contribution to the story of America. And for most Americans, the story ends there. Yet, that isn't the end of the story; as Johnson and Westin will argue in the following pages, it was only the beginning.

Historians base their arguments on evidence, at least the good ones do. There are generally two types of evidence for the Middle Ages: physical evidence, such as artifacts and other remains of human habi-tation; and written evidence, provided by texts of one kind or another.[7] It is the historian's job to evaluate and to interpret the evidence in the hope of adding a little something to the story of humankind. The

---

4.   Hendon M. Harris, *The Asiatic Fathers of America* (Taiwan, 1973).

5.   This book was originally published as *1421: The Year China Discovered the World* (London, 2002); it was retitled for its American audience in 2003.

6.   Harris' daughter, Charlotte Harris Rees, has attempted to revive her father's theories. She published *Secret Maps of the Ancient World* (2008) and speaks frequently on the topic.

7.   Those historians who study modern history also have audio records at their disposal.

difficulty lies therein—how do you evaluate evidence that contradicts everything you "know" to be true?

The textual evidence for the discovery of America by the Norse is varied and generally believed to be unreliable. The first mention of Vinland—the Norse name for that part of North America they first encountered—occurs in Chapter 38 of Book 4 of Adam of Bremen's history of the Hamburg bishops, which he wrote between 1075 and the mid-1080s.[8] Book 4 deals with the geography of Scandinavia and other northern lands, including Iceland, Greenland, and to the west, Vinland. Unfortunately, it incorporates many Greek and Roman "myths" concerning the far reaches of the world, and scholars argue over what is "fact" and what is "fiction."[9] The Icelandic sagas are no less problematic, for while they relate events from the late tenth century into the twelfth, they were by and large not written down until the thirteenth and fourteenth centuries.[10] They, too, challenge scholars attempting to separate myth from historical reality.

Perhaps the most controversial of all of the textual evidence is the Vinland Map, which purports to be a pre-Columbian map that depicts Vinland on the northwestern edge of the Atlantic. Now owned by Yale University, the Vinland Map first came to light in 1957, three years prior to the discovery of the settlement at L'Anse aux Meadows. Although initially declared to be genuine by experts in 1965, the map has since sparked a somewhat rancorous scholarly debate, with those declaring the map to be a fake taking the lead until just recently.[11]

---

8.   Adam of Bremen, *Gesta Hammaburgensis ecclesiae pontificum*, ed. B. Schmeidler. *Monumenta Germaniae Historica. Scriptores rerum Germanicarum in usum scholarum Separatim editi*, 2 (Hannover, 1917). In English: *History of the archbishops of Hamburg-Bremen* (New York: 1959; revised ed. 2002).

9.   For a recent discussion on Adam's work, although focused on Frisian voyages, see Donald D. Hogarth, "An Eleventh-Century Frisian Voyage to Labrador: Possibilities and Probabilities," *Terrae Incognitae* 43.1 (2011): 41–53.

10. The *Flateyarbok* (GkS 1005 fol. or Codex Flateyensis), for example, which includes the Vinland saga, was recorded on parchment over the course of several years, from ca. 1387–1394 by two members of the clergy. It currently resides in the Arni Magnusson Institute for Icelandic Studies, an independent research institute established in 2006 under the auspices of Iceland's Ministry of Education, Science and Culture in Reykjavik.

11. See R. A. Skelton, *The Vinland map and the Tartar Relation*, 2nd ed. (New Haven, CT:

Until the discoveries at L'Anse aux Meadows, many serious scholars were skeptical as to the actual existence of this land to the west of Greenland: Vinland.

However, the archaeological evidence found in Newfoundland in the late 1960s offered a certain validation to the problematic written record. In the 1990s, additional excavations of a farm complex in Greenland at Gård Under Sandet also reveal contact with North America. The farm, established ca. 1000 and abandoned ca. 1350, consisted of numerous buildings, including a weaving room, dating from the fourteenth century. In this weaving room, excavators found fibers from bison and brown bear fur, which "suggest that these Greenlanders traveled to North America."[12] Archaeology also may provide evidence of Norse in arctic Canada on Ellesmere Island in the fourteenth or fifteenth centuries.[13]

In general, scholars are not debating whether Scandinavians landed in North America in the Middle Ages. The root of the controversy lies in the idea that Norse explorers may have ventured inland, perhaps as far as Minnesota or North Dakota, just at a time when the Greenland settlements were failing.[14] Artifacts such as the Spirit Pond stones, found in Maine, and the Kensington Runestone of Minnesota have met with both acclaim and derision. Sensible scholars tend to weigh in on the side of forgeries and fakes. Those who support the

---

1965; new edition 1995). For more recent arguments, pro and con, see: Kirsten A. Seaver, *Maps, Myths, and Men: The Story of the Vinland Map* (Stanford, 2004); René Larsen and Dorte V. P. Sommer, "Facts and Myths about the Vinland Map and its Context." *Zeitschrift für Kunsttechnologie und Konservierung* 23.2 (2009): 196–205; Katherine L. Brown, Robin J. H. Clark, "Analysis of Pigmentary Materials on the Vinland Map and Tartar Relation by Raman Microprobe Spectroscopy," *Analytical Chemistry* 74.15 (2002): 3658–3661; K. M. Towe, R. J. H. Clark, and K. A. Seaver, "Analysing the Vinland Map: A Critical Review of a Critical Review," *Archaeometry* 50.5 (2008): 887–893. For a good review of the arguments, see this interactive website: http://www.webexhibits.org/vinland/about.html.

12. Julian D. Richards. *Vikings: A Very Short Introduction* (Oxford: 2005), p. 107.

13. Peter Schledermann, *Crossroads to Greenland: 3000 Years of Prehistory in the Eastern High Arctic* (Calgary: 1990); and Schledermann, *The Viking Saga* (1997).

14. Kirsten A. Seaver, *The Frozen Echo: Greenland and the Exploration of North America ca. A.D. 1000–1500* (Stanford: 1996), 205. More recently, see this scientific report that dates habitation to the 1430s: J. Arneberg, J. Heinemeier, et al, "C-14 dating and the disappearance of Norsemen from Greenland," *Europhysics News* (May/June 2002): 77–80.

authenticity of the stones are often labeled cranks or conspiracy theorists or, more kindly, hopeless romantics who want to believe in the untold adventures of medieval warriors. Books have been written to represent every category.[15]

It is important to note, however, that very few American scholars pay any attention to Scandinavian history at all, and even fewer to the question of Norse settlement in North America. The current Norwegian population of Minnesota consists mainly of immigrants who left war-torn Europe as children during or following World War II. Now in their seventies and eighties, they are the backbone of Norwegian heritage lodges, choral groups, and other organizations that promote and celebrate their cultural heritage in this new land. Yet, they travel back to Norway once or twice a year and many still call it home—the place where their hearts are, the place where they were born. Knowing many of these Norwegian immigrants as I do, it is not difficult to imagine their ancestors braving the North Atlantic in small ships to settle Iceland, Greenland, and North America. In many instances, their own descendents, their American children, grandchildren, and great-grandchildren, continue to celebrate and embrace their Norwegian heritage. Yet, there are few places in Minnesota, much less in the rest of the country, where one can study Scandinavian history. At the University of Minnesota, one can study Old Norse, Scandinavian literature and mythology, and the immigrant experience in the Department of German, Scandinavian, and Dutch, but the History Department offers only one course on a periodic basis.

Thus, it is left to interested people like authors Johnson and Westin to attempt to make sense of the evidence and interpret it for us. This book is the result of intensive study and time-consuming effort on their part to understand the arguments, weigh the evidence, and offer an explanation grounded in their own areas of expertise: geophysical analysis, calligraphy, stone letter-carving, and sculpting. It is up to you, the reader, to decide if they made their case, if the evidence they

---

15. For example, Erik Wahlgren, *The Vikings and America* (London, 1986; rprt. 2000) for the fake/forgery view. Graeme Davis, *Vikings in America* (London: 2009), whose interpretation follows lines similar to those of Johnson and Westin.

present supports their argument. I'll leave you with this: Archaeologists investigating the L'Anse aux Meadows site discovered butternut husks. The butternut tree is not native to Newfoundland; the closest natural habitat is the St. Lawrence River Valley, east of Quebec in northeastern New Brunswick—and L'Anse aux Meadows was situated conveniently to the Gulf of St. Lawrence. L'Anse aux Meadows was an impermanent settlement; the archaeological evidence suggests that it was used for only one or two seasons, and was perhaps never intended to be an actual settlement. Could it have been a gateway to a larger territory known as Vinland? That is the conclusion of Birgitta Wallace, who led a Parks Canada team of archaeologists to the site in the 1970s, and other members of her team. They suspect that Vinland actually referred to the coastal region all around the Gulf of St. Lawrence, with L'Anse aux Meadows as a gateway.[16] Coupled with the artifacts and trade materials found in the Canadian arctic, it seems increasingly likely that there was a larger Norse presence in North America than originally believed. Johnson and Westin suggest that we consider an even larger archaeological footprint. I urge you to keep an open mind.

—*Marguerite Ragnow, Ph.D.*
curator of the James Ford Bell Library, University of Minnesota
editor of Terrae Incognitae, the journal of the Society for the
History of Discoveries http://www.sochistdisc.org/

---

16. William Fitzhugh, "Early Encounters with a 'New Land': Vikings and Englishmen in the North American Arctic," in *Unlocking the Past: Celebrating Historical Archaeology in North America*, ed. Lu Ann De Cunzo and John H. Jameson, Jr., 53–61 (Gainesville: 2005), 53–56.

ACKNOWLEDGMENTS

This saga of medieval Scandinavian and North American history is the result of nine years of research that has been aided by many contributors. Suzanne Carlson, a long-time editor of the *New England Antiquities Research Journal*, gave us copies of her material on the discovery and the controversy surrounding the Spirit Pond runestones, and a copy of the 1354 proclamation by King Magnus that was relevant to a planned expedition to Greenland and the Western Lands. She was also the first to recognize the poetic character of the Spirit Pond inscription, a necessary clue leading to our rigorous translation. The accurate analysis of Magnus's proclamation was aided by our associate, Charlie Hughes, who read an earlier translation of the proclamation with more careful insight than anyone had before. Malcolm Pearson gave us permission to use his high-resolution pictures of the Spirit Pond inscription. A comparison of Malcolm Pearson's photos with those taken by Scott Wolter under different lighting conditions helped us to make an accurate transliteration of the Spirit Pond inscription.

We thank Bruce Kunze and Judi Rudebusch for their map of hole-stones in the Whetstone River area of eastern South Dakota. Likewise, we thank Leland Pederson for permission to use his map of twenty-five holestone sites scattered over Pope County, Minnesota, east of the Whetstone River. Richard Nielsen's insightful papers that deal with the Kensington runestone's inscription and other aspects of medieval Norse presence in North America provide strong support for the thesis of this book. For the discussion of the location of the Kensington runestone discovery, we are indebted to Al Lieffort, Superintendent of Douglas County Parks, and Darwin Ohman, who supplied pictures from Darwin Ohman's family file. In 1996, John and Diane Erdmann participated in our early investigation of the site of the massacre of the ten Norsemen on Big Cormorant Lake.

Our investigation of the previously unrecognized island, mentioned in the Kensington runestone inscription and located two hundred yards north of the runestone discovery site, was greatly aided by the assistance of Ruby and Arlen Sabolik who owned half of the island. We owe a debt of thanks to a long list of landowners in eastern South Dakota who kindly allowed us to examine their holestones and carvings. To minimize unwelcome investigations of these artifacts we do not name property owners. Judi Rudebusch was both host and guide in our inspections of the artifacts. She and Valdimar Samuelsson of Reykjavik, Iceland, did the historical research, which told us that the holestones found on Iceland had been used to mark property boundary lines from the time of Icelandic settlement. That medieval legal custom for marking Icelandic land boundaries is a key part of our story. Valdimar also sent us a copy of the *Landnámabók* of Icelandic history, and assisted in the translation of the part that says that Ari, an Icelandic trader, had a land claim in Whitemansland, and was baptized there, probably in the mid-eleventh century.

Marly Cornell, our editor, made suggestions that substantially improved the book. We owe a special thanks to Dr. Marguerite Ragnow of the History Department and the curator of the James Ford Bell Map Library at the University of Minnesota for her advice and counsel. In particular she cautioned us to make sure that our translation was grammatically consistent with the word endings of the words in the inscription. This advice enabled us to make the first rigorous translation of the long inscription on the Spirit Pond runestone. Similar strict attention to the grammar also enabled us to make an improved translation of the Kensington runestone's inscription. History

ACKNOWLEDGMENTS

Professor Herb Cederberg read the manuscript in its entirety and made valuable suggestions that improved the flow of the narrative. Wendy Skinner and Burgess Johnson read the Introduction critically. Elizabeth G. Johnson made available a liberal supply of reference books and a stimulating exchange of ideas.

Finally, beyond the usual pale, we acknowledge King Haakon's skald, his poet. He was a man who probably had served in English courts as well as those in Scandinavia, because some Anglo Saxon and Middle English words are found among the many abbreviations used to achieve the rhyming and couplet rhythm of the poetic Spirit Pond inscription. The poem was probably to have been recited in Norway by King Haakon himself or by his skald at a memorial service months after it was composed at Spirit Pond in the winter of 1361–1362. The abbreviations that made our translation a difficult task would have been no problem for the king or his skald, who would have been reading an already-familiar text. The skald pays tribute to King Haakon's explorations in the "trade empire." He memorializes the Norsemen who were lost in the great storm, and he salutes the mourning kinsmen of the lost men. In this "Saga of a young Folkung," he leaves to us a priceless record of a piece of Norse history that otherwise would have remained forever unknown.

INTRODUCTION

The story of American history from 1492 onward is old and well worn from the telling. In contrast, historians neglect the preceding four medieval centuries, despite the significance of the widespread trade in North American furs that were collected by the Greenland Norse and marketed in Norway during that time. This lucrative trade resulted in Greenland's annexation by Norway in 1261, and may have been a factor in the "discovery" of America in 1492. But around 1340, Greenland's climate became colder and the fur trade ceased.

In *The Last Kings of Norse America*, our subject is a Norse expedition to North America in 1356 that came about partly because of struggles for power and control of trade in fourteenth-century Scandinavia. At the heart of our story are young King Haakon VI of Norway (b. August 1340, d. 1380); his father, King Magnus of Norway and Sweden (b. 1316, d. 1374); and Magnus's expedition to regain the lost fur trade that had been carried on by Norse traders living in Norway's trade empire in the Western Lands. Historically, this expedition is documented only in a single 1354 proclamation by King Magnus, which is addressed to an unnamed "you" and says that the Honorable Paul Knutson shall be the chosen commandant.

Although the expedition was said to be a "före" or førre," a trading voyage, for political reasons the proclamation's emphasis was on the restoration of Christianity to the Greenlanders who had left their homes to live in the Western Lands, that is: in northeastern North America. From several lines of evidence we infer a wide distribution of Norse enclaves on the continent of North America. These people had been connected to Greenland and Norway by trading ships that were operated mainly by merchant Greenlanders, most of whom were based on their farms in the West Greenland colony.

The most valuable component of the trade was fur, pelts that were collected by resident Norse who traded with the Indians. We know that the hides of deer and the pelts of black bear, sable, and marten that were mentioned in the Bergen port records of the Greenland trade were obtained from North America because those animals did not live on Greenland. However, less than a century after the annexation, the Greenland trade ceased because the merchant traders lost their home base for their operations. A strong climate cooling, possibly combined with oppressive taxes and competition from the migrating Thule Eskimos from the north, forced those West Greenlanders to abandon their homes.[17] They left their farms and their facilities for shipbuilding behind, and emigrated to live with their friends at trading sites on the continent. Although contemporary historians have paid little attention to this event, it received the full attention of King Magnus, who decided to send an expedition to the Western Lands to take back the trade.

Two American runestones resulted from this expedition: the Kensington runestone found in western Minnesota in 1898 and the Spirit Pond runestone found on the coast of Maine in 1971. After three years of effort, we have now achieved rigorous translations of these two inscriptions, translations that are included in the appendices of this book. However, historians have thus far refused to consider our translation of the Spirit Pond inscription because the conventional opinion among the authorities is that both runestones are hoaxes. Nevertheless, in each case a competent investigation has found that the discovery of the stone was an honest and authentic event. The

---

17. K.A. Seaver. *The Frozen Echo, Greenland and the exploration of North America ca A.S. 1000-1500*, (Stanford, CA: Stanford University Press, 1996), 138.

belief that the runestones are hoaxes is deeply entrenched in the minds of most authorities of history, but underlying their negative arguments is the fact that no acceptable explanation for a Norse expedition and the runestones' presence in America has ever been proposed.

A similar problem involving a lack of an acceptable explanation is described by Stephan Jay Gould, an eminent scientist and a master of science writing, in one of his famous essays, "When the Unorthodox Prevails," *New Scientist*, 28 September 1978. Gould discussed the reluctance of authorities of geology to accept the flood origin of the scablands formations in eastern Washington State. These spectacular valley chasms were clearly the result of water erosion, but most authorities insisted that conventional slow river flow should explain their formation despite the obvious deep canyons that geologist Harlan Bretz correctly interpreted as the result of massive flooding. Gould noted that, until a valid explanation for the flood was found (water released suddenly from giant Lake Missoula when a glacial ice dam broke), the authorities could not believe what they saw: the obvious physical evidence of the great scablands megafloods. The psychologies of the scablands quandary and the runestone quandary are remarkably similar.

In the case of the Kensington runestone the facts of its honest and authentic discovery have been known from the day it was removed from the roots of a poplar tree in 1898. It was found face down, with bleached root lines on the top surface that were caused by many years of tree growth. The relatively older (medieval) age of its inscription, inferred from weathering differences on the surface of the stone, has been repeatedly noted by reliable and well-qualified observers over the last hundred years. Yet, in the absence of an acceptable historical explanation for a Norse expedition, historians could not believe that evidence. A similar argument can be made for the Spirit Pond runestone. But an acceptable explanation for both runestones is now at hand.

The key to the explanation is the identification of the man "Haakon" in the Spirit Pond inscription as young Haakon VI of Norway, the unnamed "you" in the enigmatic proclamation that

Magnus made in 1354. From that identification and with the aid of publications by historians Karen Larsen, Vilhelm Moberg, Lars Warme, and other sources, we have found the reasons for the expedition to Greenland and the Western Lands. In this search we have uncovered a saga of violence, political intrigue, and fraternal and parental jealousy that reached a peak when Magnus assigned his second son, Haakon VI, to the expedition instead of Haakon's older brother, Erik XII. There in the Western Lands the young Haakon spent the latter half of his teenage years with Commander Paul Knutson in an attempt to restore the lost fur trade. Their attempt to take back the trade failed, but centuries later the two runestones they left behind triggered the historical research contained in this book.

However, like the historians, linguists have also actively opposed the authenticity of the Kensington and the Spirit Pond inscriptions. We touch only briefly on that controversial aspect of the stones because strong physical evidence and reliable documentation exist to support their authenticity, and the opposing arguments of the linguists are logically flawed (see Appendix J). Therefore, we do not hesitate to make the historical connections implied by the content of the inscriptions. In his 1354 proclamation, Magnus authorized Haakon to choose the young men of his retinue and any other companions he wished to take on the coming voyage. Although fourteen-year-old Haakon was acclaimed as king in 1350, in 1354 he had not yet come of age and was not yet formally empowered. Thus Magnus was legally able to assign him to the expedition.

This identification of Haakon connects the runestones to all the documented events that preceded the expedition that sailed to the Western Lands in 1356. This history includes the bitter struggle of the three Folkung brothers for the throne of Sweden, a struggle that preceded the checkered reign of King Magnus in which he was forced into a delayed abdication. His misfortunes were compounded when the plague struck Scandinavia and forced him to abort his war with Russia that would have enlarged his empire and improved Norway's trade. He was always short of money and he needed more trade, but the restoration of the "Greenland" trade, with its associated religious mission, was not the only reason that the ambitious Magnus sent his ships to the Western Lands. His motives are of great interest and form a pivotal part of our story.

A web of facts connected by logical arguments supports the reality of Magnus's expedition. It is indeed a web, not a chain, and if a thread in the web were later found to be incorrect, the web would survive. Although our case for the expedition is strong and factual, the details of the expedition as described here are reconstructions based on clues in our translations of the two runic inscriptions, on our own years of field work, on the analysis of known historical events, and on the evidence of a Norse presence on the continent. That evidence includes Norse names, blond genetic characteristics found in Indian tribes, the Newport Tower in Rhode Island, which was constructed as a medieval church, and widespread occurrences of holestones: boulders containing inches-deep holes of a somewhat cylindrical shape, hammered out with a broad blade chisel. Similar holestones were often used as mooring stones along Scandinavian waterways, and evidence points to their use also as marking stones that defined medieval Norse property boundaries in the Dakotas and Minnesota, just as similar holestones did and still do in some pastures on Iceland.

The idea for this book was conceived after various lines of evidence coalesced into a valid, credible theory: The medieval Norse had not only traded for furs in central and northeastern North America, but had also lived there in significant numbers. There is evidence for substantial groups of medieval Norsemen who lived in New England, on the St. Lawrence River, and in South Dakota and Minnesota. And it was our investigation of the Norse artifacts along the Whetstone River in South Dakota that led to the historical research and results embodied in this book.

If our story were limited only to Magnus's expedition, the picture would not be complete. We have two partly interlocking stories, one in the past and one in the present. They interlock because the story of the Last Kings grew out of the authors' discoveries in Minnesota and South Dakota. Therefore in one logical sense we should tell the story of our discoveries first. On the other hand, the connection between documented history and the two American runestones that were left behind by the expedition is the most important part of the book. That story can stand alone, and we tell it first in Part A, "The Epic of the Last Kings." There we describe the turbulent years that preceded the expedition to the Western Lands. Then, using information from the translated runic inscriptions, we reconstruct the expedition and its tragic events that are memorialized on the runestones. In Part B, "Discoveries on the Graenaveldi," we take the reader forward in time to tell a strictly factual story of how the skeptics' last legitimate criticism of the Kensington runestone was overcome, and how, step by step, the fact of medieval Norse settlements on the central plains of North America was established.

A narrative voice makes this book easy to read, and in Part A, we have somewhat relaxed rigid scholarly rules of evidence to describe some details that are only inferred from historical documents or are suggested by the runic inscriptions. The text also includes fictional versions of what the actual characters of history might logically have said, thought, or done, and this breathes life into the spirit of the narration. For those who read for pleasure: Enjoy the book. For those who are looking for new historical insights: You will not be disappointed.

PART A

THE EPIC
OF THE LAST KINGS

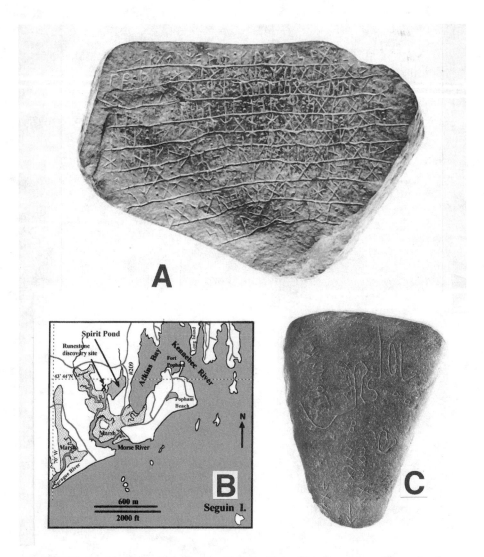

FIGURE 1: A: Side #1 of the Spirit Pond runestone inscription. The stone is about eleven inches across, and contains a total of 273 runes on both sides. The inscription is a chivalric poem containing about ninety words, half of which are abbreviated in various ways. From Collections of the Maine State Museum, mainestatemuseum.org. B: Spirit Pond and vicinity. C: The Spirit Pond mapstone, the size of a man's fist. Malcolm Pearson photo, used with permission. The mapstone is also now in the collections of the Maine State Museum. See also Figures 37 and 38 (pages 205 and 206).

PROLOGUE

On a warm day, 27 May 1971, Walter Elliott drove southward on the coast of Maine on Highway 209 to the edge of Spirit Pond, put his rubber boat into the water, and paddled across to the point where Spirit Pond drains into the small Morse River. Walter was an avid hunter of old arrowheads and Indian pots, and for some time he had wanted to examine the area around the pond outlet, a possible old Indian camp-site, where he thought he might find arrowheads. As Walter himself described it in a taped interview,[18] his first inspection of the site did not produce any arrowheads, so he sat down on a boulder and smoked a cigarette to enjoy the pleasant day, ". . . and I got up and started over again and when I did I just kicked the grass and I saw this stone down there . . ." The stone was flat and only eleven inches across, and appeared to have some markings on it. Walter picked up some weedy growth and scrubbed it clean. To his amazement he saw that it was nearly covered with neatly laid out rows of Norse runes, Figure 1. Beneath the first stone he found two others, one with a crudely drawn map of the Spirit Pond area, and the other with only a few odd runes.

Walter knew he had something unusual, and in the following

---

18. S. Carlson. "Stumbles and Pitfalls-Indeed!" in *New England Antiquities Research Association (NEARA) Journal*, Vol. 34, No. 1, 15-32, 2000, 21. In this tape-recorded interview with Walter Elliott, conducted by Professor Einar Haugen and witnessed by others, Walter describes all the details of his struggle to find someone to translate the long inscription, together with the offers he received to buy the inscription stone and his frustrating correspondence with the Maine State officials who claimed title to all three stones. In the opinions of all those who were in contact with Walter on the matter of the runestones, his honesty was not questioned.

weeks he made vigorous attempts within academia to find someone who would translate the runes and tell him what the inscription said. For some time no one took him seriously and his efforts failed. Then word of his discovery reached the newspapers and his story began to attract wider attention. He was offered $10,000 for the stones, but he refused the offer because he was still obsessed with what the runes might say, and the prospective purchaser was a collector, not a linguist.

Although Spirit Pond had once been on private property, a few years before Walter's discovery the land had been donated to the State of Maine. Consequently, when the newspaper publicity excited the interest of state officials, they served Walter a rather arrogant legal notice, saying that because he had found the stones on State land, he had to turn them over to the State of Maine. By then Walter had some of his own money invested in the efforts to find out what the long inscription said, and he was not willing to give up the stones. Fearing they would be confiscated by a court order, he took them back to Spirit Pond and buried them at a location somewhat distant from where he had found them. After learning of this, state officials tried to locate the stones by digging around the discovery site. They found nothing, and only got bad cases of poison ivy from their digging.

This impasse was finally broken by negotiations conducted by Richard Card, a local banker who acted as an ombudsman for Walter in the dispute. It was agreed that Walter would be reimbursed in the amount of $3,000 to cover his expenses. The money was donated by Lawrence M. D. Smith, who had originally owned the Spirit Pond land. Walter then dug up the stones and Smith transferred them to the State of Maine, where they are now curated at the Maine State Museum in Augusta, Maine.

The museum curator enlisted the aid of Einar Haugen, a Harvard University professor of linguistics, who was asked to examine and translate the runes. Over a few months, Haugen made a weak attempt to do this, but he was apparently unaware of the great number of abbreviations used in the runic inscription. His verdict was that the inscription consisted of "a few Norse words in a sea of gibberish," and he said the inscription was an attempted hoax by some unknown person, not Walter Elliott.[19] Haugen did not try to explain why a hoaxer would have buried his work in such an isolated location on the far side of Spirit Pond where the stones might never have been discovered. But how could a Harvard professor be wrong? So the runestone stood as a fraud in the eyes of all the authorities, and Walter Elliott died many years later without ever learning what the mysterious inscription said.

Haugen's "sea of gibberish" was not to remain an enigma forever. The runic inscription eventually came to the attention of authors Westin and Johnson, who devoted nearly three years of historical research, etymological detective work, and rigorous application of the Norse grammar to obtain an accurate translation of this chivalric poem, as discussed in Chapter 10 and the Appendix. Here is what the poem says:

> *Fallen kinsmen, ever valiant fellows. A roaring sea struck seventeen*
> *   dead.*
> *Hail to you, Weeping Fountains!*
> *Year 20, We lost the company of twelve companions*
> *12 daghrise westward (900 miles), 10 daghrise northward (750 miles).*
> *The saga of a young Folkung.*
> *Bearded chief-man Haakon discovered a circle by being able to sail*
> *   toward the west on the lakes ("laaga") of the trade empire.*
> *Weeping Fountains! Year 21.*
> *A shout into the burning lights! Blessed Maria! Alas!*
> *Powerless those on the Sealship to proceed*
> *to obtain an edge to devote attention in regard*
> *to win the ship against the terrible storm.*
> *Seventeen presage their inevitable battle stroke, accept the sinking,*
> *   the bane of their approaching death.*
> *Hail to you, Weeping Fountains! Year 21.*

---

19. Ibid., 18.

This runic inscription provided a rare thrill of discovery when we laid out the westward and northward distance coordinates from Spirit Pond on a world globe map and found that the loss of the ship and seventeen Norsemen had occurred off the southern coast of Hudson Bay.

CHAPTER 1

THE BANQUET

When the dungeon door clanged shut that December night in 1317 in the castle of King Birger, Duke Erik knew that he and his brother, Valdemar, would never again see the light of day. In the darkness Erik thought for a few moments of his young wife, fifteen-year-old Princess Ingebjorg of Norway, and their year-old infant son. But that thought soon gave way to a raging frustration that he had been duped by King Birger's invitation to set aside for the moment his ambition to own the crown of Sweden, and to join with Valdemar at a banquet in the Great Hall at Nyköping. What could be more harmless than the three brothers celebrating the Christmastide by joining together in a fine banquet? But the banquet was a trap set by King Birger, a trap that was sprung after the fifth toast when Erik's and Valdemar's armed retinues had already been encouraged into a state of happy inebriation in the town away from the castle[20] at Nyköping, Figure 2. They were in no position to come to the Duke's aid when Birger's minions swarmed into the Great Hall. With a single command from Birger, his men had

---

20. V. Moberg. *A History of the Swedish People*, Vol 1. (Minneapolis, MN: University of Minnesota Press, 2005 edition), 102-109.

chained Erik and Valdemar and hustled them off to the dungeon.

The three brothers—King Birger, Duke Erik of Södermanland, and Duke Valdemar of Finland—were members of the Folkung clan, and their bitter rivalry for the Swedish crown had been a painfully disruptive factor in Sweden.[21] In 1310 in an attempt to keep the peace, the nobles of Sweden divided the provinces three ways among the brothers. Each brother had nobles backing him, because the custom of the crown being inherited by the first son of the previous king had not yet become firmly established, at least not in Sweden. The line of inheritance was not always clear, and the crown was sometimes worn only by the man who had the strength to seize and keep it. Erik and Birger, the nominal king at the time of the Nyköping banquet, were the main contenders, although Valdemar of Finland also desired the crown.

Södermanland was a major Swedish province, and Erik had the strong support of many active followers. When it became known that Duke Erik had been captured and imprisoned at Nyköping, his people would not have known immediately what to do about it. In the usual course of such hostilities, a chieftain's capture was often followed by a request for ransom. But no such request was ever received. They waited as the days stretched into weeks. Word leaked out that Erik had asked for writing materials and had written his will while incarcerated at Nyköping, and this was viewed as evidence that he had not been killed, yet. In retrospect, it was learned that Birger was starving Valdemar and Erik to death. No one could ever say that Birger had slaughtered the brothers. They had died quite naturally while imprisoned, an argument later rejected by Erik's faithful followers.

When it became known that Erik was dead, the rallying call went out to all his people in Södermanland and elsewhere in Sweden. Some people in other provinces had supported Birger because, by inheritance, he was probably entitled to the crown. But the evil way in which Birger settled the rivalry turned most of Sweden against him. Many joined Erik's supporters. They chose Mats Kettilmundson as the regent. Mats enlisted the aid of King Haakon V of Norway, the

---

21. L.G. Warme. *A History of Swedish Literature*, Vol 3. (Lincoln & London: University of Nebraska Press), 29.

grandfather of Erik's infant son, and in the summer of 1318 their army began to take King Birger's fortified towns. In August they stormed the Nyköping castle and took it, and with it they captured King Birger's son. Birger himself managed to escape to the protection of friends in Denmark. He never returned to Nyköping. By inheritance, Birger's son might have succeeded him as King of Sweden, but after the infamous Nyköping banquet, the name Birger was a poison to the royal politics. The Swedes who might have favored him were in the minority, despite the general feeling among the nobles that the crown should pass by way of inheritance. Then, to ensure the future stability of the regime, the Swedes executed Birger's son to eliminate any possible future claim by him to the Swedish crown. Thus, for a short time Sweden was without a king.[22]

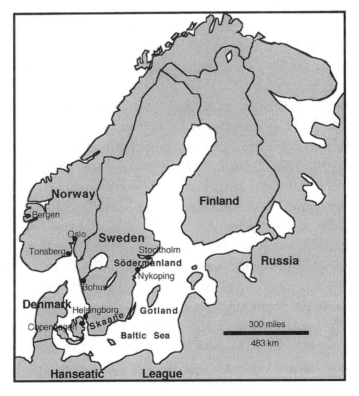

FIGURE 2: Scandinavia about 1317. National boundaries are modernized.

---

22. Ibid., 30.

In 1316, a year before the Nyköping banquet, Princess Ingebjorg had given birth to a boy named Magnus Eriksson. There was no doubt as to his parentage, for the marriage of Duke Erik and ten-year-old Ingebjorg had been carefully arranged by her father, King Haakon V of Norway, to ensure the continuation of his Norwegian dynasty, a wise move because Haakon V died soon after Birger was deposed and his son was executed. Therefore, Magnus was in the dynastic lines to claim both the Norwegian and Swedish thrones. This was legally confusing to both Norwegians and Swedes, for neither country could exclusively claim Magnus as their king. After considerable deliberation, the noblemen of Sweden and the royal Council of Barons of Norway reached a friendly agreement in 1319 in which Magnus was to become King of both Norway and Sweden when he became of age, and was to spend his time equally in the courts of the two countries. The nobles of both countries swore allegiance to Magnus, and so his reign began at age three. For the first time two of the three major Scandinavian nations were joined in a loose union by means of a shared king.

In the year 1319 the child King, Magnus, was destined to rule a large empire loosely connected by culture and trade. That empire stretched wherever ships could sail: from Finland on the east, through the other provinces of Sweden and Norway, across the sea to Iceland, and on westward to the large glacier-covered island of Greenland. The name "Greenland" was sometimes used broadly to include Vinland and other areas on the nearby continent. Icelanders had begun to settle on Greenland about 985 AD. There were two small areas free of glacial ice along the south coast where pastoral farms thrived in the warmer climate of those early times. All the good land was quickly occupied and the population soon exceeded the capacity of the land to support the people. On the island of Greenland there were few other resources. But the Greenlanders, particularly those in the West Greenland colony, had easy access to vast areas on the nearby continent that were occupied by a population of Indians, or Skraelinges, as the Norse called them.

After the first Norse explorations that were documented in the sagas of the Vinland Voyages shortly after AD 1000,[23] the shrewd Norsemen developed trade relations with the natives. The young Greenlanders who would not inherit land or ply a trade on Greenland often migrated to the continent. They brought their wives with them or, as was often the case, took Indian wives from the tribes with whom they traded. They lived along the coasts and the major rivers, Figure 3, where they acted as middlemen who collected the furs from the Indians and then traded them to their seafaring merchant country-men who were based on Greenland, and who would carry the goods back to the market in Norway to be sold.

Evidence for medieval Norse trade and settlement on the north-eastern coasts of continental North America is found at the L'Anse aux Meadows site on Newfoundland, Appendix A, in the Icelandic *Land-námabók* and in place names on Labrador, Appendix B, and in the voyage of Bishop Eirik Gnupsson to Vinland about AD 1117, Appendix C. The trade goods obtained on such voyages were delivered to the port of Bergen in Norway, and were eagerly received by the King and Church, who levied taxes on the goods.[24] The Greenland trade was monopolized by Norway, and the tax income was so important that it led to the formal annexation of Greenland by Norway in 1261, a year or two before the death of King Haakon IV of Norway. Because he taxed and formally annexed the widespread Norsemen living on the continent, Haakon IV was in a unique sense the first King of the Norse trade empire in North America.

The income from the Greenland trade was particularly important for Norway because Norway was less favorably located than its rivals to participate in the Baltic trade. By 1300 all the Norwegian trade in the Baltic had been taken over by Hanseatic merchants, the Germans.[25] In the Baltic region, the early fourteenth century was a period of

---

23. K. Kunz. translator, *The Sagas of Icelanders*, (New York: Penguin Books, 2001), 626-652.

24. H. Ingstad. *Westward to Vinland, The discovery of pre-Columbian house-sites in North America* (New York: St. Martins Press, 1969). Helge Ingstad notes that the Bergen tax records showed commodities imported from Greenland included items such as skins of black bears and martens, animals not found in Greenland but common in North America.

25. K. Larsen. *A History of Norway* (Princeton & New York: Princeton University Press, 1948), 175.

population growth accompanied by ever-increasing exchanges of goods between the nations and city-states bordering the Baltic and the North Sea. This sea trade grew hand in hand with the development of much larger ships.

By 1350, the smaller knorrs of Viking times, with their side rudders, had been replaced by large cog ships with the rudder centered at the stern.[26] These ships carried products such as dried cod from Norway, wool from England, cloth from the Flemish area, salt from the mines on the south Baltic coast, furs from the outlying Finnish and Russian wilderness, beeswax, timbers, grain, ironwork, and weapons. A thriving trade meant wealth and power to the people of the nations and city-states in the Baltic region, and they took great pride in their ships. An image of their largest vessel was often placed on their official seal, and that ship was known as the Sealship. These larger cog ships had decks that enclosed the cargo spaces. They also had high castle-like decks on the bow and stern where armed men were stationed to repel pirate attacks, because competition for the trade was not always a peaceful activity.

The maps tell us that Norwegian captains could sail easily to England and across the North Sea to the low countries, but within the confines of the Baltic Sea they had no home port, and the aggressive Germans dominated the Baltic trade. Norway's trade was of considerable economic importance, but Norway is a rugged, mountainous country and lacks the agricultural lands like those of southern Sweden and other countries along the Baltic coasts. Consequently, Norway was the poorer of the two nations Magnus was to govern. Of course, as a child, the affairs of state and the inferior conditions of the Norwegian economy concerned him only indirectly. His first years were apparently spent mostly in Norway with his mother, Ingebjorg. She was the regent with the authority of the royal seal, and we are told by historians that unwise military actions by Ingebjorg drained the funds from the Norwegian treasury.

---

26. B. Greenhill. *The Evolution of the Wooden Ship* (New York: Facts on File, Inc., 1988). The larger cog ships were developed in response to the needs of the merchants in the rapidly expanding trade of the early fourteenth century.

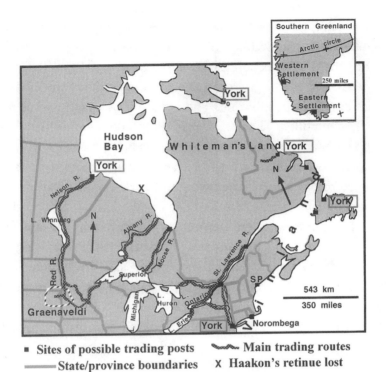

- ■ Sites of possible trading posts   ≈≈≈ Main trading routes
- ═══ State/province boundaries   X Haakon's retinue lost

FIGURE 3: King Magnus's trade empire. Black squares: Locations where some type of evidence suggests a medieval trading post. Dotted lines: Inferred trading routes on rivers. SP is the Spirit Pond site. York: The anglicized version of "jorvik," the Norse term for a trading site inland from the sea on a stream. See "The Bishops voyage " in Appendix C. The three recognized parts of the old Greenland trade empire in the Western Lands were the two coastal areas, Vinland and Whitemansland, and the interior, the Graenaveldi. North Autlatsivik Island, the black square at the north end of the Whitemansland coast, is a fast four-day sail directly westward from the Eastern Settlement on Greenland.

With Duke Erik deceased, Duchess Ingebjorg became attached to Knud Porse, a Danish nobleman who acted also as her advisor. Together they hoped to form a central Scandinavian state that would include the Danish province of Skaane, which was the southernmost province of Sweden, Figure 2. Skaane was a productive agricultural province, and in Danish hands it enabled the Danes to control the principal sea channel between the Baltic and the North Sea. Ships going from one sea to the other pass through the strait between Helsingor in Denmark on the west and Helsingborg on the Skaane coast to the east. These two port cities are hardly more than two miles apart, and as long as Denmark controlled Skaane, Denmark could force ships passing through the narrow strait to pay tolls. This lucrative tax was resented by ship owners of other nations on the Atlantic side of the strait who were forced to pay a toll if they wanted to trade in the Baltic area.

Backed by Ingebjorg's access to the royal treasury, Knud raised an army and declared war on Denmark. The campaign was a failure. Denmark retained Skaane and the Norwegian treasury became so depleted that it was said to have been "impossible to provide decently for the child king."[27] The campaign did not have the support of the Norwegian Church and Council of Barons, and in the aftermath of Knud's little war, the nobles authorized the archbishop to name a viceroy to run the government. He selected a strong and respected nobleman, Erling Vidkunnsson, to fill this position. Ingebjorg was forced to give up the royal seal, and the royal financial affairs were stabilized. She then married Knud Porse, and no longer participated in the government. Erling made peace with Denmark, and negotiated a treaty with Russia that settled the disputed Finmark boundary. With the disastrous experience with the Dane, Knud Porse, in mind, he followed a consistent policy of excluding foreign office holders from the government. He also attempted to keep the Hanseatic merchants from expanding their activities in Norwegian and Swedish cities, but trade considerations forced him to allow the merchants some new privileges.

Thus it was that when Magnus came of age he took over Norwegian and Swedish governments that were plagued by trade problems associated with the aggressive Hanseatic traders who had footholds in the main ports of Bergen in Norway and Stockholm in Sweden. Magnus's desire to increase the trade to better his financial condition

---

27.   Larsen. *A History of Norway*, 1948, 193.

occupied his mind during most of his reign. This obsession led him into undertakings that were not always favored by his supporting nobles in Norway and Sweden. One such project is the subject of this book.

CHAPTER 2

KING MAGNUS AND THE PLAGUE

In 1332 at age sixteen, Magnus was declared to be of age and was acclaimed as King of Sweden and Norway. He was said to have been a headstrong young man and seemed to lack some of the characteristics of personal diplomacy that are so important to a ruler's success. This might be explained by the absence of a kingly father figure during his formative years, because then he would have been surrounded by royal attendants and friends who were not in a position to say no to his youthful impulses. Although as a child he may have spent much of his time with his mother in Norway, it appears that as he matured he developed important and loyal friends in Sweden, perhaps because of the high esteem the Swedes had for his father, Erik of Södermanland. His friends in the western parts of Sweden stood by him even during the troubles of his later years.

Although the ill-advised actions of his mother had drained the Norwegian treasury, the wiser management of Erling Vidkunnsson somewhat improved the finances, and Sweden's resources were not as limited as Norway's. This enabled Magnus to make his first important venture after he was acclaimed in 1332. This came about because the King of Denmark had become indebted to the Count of Holstein to the amount of 34,000 marks of silver, or 170,000 marks in money. Magnus and his advisors negotiated to pay the debt to the Count of Holstein as the purchase price for the Danish provinces of Skaane and Blekinge. This was a move favored by both Norwegians and Swedes because geographically these provinces were part of Sweden, and the Swedish control of the Skaane port of Helsingborg prevented Denmark from forcing Norwegian and Swedish ships to pay a toll when sailing between the North Sea and the Baltic. The Swedes also occupied Copenhagen, which may not have been strictly part of the purchase. Thus, although the price may have been viewed as high, on the whole the purchase would have been seen as a major accomplishment by Magnus.

Not everyone was pleased with the purchase, however, because it is said that he raised taxes to make it possible,[28] a move that made him no friends. His seeming lack of good political instincts was also working against him. From the time he was acclaimed as king, his favoritism for Sweden was obvious because he did not spend equal time in Norway. When he was not in Norway he did not delegate authority to handle the routine kingly affairs, which made Norwegian administration difficult. In 1335 he married beautiful Blanche of Namur, and as his "morning gift" he gave her title to the Tonsberg castle and fief in Norway, an autocratic move that further irritated the Norwegians.

Magnus also attempted somewhat autocratic reforms that did not sit well with some of the Swedish nobility. He issued a decree that abolished hereditary slavery in Västergötland and Värmland, thus eliminating the automatic renewal of the labor supply in the fiefs of these districts. He also issued a decree to limit the custom of forcing the peasants to host without compensation the large traveling parties of the nobility and Church, an odious custom for farmers on frequently

---

28. B. Sawyer and P. Sawyer, *Medieval Scandinavia: from Conversion to Reformation, circa 800-1500*, (Minneapolis, MN: University of Minnesota Press, 1993), 70.

traveled routes. Such reforms that disadvantage powerful people always have a political cost.

But times change. In 1340, Valdemar, the new King of Denmark, drove the Swedes out of Copenhagen and threatened to force a recovery of the provinces of Skaane and Blekinge for Denmark. Duke Albrecht of Mecklenberg negotiated a treaty that recognized Sweden's right to the two provinces. In 1343, the Treaty of Varberg recognized Skaane, and neighboring provinces of Blekinge and Halland, as being under Swedish domain, and the Danish claim was set aside. Valdemar was not a man to give up his goal easily, however, and the loss of Danish control of the Helsingborg strait and its lucrative tolls was not forgotten. The year 1343 was also a fateful year for the reign of Magnus. After ten years of increasing friction between Magnus and the nobles who had "elected" him, the nobles agreed to "sever the dynastic union" of the two countries by forcing the abdication of Magnus. It was in effect a delayed abdication that preserved the ruling dynastic line.

Magnus had two sons: Erik XII, born in 1339, and Haakon VI, born in August 1340. The Swedes were less unhappy with Magnus than were the Norwegians, and it was agreed that Magnus would remain as King of Sweden until his death, when he would be succeeded by Erik XII. But the Norwegians wanted Magnus out sooner if possible; and, in the terms of the abdication, they were to acclaim Haakon VI as King of Norway when Haakon came of age at fifteen in August 1355. At that time they expected that the role of Magnus in the government would be severely reduced. Between 1343 and 1355 Magnus was to hold the position of King of Norway "in trust." In 1344 when Haakon was not yet four, the Norwegian nobility swore allegiance to him at "a unique meeting at Baahus."[29] After being given his delayed walking papers, Magnus was probably even less inclined to interact with the Council of Barons, and they with him.

For the next eleven years from 1344 to 1355 Magnus could continue to rule in both countries, and he must have given much thought as to what he might accomplish during that time. Magnus was in a difficult position because his trade income had diminished and the royal

---

29. Larsen. *A History of Norway*, 194.

treasury was depleted. The Hanse traders had the upper hand in the Baltic, and the Norwegian trade had suffered a serious loss because the Greenland fur trade had decreased in recent years, and nearly ceased around 1342 when word was received that the West Greenland colony had been abandoned because of colder summers and hostilities with Eskimos who were migrating southward along the West Greenland coast. The merchants who had been based in West Greenland no longer brought furs to the market in Bergen. It was said that the merchants and farmers had all migrated to the Western Lands to live with their fellow Norsemen who had established trading villages along the coasts and rivers.

Faced with the severe decline in Greenland trade, Magnus felt compelled to find some way to improve the situation. His attention was drawn to the Russian provinces at the far eastern end of the Baltic Sea adjacent to the Swedish province of Finland. These provinces were not as populous as Norway and Sweden, and Christianity was not yet established there. If Magnus were to make war on them successfully, he would add substantially to his trade domain, and the Church would increase its tithe income when the people there were forced to become Christians.

Such a war would be costly, however, and Magnus's royal finances had not yet fully recovered from Knud Porse's war with Denmark and his own later expensive purchase of the Skaane and Blekinge provinces from Denmark. He and his advisors gave much thought to the cost problem. Special assessments were opposed by the nobles who would have to pay up the money, and they therefore opposed the war. But Magnus thought of a unique way to fund his proposed campaign. He reasoned that Christianizing the Russian provinces would add also to the pope's income, and the pope therefore might be interested in funding the war.

Negotiations with the pope were initiated, and in the outcome the pope agreed that for five years the pope's tithe moneys collected from Norway and Sweden, the so-called Peter's pence, would be used to finance the war. This result was relatively painless for the nobility. The fiefs always had an excess of young men, and the nobles were quite willing to commit their men to war, but were less willing to commit their money. With the pope's tithes to come into the treasury, they withdrew their objections, although their's was still a grudging support for Magnus's military project. The negotiations with the pope required some time, as did the war preparations. The first of the tithe income was probably diverted to the royal treasury in about 1348 when the first part of the planned campaign could begin. The details are not discussed very much by historians, apparently because fate stepped in and destroyed Magnus's hopes for a successful conquest.

In August 1349, a "ship of death" from a country to the south arrived at the port of Bergen in Norway.[30] Although the ship entered the harbor and anchored, no one disembarked. When the port authorities boarded the ship to investigate, they found the crew all dead of the bubonic plague, or so the story goes. From the ship the plague spread rapidly through Bergen and over all of Norway. By October the disease was also raging in Sweden.

The probable origin of the plague outbreak was somewhere in central Asia, with overland traders carrying it to the ports on the eastern end of the Black Sea. From there it went by ship to Italy, France, and England, reaching Scandinavia in the summer of 1349. This was not the only outbreak that had occurred in medieval times, but it was perhaps more severe this time in that urban populations were larger and transmission of the infection was rapid. The plague appeared with different symptoms at different times, and with varying numbers of days between becoming infected and dying. It is popularly thought to have been spread by infected fleas that live on rats until the rats die, after which they jump to another host—often the nearest human. That method of transmission has been validated by laboratory experiments showing rat-to-rat transmission, and ships carried rats in their cargoes. This kind of plague causes the swelling of the lymph glands, the buboes that gave the bubonic plague its name. On the other hand, some records indicate that a different form of the disease also occurred in which rats were not involved. This affliction resembled the dreaded ebola disease of hemorrhagic fever in which extensive

30.   Moberg. *A History of the Swedish People*, Vol. 1, 2005, 123–150.

bleeding occurs. It is spread as a result of personal contact, with several days between the infection and the resulting death, time enough for a ship to sail between coastal ports before the crew sickened and died.

Whatever the precise mode of infection, the plague spread rapidly from the ship of death into the whole of Scandinavia. In Norway and Sweden a third to a half of the people died within a few months. In many districts the clergy were all dead because, when ministering the last rites, they too would become infected. Magnus's family, the nobles, the merchants, and other upper-class people often escaped the infection because, at the first sign of the disease, they traveled away to some district that had not yet been struck. The peasants could not move, however, and entire villages were often wiped out, leaving the farms untended.

Early in 1350 the plague reached the Russian provinces east of the Baltic Sea and Magnus's campaign there abruptly stopped. We do not know how many men in his army were lost to the plague, but it made no sense to continue the war with the prospect of wholesale death by contagion. His support for the campaign vanished at home in Norway and Sweden. There was no longer an excess of peasants to put into the army, or to till the fields, and the tithe income was greatly reduced. Magnus was forced to pull back and try to do what he could to keep his rule intact amid the chaos in society left by the panic and death of the plague.

The men on the Norwegian Council of Nobles were even less happy with Magnus than before. The Russian campaign had failed, and the men lost there would have been useful on the farms at home now that manpower was in short supply. As in contemporary politics, the blame for the disaster must fall on someone, and it had been Magnus's war from the beginning. Although the Council was not willing to remove Magnus, they apparently decided to send him at least a symbolic message of their disapproval. This took the form of elevating Haakon, at age ten, prematurely to the official position as King of Norway. Consequently, late in 1350 at a meeting "attended by all the royal family," the nobles, with the customary shout, acclaimed ten-year-old

Haakon VI as King of Norway, with his reign beginning in 1350,[31] although the power of the position was yet to remain with Magnus until Haakon came of age in August 1355.

After a deadly year of the plague, the people of Scandinavia slowly began to put their disrupted society back together. The empty farms were given to survivors, who for a time bargained for higher wages due to the scarcity of labor. New priests were found to serve the depleted parishes, and other survivors replaced the dead officials who had governed the cities and collected the taxes. Although the tithe income was now less than before, it still was being collected, and Magnus retained it in the royal treasuries.

It is likely that when the pope learned of the failed Russian campaign he requested the return of the five-year grant of the tithe portion that he had made to Magnus to fund the war. But Magnus seems to have refused, perhaps arguing that a bargain was still a bargain. The pope was not accustomed to having his requests refused, and he reacted by doing the only thing within his power to do—he excommunicated Magnus.[32] Perhaps Magnus was not particularly devout, because the pope's action had little effect on him or on the retained tithes, for which Magnus had other uses in mind. In the next three years he began to develop a grand plan to effectively enlarge his empire and retain his control as King of Norway beyond the year 1355 when, according to the terms of the abdication, Haakon VI was to be empowered as Norway's King.

---

31. Larsen. *A History of Norway*, 194.

32. Seaver. *The Frozen Echo*, 111.

CHAPTER 3

THE PLAN, THE PROCLAMATION, AND THE REBELLION

Magnus had always been a strong-minded person and an autocratic ruler who preferred to ignore unwanted advice when promoting his projects. It is easy to imagine his state of mind when he considered the coming empowerment of his second son, Haakon. He would then no longer rule Norway without constraint. He would lose his authority to, or at least have to share it with, a fifteen-year-old youth with no experience as king. Haakon would be entering the rebellious mid-teen age when the father's ideas are often rejected just because they come from the father. And Haakon would surely be influenced by the wishes of the nobles who did not agree with Magnus on matters of royal business.

For Magnus, the situation was almost intolerable. In 1352 after busy days working on the problems in the aftermath of the plague, Magnus spent many sleepless nights considering all the possible consequences of the coming transfer of power, and what he might do to minimize its effects on his position. Certainly he would not be totally powerless, for he would still be King of Sweden. He had many friends there, and Sweden was in many respects a stronger nation than Norway, but Haakon's accession to the crown of Norway would greatly complicate Magnus's royal administration.

Those sleepless nights were not spent without results. Or perhaps with his intense concentration on the problem, a solution occurred to him suddenly as he awoke in the early dawn hours. Such flashes of insight often occur after the subconscious mind works on a puzzle while the conscious mind is rested by sleep. His brilliant idea was this: Why not send Haakon away from Norway on a mission to reactivate the lost fur trade with the Greenlanders who had migrated to the Western Lands? This would keep Magnus free to rule Norway for several years, and when the mission was over and Haakon came back— if he came back—he would be a mature man and much better equipped to take on the role of King of Norway in a way that his father could respect. The mission, if successful, would revitalize Norway's trade, which had languished for a decade since the Greenland fur trade had ceased. And above everything else, a successful mission would lay the foundation for a future empire of Norway that would dominate all the other rival nations and city-states of northern Europe.

The more he thought about the idea, the better it looked. The mission would be a strong expedition with four large trading ships, fully manned with all the men needed to complete the mission successfully. He would have the money to finance it because by 1354 all of the pope's five years of tithe money would be in the royal treasuries of Norway and Sweden. No additional taxes would be needed from the people and no contributions of money would be needed from the nobles of either country. The mission would be under Norwegian command, and Magnus knew just the right man to be the commandant. He would choose Paul Knutson, who was a widely known and respected young law speaker and administrator in Norway, and who had been a great help to Magnus in the post-plague period. The mission would be primarily a Norwegian venture. Nevertheless, the Church hierarchy of both Norway and Sweden would support the mission because, in addition to restoring the fur trade, Magnus would establish the goal of returning formal Christianity to the migrant Greenlanders, an important part of the politics of firmly re-attaching the lost trade empire to Norway. He could easily promise that the Swedish Church Archdiocese would also share in a renewed trade tax. Restoring Christianity in the Western Lands would necessitate the construction of at least one church building there, and would even improve his relations with the pope who would also benefit when the Norse population there resumed their tithing. To further solidify his support in Sweden, some of the personnel of the expedition could be Swedes, and certainly the expertise for church construction could be drawn from both Sweden and Norway where in recent decades many new substantial stone churches had been built.

The assignment of Haakon to the expedition would be a delicate matter, because sending him away from Norway might be viewed as contrary to the terms of the abdication, and Magnus did not want a confrontation with the Council of Barons in an abdication dispute. But with a little more thought, Magnus soon resolved that problem. He could legally assign Haakon to the mission at age fourteen in the year before Haakon was to become empowered as King. Then the expedition could depart in the spring of 1356 soon after Haakon's empowerment, and Magnus would point out that having the King of Norway on the mission to expand the Norwegian empire would enhance its prestige with the Greenlanders in the Western Lands and would surely contribute to the success of the mission.

Furthermore, young King Haakon would, of course, need a retinue to accompany him. The customary twelve high-ranking companions for the retinue would be drawn from the young men in Magnus's court. Although Magnus had courts in both Norway and Sweden, the retinue would of course come from Norway. Since becoming king, Magnus had always shown much favoritism for his friends in the Swedish court,[33] a practice that had contributed greatly to the displeasure of the Norwegian Council of Barons and that had led to his forced

---

33. Holand, *Westward from Vinland*. 134, 135.

abdication. But now he viewed the choice of a Norwegian retinue as an opportunity to painlessly improve his relations with the barons. Haakon himself could select his future retinue of twelve high-ranking companions from among the sons of the barons serving in the Norwegian court. Many of them would have been his friends since childhood when he was part of his mother's household in Norway. An all-Norwegian retinue would be a master stroke, for how could the Barons of the Council then object when their sons had the opportunity to serve with the new King Haakon and win fame in an adventurous conquest of new lands? Thus, Magnus envisioned that he would have the support of all the upper echelons of Scandinavian society, and a successful mission would ensure his control over Sweden and to some extent over Norway, for who would dare argue against his success?

Magnus was confident that if he handled it right, there would be no problem in assigning Haakon to the expedition as second in command. Haakon was a dynamic and intelligent early teenage young man with many friends both in and out of the Norwegian court, and as far as Magnus knew, Haakon had no particular desire to jump into the role of king of Norway just to exercise power. What fifteen-year-old fellow would not enjoy the prospect of a sailing adventure in which he would command a retinue of his friends, with all of the really hard work and difficult decisions made by some other well-respected commander? It would be a far better prospect for a teenage prince than being compelled to stay home and worry about the nation's politics and endure all those dull administrative duties. Thus, Magnus thought out his plans, and finally began to get a good night's sleep.

In the year 1354, Magnus quietly laid some of the groundwork for the combined trade expedition and religious mission by discussing the matter with the Scandinavian Church officials who then fully approved of the plan. He also floated the idea in the minds of the nobles of Norway, although no details were yet specified. Better that they think a little about the good points of the plan before learning the details. Any improvement in the trade picture would be good for the whole of Norway, but the precise financial benefits for the nobles might be hard to see.

We speculate that in August Haakon marked his fourteenth birthday with a celebration hosted by his father, to which all the young men of the Norwegian court were invited. There was much talk that evening about the upcoming trade foray to the Western Lands, who would command it, and what it would mean for the members of the court, and for Haakon himself who a year hence would be empowered as king. It was the first such social affair for Haakon. In every respect it was a great success, and it resulted in a subtle rise in the status of both Haakon and his father in the eyes of the court.

After the birthday celebration, Magnus began to put the expedition together. He identified the priests and supervisors who would be charged with building a new church in the Western Lands. He negotiated the purchase of the needed cog ships, and designated Norway's largest "Ship of the Seal" as the commander's ship.

On the third of November 1354, he sat down with Haakon and the royal scribe, Orm Østenson, to dictate the proclamation that assigned Haakon to the expedition. He had already told Haakon that if he wanted to join the expedition, Magnus not only approved, but urged that he do so. The meeting with the scribe was to formalize the assignment and to authorize Haakon to choose his retinue and any other companions he might desire. The proclamation had both legal and political implications, and would also name the commandant for the expedition. The original document of the proclamation was lost in a fire in Denmark in 1728, but a Danish copy[34] survives. Our word-by-word English translation from the part of the copy between the double asterisks is given in Appendix D. The entire translated proclamation reads as follows:

"Magnus, by the Grace of God, King of Norway, Sweden, and Skaane, sends to all men who see or hear this letter good health and happiness. **We desire that

---

34. Our source for the 1354 proclamation is *Grønlands Historiske Mindesmaerker, III*, 120-122, Copenhagen, 1838-1845. We use the first of two slightly different Danish versions of the proclamation: (1) Projekt Runeberg at http://runeberg.org/gronland/3/0145.html and (2) Dokumentasjons-prosjektet at http://www.dokpro.uio.no/perl/middelaldere/ diplom_vise_tekst.prl?b=16908&s=67&str=Po ... (accessed April 2011).

you pledge that you, on your part, take all those men who, in the choosing, desire to journey with, all from wheresoever, either they be titled or else not titled, (from) my personal attendants or else other men's attendants, and also any other men, those *who would be acceptable to us* on the 'före' (trading voyage). With that said, Honorable Paul Knutson, the Honorable Commandant, shall be, upon (his) choosing, fully authorized to name those men in the choosing (men of his choice) who would be the stouts (strong men) best suited for him, both for masters (officers) and journeymen (crew). ** We ask for the acceptance of this our command with a right good will for these matters because we do this in honor to God and for our soul's and forbearer's sake, who on Greenland established Christianity and upheld it to this day, and we will not allow it to perish in our days. Know this for truth that whichever who defies this our command (anyone who refuses to serve on the expedition) shall meet with our true harshness and shall reply to us a complete letter of resignation." Executed in Bergen, Monday after Simon and Judah's day in the six and XXX year of our rule. By Orm Østenson, our regent, sealed.

The emphasis is ours. The only mention of trade in the Western Lands in this proclamation is the "före," a trading voyage, which implies that the document was mostly a political statement intended for the eyes of the pope, and Magnus did not want to dilute its effect on the pope by emphasizing the trade motive. Notice that Haakon is not named in the proclamation. Haakon was probably seated at a table with Magnus and the scribe when Magnus dictated the proclamation; Magnus would therefore have addressed him as "you" rather than "Haakon." Nor was it necessary to name him because Haakon would be carrying the proclamation when he personally invited his young friends in the court to join his retinue. The absence of Haakon's name has led many historians to assume that the "you" in the proclamation was referring to the named "Paul Knutson." But neither the wording nor the grammar conveys that meaning. Instead, the "you" is first addressed in the present sense: "We desire that you pledge . . ." Then Paul Knutson is referred to in the future sense: " . . . Knutson . . . shall be . . . authorized to name . . . the stouts . . . " Finally Magnus returns to the present sense: "We ask for the acceptance of this our command . . . ," clearly again directly addressing Haakon, sitting across from Magnus at the table. But the "you" could only be Haakon because that name appears with a unique title: "bearded chief man Haakon" in the poetic inscription that Walter Elliott discovered on a runestone more than 600 years later at the edge of Spirit Pond in Maine.

The following year of 1355 was a busy one for Magnus, Knutson, and the others charged with making the preparations for the expedition. Then, in August on Haakon's fifteenth birthday, he was ceremonially empowered as king of Norway. The final tasks to make ready the expedition were completed that winter. At the first full moon in the spring of 1356 the fleet set sail from Bergen, and Haakon's great adventure began. As Haakon sailed away, neither he nor his father could have foreseen that Magnus's careful plans to retain his own rule were soon to encounter a snag.

Erik XII, Haakon's older brother, was perhaps a less gregarious fellow than Haakon, but not less intelligent. History reveals little about his character, but it can be inferred from the events of that time that he did not take kindly to Haakon's assignment to the expedition to the Western Lands. As the firstborn son of Magnus, he no doubt thought the assignment should have been his, and that he was unjustly being denied the opportunity to take a commanding role in the great foray to restore the trade empire. His ambitions were also frustrated in another way. Although he expected to be king of Sweden someday when his father died, Magnus was in good health and there was no foreseeable possibility of Erik becoming a king in the near future. In his mind he seemed to be stuck in some unending purgatory, with no way of getting out into one of life's adventurous main streams that would befit a king's older son.

As all the exciting preparations for the expedition were going on, Erik became continually more irritated by his perceived neglect, and decided to do something about it. He was well aware of the political forces that had been opposing Magnus in recent years. Even the grand project to bring back the trade empire for Norway seemed to have little direct benefit for Sweden, and was taking much of Magnus's attention that should have been devoted to Sweden's affairs, or so it was viewed by those in Sweden who were not his friends. Erik had come of age in 1354, and in 1356 at age seventeen he approached the Swedish nobles who were unsatisfied with Magnus, and proposed that they make him King of Sweden and thus replace Magnus, an action similar to what had happened legally in Norway in 1355 when Haakon was empowered as King.

Erik's rebellion was largely successful, but the Swedish nobles were not unanimous. Magnus had strong friends in provinces in southwestern Sweden, friends who did not forget that he had returned their coveted province of Skaane to the Swedish domain, and they insisted that he remain as their king, while the majority of Sweden accepted Erik XII. As part of the final agreement it was specified that if Erik died without issue, Haakon would be his successor.[35] This was a prescient provision and an important detail in our story, a detail that assured most of the Swedes that Magnus would not again be king of Sweden.

Although Magnus was not happy with the decision of the Swedish nobles, it was nevertheless his son who was the new king of most of Sweden. And Magnus, like his grandfather Haakon V, had a large amount of dynastic pride. He could therefore reluctantly accept the results of the rebellion and focus his attention on Norwegian affairs. How fortunate it was, he thought, that he still had a free hand in Norway now that Haakon was in the Western Lands on a mission that would probably not be completed for many years.

---

35. Larsen. *A History of Norway*, 195.

CHAPTER 4

TO NOROMBEGA
AND BEYOND

How large was Knutson's fleet of trade ships that sailed away from Bergen early in 1356, heading for the Western Lands? Historians have nothing to say on this question because documented evidence is not to be had. Later in the expedition, events tell us that the fleet consisted of at least three ships, and probably four. The commander's ship carrying Knutson and Haakon was the large Norwegian Sealship—or the "Ship of the Seal," like those depicted on the wax seals of many documents of medieval nations for which the sea trade was vitally important. One of the other ships carried Haakon's retinue of twelve young men plus a crew of five. All of the ships were loaded with tools, provisions, and other supplies, including trade goods. The ships also carried construction tools and equipment, because Knutson knew they would be spending winters on shore, and in addition to the construction of a stone church building in which to worship when establishing Christianity, they would need houses to live in during the construction process. For navigation purposes, they may have had crude magnetic compasses. Certainly they also had sextants for measuring the altitude of the noontime sun, from which their latitude could be determined after making the correction for the sun's varying northerly position that depended on the time of year.

Their first port of call was at Reykjavik in Iceland. There they picked up current information about the East Greenland colony that was still occupied, and anything the Icelanders could tell them about the Western Lands. Their next port was at the settlement of Brattahlid in the East Greenland colony, Figure 3, at the head of a long fjord where Erik the Red had first settled more than three hundred years earlier. Significant numbers of people still lived there, although the trend of colder summers was making life more difficult for the farmers who were often short of winter hay for their sheep, cattle, and horses.

The East Greenlanders had not been as directly involved in the fur trade as the men of the now abandoned West Greenland settlement. But a few of the Western Settlement men now lived at Brattahlid, and Knutson obtained valuable information from them. Although no maps have survived to our time, Knutson's subsequent actions suggest that he surely had obtained simple maps of the old trade empire in which the coasts and the major river routes used by the traders were depicted. Even the Icelanders could have given him such maps, for Icelanders had also traded and lived in the Western Lands, as noted in the Icelandic *Landnámabók* account of Ari of Holum who lived for a time on the coast of Labrador and who also traded in Ireland (see Appendix B).

Although the fleet no doubt touched land more than once on the voyage to the southwest from Greenland, they probably did not find a significant population of ex-Greenlanders until they arrived in New England. Norsemen could have been living at one attractive site on the northeastern coast of Massachusetts at an enclosed bay, or a "hop" as it was called by the Norse, where the current city of Newburyport is located. This bay, connected to the sea by a shallow channel across a long sandbar, matches the description of the place where Thorfinn Karlsefni spent a pleasant winter and traded very profitably with the nearby Indian population, as described in one of the earlier Vinland

Voyages about AD 1015.[36]

However, the site for which there is the most convincing evidence of a Norse settlement is on Narragansett Bay in Rhode Island. Giovanni Verrazzano, a sixteenth-century sailor, was the first European explorer of that time to visit this location. He was sailing for the king of France, and spent fifteen days at Narragansett Bay in 1524. He described the natives there as being taller than his own sailors, and as having white or bronze complexions. They called their home Norombega, Figure 4. These people were the descendents of a mixed Norse-Indian population whose ancestors were the migrant Greenlanders who had resettled with their fur-trading friends almost 200 years earlier.

Even the name of their settlement clearly betrayed their Norse ancestry. When the name is parsed, "Nor" is "North," and "om," or "um" in many old maps, is a Scandinavian preposition meaning "past" or "beyond," and "bega" is likely a native pronunciation of "vegr" or "vegé" in the native dialect that had no "v" sounds, similar to Japanese, for example. "Vegr" has the meaning of a "way, direction, road." Allowing for the word inversion, there is a similar modern English idiomatic expression of extreme distance in which a New York City resident might say: "Chicago is 'way beyond' Pennsylvania." Similarly, if a fourteenth-century Norwegian mentioned "Norumvegé, the country way beyond the North," he would have understood "the North" to be the well-known Norse territories of Greenland and Iceland. An alternative interpretation is possible if the word "bega" represented the Norse word "byggja," a dwelling place or home. The two words have similar pronunciations. If so, the settlement would have been called Norombyggja, the "dwelling place beyond the North." In the 1600s, faint echoes of Knutson and Haakon's years at Norombega are found in the names of two chiefs of the descendents of the fourteenth century Norse and Indian residents of the Narragansett Bay area, Magnus and Canonicus. These names, as anglicized from the Indian pronunciations, show the cultural impact of Paul Knutson's expedition and the Catholic Church structure that he built high on a

---

36. Kunz. *The Sagas of Icelanders*, 669–671.

peninsula in what is now Newport, Rhode Island.[37]

When the fleet arrived at Narragansett Bay, Knutson and Haakon were given a mixed welcome by the Norombega residents, some of whom had bitter memories of the oppressive tax and tithe requirements that had marked their last years on Greenland fifteen or twenty years earlier when they were starving because of the cold summers. The younger Norse people had not experienced those times. They were curious and were properly impressed by the ships, larger than any they had ever seen, and by King Haakon's outgoing and cordial interest in their village and its history. In the end it was the novelty of the expedition that carried the day because it was an exciting interruption in the rather routine lives of the Norse youth. Then with friendly Haakon as Knutson's ambassador, the population as a whole was won over to the prospect of future regular trade visits by ships from Norway, and by the prestige of having an established church at Norombega.

---

37. In Chapter 9 of the book *King Philip's War* by Ellis and Morris (New York: Grafton Press, 1906), the authors tell of events during King Philip's War during the winter of 1675–1676. The early New England colonists were at war with the native Narragansett peoples of what is now Rhode Island. In footnote 12, the authors discuss a defeated leader of the Narragansetts known as Magnus. Queen Magnus was the sister of the great Niantic chieftan, Ninigret. She was the widow of Mexanno, a Narragansett chief whose father was the chief Canonicus, and she became chief of the Narragansetts after the death of Mexanno. Her last stronghold was the "Queen's Fort" on the Patuxet River west of Narragansett Bay where she was killed by Major Talcott and his forces in 1676. A contemporary colonist, William Harris of Providence, in 1676 wrote of her personal character: "A great woman; yea, ye greatest yt ther was; ye sd woman, called ye old Queene." *The Lands of Rhode Island*, Sidney S. Rider, 240, 241, 1904, also 155, 156 of the same book, 2009 edition (La Vergne, TN: General Books, 2009). The names of the chiefs, Magnus and Canonicus, suggest the influence of the Knutson expedition of the 1360s and the resulting interval of the practice of the Catholic Christian faith. "Magnus" was from the Norse King Magnus, and "Canonicus" is a Latin term for "one living under a rule" in the context of the Catholic Church. The meaning of "Canon" that applies best here is "A member of a religious community living under common rules and bound by vows." These names were not derived from the English colonists, because the English were not Norse in the seventeenth century, nor were they Roman Catholic, thanks to King Henry VIII. The connections of the Iroquois, Algonquians, and other tribes to their ancestral Norse, as proposed by eight earlier writers, are discussed in an article by Erik Drilen ("Maybe the Vikings made it Norse America." Minneapolis *Star Tribune*, 24 May 1992, 21A).

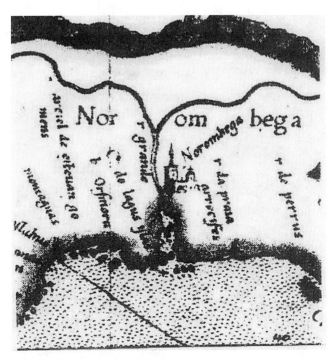

FIGURE 4: "Norombega" as first reported by Verrazzano after his visit in 1524. This is a magnified portion of the Mercator world map of 1569. It shows Narragansett Bay with a stylized Newport Tower on the east side of the bay.

Following the getting-acquainted negotiations when the expedition arrived late in 1356, a site for the new church building was selected. The church would always be occupied by priests or other people serving Church functions. Consequently, the decision was made to place the building where it could also serve as a lookout tower to alert the general populace to any new ship arrivals. The chosen site was therefore on the crest of land on a peninsula with clear views of Narragansett Bay to the west, and the open sea to the south and east. It is there at a site in the town of Newport, Rhode Island, that the first church ever built for Christian worship in North America can be found. We know it as the Newport Tower,[38] Figures 5 and 6. Hjalmar

---

38. C.F. Waidmann. "Who Built the Newport Tower? The cartographic evidence." In
   The Newport Tower, Arnold to Zeno. (Edgecomb, ME: New England Antiquities Research

Holand analyzed the details of the construction to show that it was a Catholic church,[39] but the age of the structure has not been reliably measured (see Appendix A).

FIGURE 5: The Norombega church in Rhode Island, now known as the Newport Tower. In the completed church there would have been an ambulatory, a larger wooden structure that surrounded the central stone tower. Postcard photo.

Commander Knutson was told by the resident Norsemen that, although life was usually peaceful in Norombega, there had been occasions when roving groups of Skraelinges had attempted to rob and carry off some of their people. With that in mind it was decided to make the church building a fortified structure into which the priests and others could retreat if threatened by hostile strangers. There was a precedent in Scandinavia where similar fortified churches had been constructed in politically unstable districts. The plan of the structure

---

Association Monograph, 2006), 67–71. This monograph is a thorough summary of the controversy surrounding the Newport Tower, and Waidmann's maps make an invincible case for a construction date before the English colonial times. H. Holand in *America: 1355–1364* (New York: Duell, Sloan and Pearce, 1946) thoroughly analyses the tower structure, and cites convincing evidence that it was in fact a church.

39. H.R. Holand. America 1355–1364, (New York: Duell, Sloan and Pearce, Inc. 1946), 59–93.

therefore consisted of two upper stories supported on eight sturdy stone pillars. Access to the first upper floor would be by a steep set of wooden steps that could be easily defended. That floor would have the conventional altar for worship rituals, and a fireplace for heating and cooking. A few splayed ports in the stone walls would be made for observations and defense. The top floor would have the sleeping quarters and space for storing supplies. Like other thirteenth-century churches built in Norway and Sweden, there would be an ambulatory around the base, a wooden structure to enclose the lower stone pillars with room for ceremonial gatherings of larger numbers of people.

FIGURE 6: View of the Norombega church interior showing the altar table location with the reliquary chamber beneath the slots in the wall into which the altar table was fitted. L.J. Westin photo.

After the important decisions of building location and design had been made in the winter of 1356–1357, the arduous preparations for the construction began. It was necessary to collect and, when needed, to shape the stones for the pillars, walls, and foundations. The men had to find beds of oyster shell to be burned into quicklime for the mortar. Trees had to be cut, split, and shaped for the beams, roof, and other parts of the structure. Most of the year 1357 was devoted to these preparations before the construction could begin. The men who did this work were experts in their crafts. Haakon and his retinue from the court would have been above such tasks, and would have been doing other things.

Our translation of the Spirit Pond inscription given in Chapter 10 suggests that Haakon and his friends explored the trade empire, no doubt leaving Knutson to supervise the construction of the stone church at the expedition's base. The inscription says: "...Haakon discovered a ring (circle) by being able to go (to sail) to the west on lakes of the trade empire." This enables us to speculate that early in 1357, Haakon, his retinue, and a small force of other armed men took two of the afterboats that were carried on the trade ships and set out on a journey of trade and exploration following a large "ring" route that was found on one of the crude maps made by the much earlier Norse traders. Their boats were the equivalent of the large freight canoes of the colonial French and British traders of the eighteenth century, but were adapted for sailing on the open seas if necessary. Each afterboat could carry as many as fifteen men plus trade goods and provisions to supplement the usual diet of fish caught and smoked while en route. Haakon planned to explore, trade for furs when the opportunity occurred, and return to Norombega before the summer was over.

It was late in March when Haakon's mini-expedition set out sailing up the Hudson River, following one of the trade routes to the west that had been used by the Indians for thousands of years and by the Norse for at least two hundred. They soon reached the confluence of the Mohawk and the Hudson Rivers, Figure 7.

From there they followed the Mohawk westward up to its head-waters where they portaged into Lake Oneida, then down its outlet stream to the Oswego River and into Lake Ontario. Their plan, as they looked over their trader's map, was to follow the shore northeastward to the great river flowing out of the lake. But the traders' lore on the map told of a giant waterfall at the west end of this great lake. The summer was young, and Haakon decided to depart from the plan and see the falls. They then put up sail and moved westward along the Ontario coast until they arrived at the mouth of the Niagara River.

They rowed seven miles upstream before they were stopped by a series of turbulent rapids. Although they could row no farther, they could hear the distant roar of the falls, so they moored the boats, left two men on guard, and followed an old trail up the river.

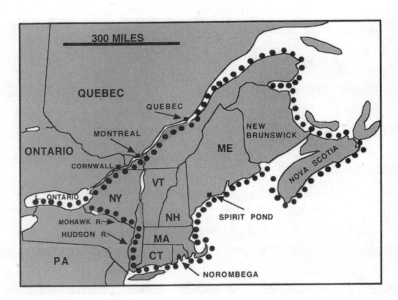

FIGURE 7: Western Vinland showing Haakon's hypothetical first exploration to find enclaves of Norsemen who might be persuaded to resume the fur trade.

They found not one, but two great cataracts pouring over a 160-foot-high cliff into the river below. The plunging water generated a deafening roar and a billowing mist that occasionally obscured part of the view. None of the men had ever seen anything like it. The old traders had not exaggerated the story, and his seeing the falls considerably increased Haakon's faith in his map. But they had no reason to linger, and soon returned to the boats and made good time down the river and back to the lake.

Again they set sail. Driven this time by westerly winds, they moved rapidly back eastward along the coast, passed the Oswego River outlet and then northward to the islands at the entrance to the St. Lawrence River. Downstream under sail, it was a short run to the vicinity of the modern-day city of Cornwall. There on the south side of the river they visited a village with a substantial number of Norsemen living with a few Indians. Their houses were the typical communal longhouses that were common in Norway until the thirteenth century. Arlington Mallery made a twentieth-century study of the descendants of these people, known to later European settlers as the nations of the Iroquois Indians.[40] He found that the Iroquois language was remarkably similar to Old Norse in many word usages, although the rules of grammar were different. According to Mallery, the difference may have developed because children of Norsemen with Indian wives would learn simple grammar from their mothers when first learning to speak, but later in childhood many of the words learned would be those of their fathers.

Mallery's most remarkable observation was made when he was watching ironworkers who were building a bridge near Sherbrooke, Quebec. He asked the boss of the project where he had obtained all those square-jawed Norsemen. The boss's response was that all the men were genuine card-carrying Iroquois Indians from the St. Regis reservation.[41] The Iroquois are widely known as ironworkers in the construction industry, and for some of the Iroquois, the genetic imprint of the medieval Norse is quite clear, even after more than 600

---

40. A. Mallery and M.R. Harrison, *The Rediscovery of Lost America* (New York: E.P. Dutton, 1979). Arlington Mallery makes a convincing case for the settlement of a substantial number of Norse along the St. Lawrence River. In his typical scholarly approach, Mallery made a study of Norse loan words that are found in the Iroquois language. He says that a "significant percentage" of words were derived directly or indirectly from the Scandinavian language, 184–188. One of his cited examples is the root word "ok," "auk," or "auka," which had the same use in the Norse for "and," "but," "as," "when," and "also." Although the Norse and Iroquois grammars are not the same, he says the many Norse loan words imply the acquisition of Indian wives by Norse settlers who lived permanently with the tribes on the St. Lawrence River. The genetic characteristics of the Iroquois tribes of that area also suggest Scandinavian ancestry. Mallery personally observed construction crews of Mohawk Indian ironworkers in Quebec whose stature and "square-head" appearance more closely resembled Scandinavians than Indians. He describes the unique communal longhouses of the Iroquois that were in use as late as AD 1800. They consisted of long, narrow halls with hearths at intervals along the centerline and seats and sleeping platforms along the sides. These longhouses were similar to Norse houses in Scandinavia prior to about AD 1200.

41. Ibid., 54.

years of life in the Western Lands.

Haakon's visit was probably a profitable one from a trading stand-point, and he would have been able to report to Knutson the discovery of another Norse group living in the old trade empire. They then sailed on down the river with a brisk wind at their backs. At the sites of modern-day Montreal, Trois Rivieres, and Quebec, they also encoun-tered Norse settlements, where smaller rivers entered the wide St. Lawrence and gave traders access to the surrounding country. At Quebec the St. Lawrence slowed and widened still farther as it entered the Gulf of St. Lawrence. From that point, they sailed the coastline of the present day Maritime Provinces, then back along the rugged Maine coast to New England and Norombega, completing a poetic "circle to the west" with a bit of the summer of 1357 to spare.

CHAPTER 5

THE BETROTHAL OF KING HAAKON VI

Early winter, 1358. Commander Paul Knutson was always a meticulous planner and he was sensitive to the delicate relationship between himself and Haakon, who was both his king and his subordinate. Knutson did not want Haakon to become bored due to lack of a suitable activity for him and his retinue. Fortunately, circling part of the trade empire the previous summer had occupied Haakon and his men during much of the sailing season; during the winter when travel was limited, the young men had been happily occupied in socializing with the young women of Norombega. Although much more exploration of the empire remained to be done, Knutson decided that in the coming summer, Haakon and his retinue should sail back to Norway to report to Magnus on the progress made by the expedition toward their two goals of restoring the fur trade and bringing formal Christianity to Norombega. They would carry with them all the trade goods that could be collected from the Norombega region, and Haakon could spend the early part of the summer assembling the cargo. Haakon had already obtained a significant quantity of furs the previous summer, and he welcomed Knutson's proposal.

In the spring Haakon joined his retinue on their ship and they toured the coast of Vinland wherever trade contacts could be made with Norse or Indians, bargaining for furs and deer hides. The tour made them well acquainted with the coasts to the northeast, and by midsummer on their return they had an impressive quantity of traded goods. Before leaving for Norway they added to their cargo a few casks of the much-appreciated wine from the famous Vinland grapes of the region, and also some large slabs of birds-eye maple, a wood coveted by Scandinavian woodworkers who supplied the nobility with exceptionally beautiful pieces of furniture.

A few weeks after midsummer, they set sail for Norway. In this voyage they took a direct course for Norway without a stop at Greenland or Iceland. In the late summer days of weak westerly winds the voyage required about two months. When they arrived at Bergen, they received a royal welcome indeed, for the value of their cargo was by itself great enough to fund a good part of the expedition's cost, and Magnus could not have asked for a better report. Haakon was received like a hero, and his friends in the retinue were all given a similar enthusiastic reception by their families of the court. They all looked ahead to a few months of the good life of the court before they returned to the expedition in the following spring of 1359.

Magnus was surely pleased with Haakon's cargo and his report on the church construction and the exploration. However, Magnus was only willing to briefly discuss Erik's rebellion . Haakon could see that the subject was painful, and that Magnus had something else on his mind. Magnus's concern was that in Haakon's absence, no arrangements had been made for his future marriage. But now that eighteen-year-old Haakon was available, Magnus decided to start negotiations with King Valdemar Atterdag of Denmark to arrange a betrothal of Valdemar's daughter, Margrethe, to Haakon to maintain the dynastic line of Folkung rulers to which Magnus belonged.

Magnus had more than just a dynastic motive for making this move. Relations between Norway and Sweden on one hand and

Denmark on the other had always been somewhat tense, with a continuing dispute over the Swedish province of Skaane, a dispute that Magnus thought he had settled by purchasing that province from the weak Danish king who preceded Valdemar. But rumors had it that the aggressive Valdemar would like to retake Skaane, and that he might go to war to do so. Magnus hoped that a betrothal with Haakon and five-year-old Princess Margrethe would appeal to Valdemar's dynastic pride also, and would keep Valdemar from any hostile actions to take Skaane in the future. Therefore, soon after Haakon returned to Bergen, Magnus dispatched a trusted lieutenant to Denmark to explore the betrothal idea. It was well into the dark of winter by the time word came back from Denmark that Valdemar would seriously consider Margrethe's betrothal to Haakon, and would welcome a visit to seal the arrangement. With short days and long nights, little winter traveling was normally done in Norway and Denmark. But in *The history of Hâkon VI Magnusson's coinage*: (www.dokpro.io.no/umk_eng/myntherr/hvi.html), it is noted that Haakon and his father and mother made an "unusual winter journey" in the 1358–1359 winter to Denmark where the betrothal was finalized. The marriage was to take place in the spring of 1363 when Margrethe would be ten years old.

The unusual journey to Denmark surely occurred during the winter, because Haakon desired to return to Norombega in the spring as soon as sailing weather permitted. Consequently, it was not long after the betrothal that he gathered his crew and retinue, and together they sailed away. His early departure is inferred from the fact that he was not in Scandinavia when his brother, Erik XII, and Erik's wife and infant son all died suddenly in June 1359. The "children's plague" killed them, it was said.

According to the agreement with the Swedish nobles at the time of Erik's rebellion, Haakon would become King of Sweden if Erik died without an heir. But Haakon was no longer in Scandinavia, so no acclamation could occur at that time. Instead, to make the situation clear to any others who might want to claim the crown, the Swedish nobles, with the approval and consent of Haakon's mother, Queen

Blanche,[42] issued a proclamation stating that Haakon would become King of Sweden. But a proclamation written on parchment is not a shout of acclamation, and the acclamation that started Haakon's brief reign as King of Sweden was delayed until he later came back to Norway for his scheduled wedding.

As far as we know, Haakon's return to Norombega was without any difficulties, although sailing against the brisk winds of the prevailing westerlies in spring probably kept him and his men at sea until after the midsummer solstice. When they arrived at Norombega, the news of Erik's rebellion surprised Knutson, but being a Norwegian himself, he was not greatly concerned. However, he had to refocus on the goals of the expedition. His schedule for these goals now had to take into account the date of 1363 for Haakon's wedding, which, Knutson feared, might not leave enough time to accomplish the last of the expedition's tasks: contacting the Norsemen living on the plains far to the west.

On his return, Haakon noted that the church building was well on the way to completion. The builders bragged to him that their church would last a thousand years, and it should, for they were doing a very careful job. The speed of construction at that point was limited by the time needed for the mortar to set and gain strength after each course of stones was mortared into place. Not all the wooden parts and furnishings were yet made, and with these details in mind, Knutson told Haakon that he expected the church to be completed in the following summer of 1360. As Christmastide approached, they decided to plan for a special mass in the incomplete church to celebrate their progress. They had built the ambulatory, the skirting wooden structure that surrounds the arches, which provided a roofed shelter and a larger gathering area for services. The weather was mild and the event was successful, partly because after the mass a lot of the excellent Norombega wine was consumed at the Christmas feast of 1359.

The feast capped the fourth year of the expedition, and Knutson

---

42.   Moberg. *A History of the Swedish People*, Vol. 1, 2005, 118. The significance of Haakon's mother giving her consent is that Haakon was absent and that she stood in for him and legally committed him to accept the Swedes' request that he become king of Sweden.

noted that their success in restoring the trade and establishing Christianity in the trade empire seemed assured, although some problems remained. In arranging a trade commitment with the resident Norsemen, he found that they tended to be more independent-minded than he would have liked. They had no strong chieftain as their leader who could be depended on to make sure the furs were available in future trading. This was a problem that Knutson expected to be remedied by the presence of the Church and a yet-to-be-named member of the hierarchy of priests who would serve Norombega. He knew that a similar arrangement was in place on Greenland, where a dynamic priest, the Norwegian Ivar Bardson, had been assigned to Greenland to strengthen Church administration and to ensure the payment of taxes and tithes.[43]

Although Greenland had a bishop, half the time he preferred to remain in Rome rather than live on Greenland, so far from any center of culture and power. So the faithful Ivar lived on in Greenland for more than twenty years until 1364, and in the absence of a resident bishop, Ivar was responsible for collecting both tithes and taxes. That made him very unpopular with the Norse citizenry, who were only too willing to migrate to the Western Lands when the opportunities arose. But at Norombega, Knutson was not aware of Ivar's problems, and his faith in the ability of the men of the Church to carry on their duties at Norombega was unchallenged. The visible symbol of this authority was the impressive stone church, now nearing completion. With everything going well, Knutson began to think about his next task: to measure the extent of the lakes of the trade empire.

---

43. Gullov. "Natives and Norse in Greenland," Chapter 24 in *Vikings, the North Atlantic Saga*, Fitzhugh and Ward, eds. (Washington: Smithsonian Institution Press, 2000), 321.

CHAPTER 6

TO THE END
OF THE LAKES

Prologue: The poetic Spirit Pond inscription in Chapter 10 gives the east–west and north–south differences in daghrise units between Haakon's last winter camp in Maine and the location of the great storm on Hudson Bay where his retinue was lost. The north-to-south distance could easily have been obtained with an early version of the sextant that was used to measure the altitude of the noontime sun. There was no similarly easy way to measure the westward distance coordinate, which would have been estimated by dead reckoning. This reckoning could have been done best if the westward distance were traversed in one or more approximate straight lines. This chapter describes just such a probable exploration on the Great Lakes that would explain how Haakon was later able to estimate the distance coordinate of twelve daghrise westward to the location of the great storm. This exploration probably occurred the year before the voyage to Hudson Bay, which is dated to the midsummer sailing season of 1361. 1361 corresponds to the first year number (Haakon's age) on the Spirit Pond inscription, Chapter 10, when Haakon's retinue was lost off the south coast of Hudson Bay and Haakon was yet twenty years old.

Still winter, early in 1360. Although he would not have admitted it, Knutson was becoming tired of the administrative part of his command. He felt it was no longer necessary for him to closely monitor the church construction. The Church officials could finish it and carry on the missionary work among the Norombega people. For some time he had felt an obligation to develop a more accurate knowledge of the extent of the trade empire than was available in the crude maps he had obtained from the old traders on Greenland. The maps showed relative positions of lakes and rivers, but details were lacking and they had no scale for distance. After some discussion with Haakon, he decided to use the coming sailing season to see how well the old maps depicted the western extent of the big lakes of the trade empire, and in doing that they would generate a scale of distance for their best map, and would also evaluate future trade possibilities at old trading sites.

Norse merchants always spent more time traveling on the sea than on the land. Their fundamental unit of distance measurement, even when on land, consisted of the distance covered in a good half day of steady sailing—twelve hours with no stops for provisions, no interruption by storms, no portages. This unit was the daghrise, which was equivalent to about seventy-five miles. On land, experienced travelers could estimate daghrise distances by the number of days required to get from point A to point B, and by allowing for any difficulties or delays along the way. If possible it was always better to travel in a straight line on water to obtain the most accurate measurement. But the traders' routes on Knutson's old maps were never really straight lines. Nevertheless, Haakon noted that there was a trade route from Norombega to the western end of the lakes that consisted of approximate straight segments heading either north or west. Knutson decided to explore that route the coming summer. They would trade along the way and, on the return to Norombega, Haakon would have an estimate of the westward length of the Great Lakes of the trade empire and a distance scale for the maps. They would also have a better idea of how far they would have to travel to reach the Norsemen on the plains to the west, the area known to the Icelanders and Greenlanders as the Graenaveldi.

When the April sun began to warm the land, Knutson and Haakon set sail with his retinue and other selected men in two fully loaded afterboats. They started on the route that Haakon had taken two years earlier, first a smooth sail westward to the mouth of the Hudson River, a distance of about two daghrise, then a long stretch straight northward up the Hudson. They passed the outlet of the Mohawk River, Figure 8, continued on their northward course, and portaged into Lake Champlain, which is drained to the north by the Richelieu River that empties into the large St. Lawrence River. When they reached the St. Lawrence they had traveled northward a distance of four daghrise.

At the confluence of the rivers, Figure 8, they turned westward and, traveling upstream, they soon reached the mouth of the Ottawa River and the future city of Montreal, a trading site both then and now. From that point their course up the Ottawa River was almost due westward to the Indian village of Mattawa at the mouth of a small river, an added westward distance of slightly less than five daghrise. Continuing westward, they pushed onward from Mattawa up the small stream to its head, then over portages and through small lakes to the site of the modern-day town of North Bay on the eastern shore of Lake Nipissing. After a short day's sailing, they reached the outlet stream at the southwest end of Nipissing. Aided by a friendly Indian guide, they then worked their way downstream through an interlaced maze of narrow lakes to the site of the modern-day village of Pickerel River on the shore of Georgian Bay. This large bay is separated from the main body of Lake Huron by a row of islands. At Pickerel River they had added somewhat less than two more daghrise to the westward total.

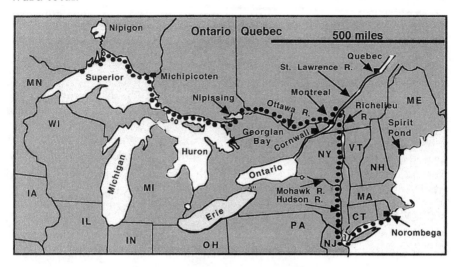

FIGURE 8: Knutson and Haakon's hypothetical westward exploration to measure the extent of the lakes of the trade empire, and to evaluate trade possibilities. This measurement also would have made possible a later estimate of the westward distance coordinate of the great storm. Explorations like this one and that in Figure 7 are implied by the Spirit Pond inscription, which says that "Haakon discovered a ring by being able to go (sail) to the west on the lakes of the trade empire."

It was a great relief to be able to again travel with the wind in their sails as they worked their way westward along the shore from Pickerel River to the short river and rapids that connected Lake Huron to Lake Superior, the largest of the lakes of the trade empire. There at the site of the future town of Sault Ste. Marie, named by the later French traders, they noted another westward addition of slightly less than three daghrise. Their course then turned almost northward along the Superior shore. A few days of leisurely sailing more northward than westward brought them to the site of a small village the Indians called Michipicoten. There they found a small group of people mostly of mixed blood living with a few old Norsemen.

These men still spoke much Norse and still traded in the region. They told Knutson and Haakon that there was a good river route from their village to a trading port that was four daghrise north of Michipicoten on the arm (James Bay) of the great inland sea. The inland sea that we know as Hudson Bay lay another four daghrise northward beyond the port. They had visited and traded there every year in the old times, until the Greenland trading ships no longer came. Since then trading only with the Indians was much less profitable, and they were happy to know that Knutson would now trade for their furs, and that, as Knutson told them, the annual visits of trading ships would come again. All the participants were pleased with the trades at Michipicoten. Then the explorers resumed their voyage, now again westward on the north shore of Superior shown on their crude map.

The shoreline was smooth for a time, but at a distance slightly less than three daghrise to the west from Michipicoten they encountered a complicated shore not shown on their map. First they entered Nipigon Bay. At the west end of Nipigon Bay they encountered another village like Michipicoten. Here, too, they found a few old resident Norse traders among light-skinned descendents of earlier Norse. These old men also had nostalgic memories of annual voyages when they would travel up the Nipigon River to the lake with the same name and from there by river down to another port on the great inland sea where they traded their furs. Again, trades with Knutson were welcomed, but the explorers did not linger this time. Sailing out of Nipigon Bay they entered Black Bay, circled it, and entered Thunder Bay.

By the time they got beyond this complex shoreline, it was clear that they had passed the northernmost part of the lake and it appeared to them that it might require three more days of good sailing before they would reach the western end. But the time had come for a decision. It was now well past midsummer and it was imperative that they return to Norombega before the storms of fall and winter began. Travel on the lakes was never at a steady pace. Weather conditions were not always favorable, and now with fewer supplies they would need to stop more often to hunt or fish. Consequently, they wisely abandoned their goal of reaching the extreme end of the lake and set their course back eastward along Superior's north shore.

It was their first summer in the continental interior, and summer storms there can be much more frequent and violent than at Norombega. Although in their afterboats they were seldom far from shore, a sudden violent storm could still have caused them serious problems. In the typical severe thunderstorm, the sky fills with an advancing wall of dark, billowing clouds with powerful winds beneath it. When the storm reaches the observer, being on the water is an invitation to disaster. It would not have been unusual to experience such a storm on their return journey in July and August that summer of 1360, with a corresponding delay to repair damaged boats or equipment. Their decision to end their westward exploration when they did was therefore a wise one.

None of the details of their exploration either westward or eastward are truly known. Nevertheless, we know that their long journey on the lakes was successful. We speculate that they learned from the old traders at Michipicoten that their village was directly south of the southern coast of Hudson Bay. Consequently, the westward distance measurement they made to Michipicoten and Nipigon Bay in 1360 enabled Haakon later in 1362 to estimate the westward distance to the location of the great storm that they were to encounter during the 1361 summer on Hudson Bay. Haakon and Knutson had traveled nearly the entire extent of the trade empire's lakes, a distance of approximately fourteen daghrise westward from Norombega, and they would have once again returned with modest cargoes of valuable furs and hides. That winter at Christmastide the celebration of their successes in the newly completed church was a really memorable event.

Now, it was only necessary to make a trade contact with the Norsemen on the Graenaveldi to reach all the expedition's goals. Many of the furs of the Greenland fur trade during the previous 200 years had come from the Graenaveldi, the name applied by the Icelanders to the almost treeless plains of the Dakotas and western Minnesota. The Norse who lived there and collected the furs made an annual journey of almost a thousand miles down the Red and Nelson rivers to the

Indian village on Hudson Bay, the site of the eighteenth-century York Factory trading post of the Hudson Bay Company. There they met the Greenland ships and bargained their furs for trade goods. Those Norsemen lived much farther westward than Knutson and Haakon had gone in the summer of 1360. Now that he had a scale of east to west distance for the trade empire, Knutson knew that his task of getting to the Graenaveldi, arranging for future trade, and then returning to Norombega would be a time-consuming effort. In this final endeavor, we shall see that fate would not be as kind to him and Haakon as it was in the first four years of the great adventure.

CHAPTER 7

THE STORM

It was well past the winter solstice and the Christmastide celebration in the winter of 1360–1361. The men who had been building the church in the summer were now working at a slow pace making wine casks and other containers for carrying goods and supplies back to Norway when the expedition would be completed. Winter was also a time for the men to socialize with the residents of Norombega, and the young women of the settlement enjoyed the competition of the more numerous Norsemen for their affections. Although Commander Knutson and King Haakon were not entirely immune to such attractions, they nevertheless maintained a substantial social separation from the men, as was appropriate for the commanders of the expedition.

In one of his occasional conferences with Haakon on the progress of the expedition, Knutson summarized where things stood: Most of the goals had been attained. Trade possibilities with the Norsemen in the Norombega area had been demonstrated by Haakon's return to Norway with his valuable cargo of furs two years earlier. Christianity had been introduced to Norombega, and the foundation had been established for a continuing presence of the Catholic Church with all of its political and trade implications that would be important to King Magnus in his dealings with the pope. Everything seemed to be going well.

Knutson had also been giving considerable thought to their final task—arranging for future trade with the Norsemen out on the plains of the Graenaveldi, the source of a large portion of the furs that had come to Norway in the preceding years of active trade. But now Haakon's royal wedding was scheduled for the spring of 1363. Consequently, Haakon would have to return to Norway in the preceding sailing season. It was clear to Knutson that the expedition would have to be divided to permit Haakon's timely return, which would occur before Knutson could complete his contact with the men on the Graenaveldi. However, Haakon was reluctant to return to Norway earlier than necessary in 1361. Consequently, Knutson decided that Haakon and his retinue should continue their trading activity until their return in 1362.

The Graenaveldi colony was, of course, much more isolated than Norombega. From what Knutson knew from the old trader's map, it might be possible to reach the Graenaveldi by traveling westward overland from the great Lake Superior, but it was an ill-defined river route. It therefore appeared to Knutson that the best way to go there would be to take three ships, sail to the port and trading post on Hudson Bay near the mouth of the Nelson River, and go directly up the river on the main trading route to the Graenaveldi, Figure 3.

Haakon could supervise the trading that they would do on the outward-bound voyage to the trading village at the mouth of the Nelson. He would take two ships immediately back to Norombega before the sailing season ended, and sail back to Norway the next summer in 1362. Knutson would leave the Sealship at the port near the Indian village over the 1361–1362 winter while he and his men would go southward up the river. It would be late in the season and they would go as far as possible before stopping for the winter along the way. After arranging for future trade the following summer, he would return to the Sealship and sail back to Norombega late in 1362. If, however, he was delayed an unexpected length of time in making his contacts with the Norsemen on the Whetstone River, his ship would return to Norombega in 1362 without him. He and his men would then find their way overland by way of rivers to Lake Superior and return to Norombega by the same lake route that they had traveled in 1360. It was, Knutson thought, a good plan.

Thus it was that Knutson's fleet of three ships departed from Norombega early in the spring of 1361, leaving his fourth ship at the base on Narragansett Bay. Knutson and Haakon were on the commander's cog ship, the Sealship, which carried a priest and a full complement of tradesmen plus armed Norsemen who were prepared for travel in the wilderness. A second cog ship carried a large quantity of supplies and trade goods and many armed men, who were also well equipped for a wilderness foray. The third and slightly smaller ship carried the twelve-man retinue of King Haakon and a crew of five, plus trading supplies.

The long route took them eastward and northward beyond Vinland and around Whitemansland, with occasional stops along the way to bargain for furs at the old trading sites on their map. Their onshore trading was usually brief because that curse of the arctic summer, the black flies and mosquitoes, made life miserable at some locations. Eventually they rounded the northernmost headland of Whitemansland and sailed southward along the coast and into James Bay, where they hove to briefly at the Moose River Indian village, located northeast of Michipicoten where they had traded the previous season. It occurred to Haakon that they had now again nearly completed a great "ring" around the trade empire. After a short trading session, they sailed back northward out of James Bay, and it was well past midsummer when they resumed their course toward the west along the south coast of Hudson Bay, Figure 3.

The little fleet was sailing slowly westward with little wind, three ships abreast with the Sealship in the middle, on one especially hot and humid day. Haakon had made one of his navigational sightings of the sun's elevation above the horizon at noon, when the man on the lookout reported an unusual line of clouds in the distance to the west. Unbeknown to the men on the Sealship, a tongue of cold arctic air was sweeping down from the north. On the line separating the colder air from the summer warmth a great storm was born.

At first the Norsemen could see only a solid line of clouds on the western horizon, and a thin, high cloud began to dim the sun. The line soon became a thick band and the clouds darkened. In the distance the faint muttering of thunder could be heard. The clouds then boiled upward and rose in a towering black mass to swallow the afternoon sun, as the storm announced its attack with never-ending lightning bolts and ever louder thunder. The ship captains ordered most of the sails to be furled, leaving only enough sail to maintain headway. At the base of the approaching black mass an ominous, smooth white wind cloud formed where the cold and heavy rain-soaked air poured down. With hurricane force, the air under the wind cloud roared eastward, blasting the little fleet with a nasty foretaste of the raging storm that quickly engulfed them.

When the wind cloud struck, the three vessels still had a little sail up, and they nearly capsized in the blast. On the ship carrying Haakon's retinue, the wind tore away what sail they still carried, together with most of its rigging. That somewhat smaller ship had also taken on a lot of water when it heeled over in the first blast of wind, and it now wallowed uncontrollably at the mercy of the wind and waves. The other two ships did not suffer major damage, but in the raging storm they could not steer across the wind to help their comrades without themselves capsizing. Haakon and Knutson on the Sealship could only watch the ship through the driving rain and the flying spume, torn from the wave tops by the roaring wind. Each towering wave poured more water over the gunnels, settling the ship deeper and deeper into the sea. Suddenly, there was a great crash as a lightning bolt struck and shattered the mast of the stricken ship. With the lightning flash, a great shout went up from the Sealship, half oath, half desperate appeal: "Beatae Maria!"

When their eyes recovered from the blinding flash, they saw the last of the doomed ship disappearing beneath the waves, carrying with it Haakon's twelve companions and their crew of five. Haakon and the other men on the Sealship were numb to the shock of the loss of their friends while they struggled to keep their own wave-battered vessel afloat in the storm. But after a time, the lightning bolts ceased, the wind abated, and the storm passed onward to the east. In the evening after the storm the two ships hove to along the shore, and their crews did what they could to repair the damage to rigging and sails. As darkness fell, the deaths of his loyal companions struck Haakon to the heart, and left him in a dark mood from which he did not quickly recover.

With the next dawn, the two ships sailed onward. Many more slow late-summer days were spent on their westward course before they arrived at the trading post near the river's mouth on the southwestern corner of Hudson Bay. There they anchored just offshore from the Indian village sitting at the edge of the estuary. After performing the usual introductory ceremonies with the village Indians, Knutson began to make preparations for his journey to the south, and Haakon started the ritual of trading for what they found to be an abundant supply of furs. Here there were no resident Norsemen. Those Norsemen had preferred the life on the southern plains to the isolation of the frigid winters on Hudson Bay. Despite the difference in language, Haakon's trading with the Indians was not difficult, because after two hundred years or more of trading with the Norse, many Norse trade words remained embedded in the native language. Knutson was even able to glean some specific information about the southward route up the river. He would have been told of locations on Lake Winnipeg where other Indians lived, knowledge that Knutson needed because he intended to winter over somewhere on that lake in the company of friendly Indians.

At this point, the expedition was divided, and likewise our story must take two paths. Before accompanying Haakon on his return to Norombega and, at last, back to his royal place in the history of Norway, we will follow Knutson on his epic journey into the heart of the continent where he inscribed a runestone three miles northeast of Kensington, Minnesota.

Chapter 8

A SEARCH AND A MASSACRE ON THE GRAENAVELDI

One of the most interesting parts of our story is Commander Paul Knutson's unsuccessful search for the Norsemen on the plains of the Graenaveldi, for which documented information is found only on the Kensington and Spirit Pond runestones. Although there are gaps between the known facts, the saga would not be complete if we failed to describe a partly fictional reconstruction of that search. We have good reasons to believe that Knutson's objective was to contact the Norse on the Graenaveldi near Big Stone Lake to restore their trade, just as we infer that he and Haakon had been doing with the Norsemen in Vinland and the Great Lakes region.

Some things we know. From the mention of the Sealship and daghrise coordinates in the Spirit Pond inscription, we believe that the expedition was sailing westward on Hudson Bay in 1361 at the time of the storm. From the Kensington runestone inscription, we know that in 1362 thirty Norsemen were traveling eastward in western Minnesota. The leader of this force was almost certainly

71

Commander Paul Knutson, who would not have delegated the respon-sibility of arranging for future trade to someone else. And it would have been Knutson who erected the runestone on Runestone Hill northeast of Kensington, Minnesota, one daghrise south of a lake where ten of his men had been killed. The inscription also tells us that they had left ten men to guard their ship over the winter, fourteen daghrise beyond "this island," that is, northward at the port on Hudson Bay. These distance amounts probably combine Knutson's own estimates with the north-to-south distance measured by his observations of the noontime sun's altitude with his sextant, giving their travel distance in terms of latitude changes.

Our conclusion that Knutson failed to find any Norsemen on the Graenaveldi is based on the direction of his travel when the massacre occurred and the Kensington runestone was inscribed. If he had found the Norsemen he was searching for, he would have made the trade agreement and immediately returned northward to his ship. But we assume that his search was unsuccessful because he was traveling generally eastward toward Lake Superior when the massacre of his ten men occurred. This suggests that he had overstayed his time during the search. He knew that he would have been unable to return northward that summer before his Sealship left the Hudson Bay port, and that he would have to use the alternate Great Lakes route for his return to Norombega.

Other facts that contribute to our reconstruction include the observed seasonal hydrology of the Red River, and knowledge of the Graenaveldi terrain and river courses. The terrain is very important, and for this we are particularly indebted to the Google Earth™ infor-mation system and the 2003 *DeLorme Atlas and Gazetteer* for Minnesota. The known facts are stitched together using logical suppositions as to how Knutson would have made the critical decisions that ultimately resulted in the inscription on the Kensington runestone. Our recon-struction is as plausible as careful logic can make it, and we begin this last part of the story at the trading site at the port on Hudson Bay, Figure 9, after Haakon departed to sail back to Norombega late in the summer of 1361.

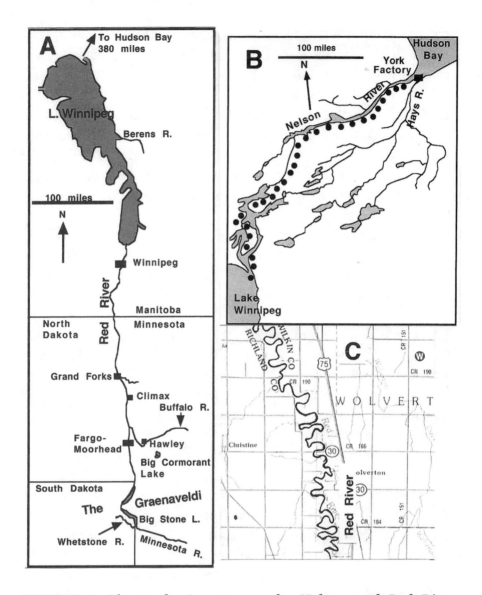

FIGURE 9: The traders' route on the Nelson and Red Rivers between Hudson Bay and the Whetstone River area on the Graenaveldi. A: From the Graenaveldi to Lake Winnipeg. B: Lake Winnipeg to Hudson Bay. C: Oxbows south of Fargo. Squares are one-mile section lines.

Knutson expected to reach the Norsemen on the Graenaveldi with no difficulty in the summer of 1362. He also assumed that he would return to his Sealship late in that same summer before its captain would have to begin the voyage back to Norombega. He had left ten armed men with the crew to guard the ship at the site of the later York Factory post, but it would not have been possible to house the men on the ship during the frigid winter. Therefore, as told on the Kensington runestone, as soon as Knutson departed up the river, the remaining men began the construction of a large house next to the ship in which to spend the winter.

Each of the two ships that survived the storm had contributed one of their two afterboats for the use of Knutson's force of thirty men. These boats satisfied Knutson's needs very well because they could be either rowed or sailed, and, as noted in Knutson's and Haakon's earlier explorations, each one could also carry a quantity of trade goods. Although the days of summer were becoming shorter, Knutson could still expect eight weeks of friendly weather before the 1361 travel season ended, and he expected to be halfway to the Graenaveldi before winter put a stop to travel. So on a warm day in late summer the miniature fleet of two afterboats pushed off, raised sail, and headed up the broad Nelson River.

Although occasionally interrupted by rapids that had to be portaged, much of the Nelson River, Figure 9, runs slowly, and by using their sails they made rapid progress upstream. Knutson easily covered the 380 or more miles from York Factory to Lake Winnipeg before serious cold began, and he probably sailed well southward on the lake. Where they spent the winter can only be guessed, but the mouth of the Berens River is a good possibility. It was a natural location for Indians to have lived, and Knutson, with a little trading, was well prepared to negotiate with the Indians to help him and his men through the winter. And they would have needed to trade for a few helpful things—like fur coats to wear, because they knew the winter would be cold. And indeed it was—like no winter they had ever seen before. With the help of the Indians, they were able to accumulate a supply of smoked fish and migrating geese and ducks for winter fare, but after that the cold came and never seemed to end. It was only by making a successful hunt later amid the snow that they avoided serious starvation.

After that cold and tedious winter, the spring of 1362 finally arrived. Knutson was pleased with the distance covered from the port to their winter camp, and he thought the Graenaveldi venture was off to a good start. He and the men were all anxious to get going again, and when the ice on the lake began to break up around the first of May, they loaded their supplies and equipment into the boats and traveled southward through scattered ice patches to the mouth of the Red River. That point is about 350 miles north of the Whetstone River area on the Graenaveldi.

They found the Red River still in its flood stage, which was an unexpected benefit. The Red River is not an ordinary stream. It meanders back and forth across the bottom of ancient Lake Agassiz, a lake formed when the great ice-age glaciers blocked the river's drainage to the north thousands of years ago. The land is almost as flat as a tabletop, and over nearly all the 350 miles to the Whetstone as the crow flies, the path of the Red River when the water level is low consists only of looping oxbows.[44] Later after the spring floods subside, these oxbows more than double the travel distance on the river.

But with the winter snows melted and the river in flood, the high water was now spread out widely over the adjacent prairie. The river had become a narrow lake with almost no current at its edges. On that lake they could sail rapidly southward in a straight line, and they would have been largely ignorant of the looping oxbows that remained almost unseen beneath the surface of the flooded land. Knutson was to bitterly regret this ignorance later that summer when the flood had subsided. In the month of May, however, they saw only a narrow lake ahead. So they set their sails to catch the brisk winds of spring blowing across the plains, and moved rapidly southward, sailing not far from the shoreline where the water was hardly moving. Stopping briefly only to sleep and hunt migrating geese, they arrived at the south end

---

44. *Minnesota Atlas and Gazetteer*, fourth edition (Yarmouth, ME: DeLorme, 2003), 50, 58, 68, 80, 90.

of Lake Traverse, the head of the Red River drainage, after only fifteen days on the river.

To this point, Knutson's map had served him well. At Browns Valley, the short portage into a south-flowing stream that took them into Big Stone Lake was the first portage they encountered that season. Traverse and Big Stone lakes are the remnants of the great River Warren, fed by the rapid melting of the monstrous ice sheet that lay across Canada to the north and formed glacial Lake Agassiz long ago when the melt water could only flow southward. The two narrow lakes now straddle the continental divide between the Arctic and the Gulf of Mexico. Again, travel was easy as they sailed the twenty-five miles to the south end of Big Stone. There, they found the mouth of the Whetstone River, Figure 9, which according to the old traders on Greenland, was the portal to the fabled Graenaveldi where life was easy and the furs were abundant. At this point, Knutson had no reason to doubt the "life was easy" part of the legend, for his journey up the Red River had not been difficult. The Red River is on the main flyway for ducks and geese between the Gulf of Mexico and the summer nesting areas in the arctic, and the hunting had been superb, with roast geese often enabling his men to sleep with full stomachs.

The Whetstone River was not a large stream, but its spring flood had not yet subsided and the current there was still significant. Consequently, progress up the river was slow. As they worked their way upstream, men were assigned to scout along the banks a short distance away, because Knutson expected soon to encounter the houses of the Norse residents. After a few miles they did encounter the first house, but it had been abandoned. Likewise the second, the third, and the fourth, all either burned down or in an abandoned state of ruin. Grimly, Knutson pushed on upstream, hoping against hope that they would find some Norse still living there.

Eventually they arrived at what had been a local Thing, the meetinghouse for the neighborhood. There they found ten holestones at the edge of the slope high above the stream, stones that had been used to tie up the Norsemens' dogs during meetings, or perhaps to hold banners on occasions of celebration. Surprisingly, the house was still largely intact, with a well-constructed roof that diverted most of the rain that was falling when they arrived at the site. For the first time in many weeks they had a roof over their heads and a fire on the hearths to warm themselves on that rainy night.

Knutson was bitterly disappointed. The Norsemen that he had expected to find had obviously been gone for some time. He decided to lay over for several days and take advantage of the meetinghouse while fishing in the stream and hunting in the surrounding prairie to replenish their supplies. All the men favored this because they needed the uplift in morale that such activities could give them. While they were enjoying the pause in their upstream travel, a small hunting party of Indians came down the Whetstone River and appeared at their camp.

Hungry for information, Knutson signed a welcome to the strangers, and initiated a sign language interview to find out what they knew about the missing Norsemen. These Indians had apparently had only slight contact with the missing residents, but they said that the "bearded ones" who had lived there had gone away "down the river." Knutson could learn nothing more from them, if in fact they knew any more than they had said by using signs. Before they moved on, they did convey the idea that not all the Indians were friendly, and that some tribes were on the warpath at that time.

Much of the Graenaveldi was located to the east on the Minnesota side of Big Stone Lake, away from the Whetstone area, as Knutson knew. Why the Norsemen had left the Whetstone River area was a mystery, but he desperately wanted to believe that there were still Norsemen somewhere in the region who could be convinced to resume the fur trade. If so, he was thinking that perhaps those who had gone "down the river" had left to join those east of Big Stone Lake. After the Indian hunting party had departed, he discussed the situation with his men and laid out a plan to explore downriver to the east in the hope of finding the missing people in a different part of the region. The next day, they reversed course and made their way down the Whetstone, now flowing more slowly, and retraced the long stretch of the stream to its outlet where it joined the headwaters of the stream we know as the Minnesota River.

The Minnesota River begins as a series of shallow lakes and swamps on the wide bottomlands where the torrent of the great glacial River Warren had swept through as it drained the great ice sheet to the north. In these broad areas of swamps the flow is now hardly detectable in the summer. They entered this mosquito-plagued stretch of water soon after they left the Whetstone River, and it was obvious that the swampy shores of the stream would not have attracted Norse settlers. So Knutson knew that he would have to find a stream like the Whetstone coming into the river from the north. For that his map was no help. It only showed the Minnesota River flowing far off to the southeast, a direction Knutson really did not want to go, Figure 9.

Nevertheless, they continued down the swampy river, threading their way through the reeds and cattails, and fighting mosquitoes all the way with never a decent place to spend the night. Toward the end of the third day, they were rewarded by finding the mouth of a stream flowing in from the north, now known as the Pomme de Terre River. This river was named by the later French traders, who knew a good fur-producing area when they saw one. With great relief, Knutson left the swamps behind and found a high and dry camp for the night along the stream.

The Pomme de Terre flows slowly across the prairie, and their progress northward upstream was easy. Three days later near the present town of Morris they found two houses that were vacant but quite intact. Another day northward and they reached a lake on which they found two more vacant houses. In Knutson's mind the question echoed again and again: Why had these houses been abandoned, and where were all the people on the eastern part of the Graenaveldi? But he was reluctant to give up the search. They continued northward up the river for another two days and arrived at Barrett Lake.

Here they found a large tribe of Indians living on the shore. Among them were a few light-skinned mixed Norse/Indian people who were able to use a little Norse in conversing with Knuston and his men. They told Knutson that the scattered bearded Norsemen had all been forced to join one of the larger tribes to defend themselves against hostile attacks. Where they had gone, no one knew, and Knutson finally was forced to accept a crushing disappointment. Norsemen were no longer living on the Graenaveldi, and the mission to restore the fur trade with the Norse people of that region had failed.

After a little trading and fishing to rebuild their supplies, they began the long journey back to the Sealship. Their return downstream was now more rapid, but the mood of the expedition was somber as they struggled back through the swamps at the head of the Minnesota River. They were a bit more cheerful when sailing northward on Big Stone Lake, and then, after the short portage, northward on Lake Traverse to the first small flowage of the Red River, also now known for a few miles as the Bois de Sioux River. Ah, yes, the French fur traders of the eighteenth century, like the Norse traders of the thirteenth century, had been everywhere.

But very soon, Knutson and his men began to encounter the series of oxbow loops in the river that had been masked by the high water of the spring flood. Between Lake Traverse and Lake Winnipeg there are more than 400 long oxbows. What had been an effortless sail southward during the flood was now a painfully slow process, with two miles eastward and westward on the loops for every mile gained toward the north. The men rowing the boats had to work, for now the lazy current of summer was of little help, and with the twists and turns of the stream, the use of the sails was not possible.

As the days went by, Knutson frequently re-estimated their arrival time at the distant port on Hudson Bay. The oxbow loops never ceased, and when the number of loops approached a hundred, it became clear to him that it was unlikely that they would be able to get to the York Factory port before his Sealship set sail for Norombega. To continue northward became a gamble he could not afford to take. If they were even a day late, they would be forced to spend another winter in the bitter cold, isolated and starving at the port, and would then have to come all the way back southward to take their alternative river route to the Great Lake Superior, an option they had seriously considered the year before at the start of the expedition to find the Graenaveldi. Even if they survived another winter in the arctic, their return to

Norombega would then be delayed another year or more.

On their way southward a few weeks earlier, Knutson had noted a substantial river that flowed in from the east to join the Red River at about the point on his trader's map that marked the somewhat uncertain route to Lake Superior. The mouth of that river, the Buffalo River in Figure 10, was now only a day or two ahead. He announced his decision to the men. When they came to the Buffalo River, they would go to the east.

From his map, Knutson could not learn much about the river route eastward to Lake Superior. The trader who had drawn it might have done so based on another man's description, for it lacked details. The map showed only a southeastward connection to a large river that flowed even farther to the southeast before the route branched off upstream to the northeast to reach the western end of Superior. Their course on the Buffalo River began close to the indicated spot on the map, and Knutson was confident that they had started eastward at the correct point.

In tracing Knutson's course from the Red River to Big Cormorant Lake, Figures 9 and 10, we initially follow the route that scholar Hjalmar Holand proposed.[45] Holand's logic was based in part on his assumption that the holestones found at water's edge along the route were mooring stones. However, we know now that an isolated mooring stone on a lake or stream would be ambiguous. It could have been used as a mooring stone, but might have been only a Norse property boundary marker, as we learned from our fieldwork described in Chapter 12. In our proposed route, the mooring stones are incidental to the logic governing Knutson's route decisions. In his mind it was always a question of "Which is the route to the southeast?" or "Have we crossed the drainage divide to an eastward flowing stream yet?" We suspect that Knutson often sent out scouts on foot when the choice of the course was in doubt. They would make a quick exploration or would climb the high hills to look over the country ahead. In the fourteenth century the Graenaveldi was largely free of trees because of frequent prairie fires, and hilltops would always have given

45. Holand. *America 1355–1362*, cover map.

the scouts long views of the terrain ahead.

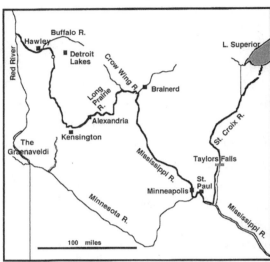

FIGURE 10: Right: Knutson's probable route across central Minnesota to Lake Superior. Left: Details of the route from Hawley to Big Cormorant Lake and beyond. The Pelican River flows due southward for twenty-three miles to join the Ottertail River after leaving Prairie Lake. Squares are mile sections.

After leaving the Red River they rowed upstream on the Buffalo River, going back and forth on oxbow loops for forty miles and traveling generally toward the southeast. Eventually when they climbed out of the flat Lake Agassiz basin, the oxbows ceased and the course of the river became less erratic. Fifteen miles and a day or more later, they found that the river turned and came from the northeast, contrary to the general direction shown on their old map. They had no other choice, however, and continued reluctantly northeastward to the site of the modern-day town of Hawley, Figure 10. Two miles northeast of Hawley there is a mooring stone that suggests a possible stop of Knutson and his men for the night. Another mile beyond that point a small stream, Hay Creek, comes from the east to join the Buffalo at a point where the Buffalo comes down from the north.

The upstream northward direction of the Buffalo River at that point did not fit the southeastward course shown on their simple map, and Knutson decided to take the Hay Creek route toward the east because it more closely conformed to the map. That was a fateful decision. Because he chose Hay Creek, we now have the Kensington runestone. But the old traders would have followed the Buffalo's temporary upstream swing to the north before it comes back to its head in Tamarack Lake, nine miles northeast of the modern-day town of Detroit Lakes. Four short portages to the east of Tamarack and the traders would have been in Shell Lake, the head of the Shell River. The Shell flows eastward and becomes the Crow Wing River, which enters the Mississippi River west of Brainerd. From there onward Knutson's map would have been quite accurate, with the Mississippi flowing far to the southeast and the old traders then taking the St. Croix River northward to Superior. But for Knutson at that time and place, Hay Creek it was. Guided more or less by the logic of lakes and streams on a current map, we continue to follow Knutson and his men.

Upstream on Hay Creek and four miles to the east, they reached Stinking Lake, where Hjalmar Holand later reported another mooring stone that tells us of a possible campsite. Hay Creek flows into Stinking Lake from the southeast, the direction favored by Knutson, of course. But the small Hay Creek was not an easy route for Knutson's two afterboats to follow. Using Google Earth™ imagery to follow the creek southeastward to its head, we see that the Hay Creek of 2011 becomes increasingly shallower and difficult to traverse. In the fourteenth century, however, streams like Hay Creek would have consisted of a long series of beaver dams and ponds. The ponds were easy, but the boats had to be dragged up and over the dams again and again, a tiresome way to travel.

Beyond the head of Hay Creek and after four more miles of laborious portaging between small lakes and ponds, Figure 10, they would have reached Leaf Lake, separated by a gravel bar from Big Cormorant Lake, Figure 11, one of the largest lakes they had seen since leaving Lake Winnipeg. They crossed the gravel bar and immediately hove to at the northwest corner of the lake not far from one of two rocky island reefs. After starting to carve one mooring hole in a boulder near the waterline, the man with the chisel changed his mind. He moved to an adjacent boulder at a better location to the left and succeeded in finishing a suitably deep hole there. After securely mooring the boats, they set up a camp a short distance up the hill from the shore among the scattered oak trees that dotted the slope.

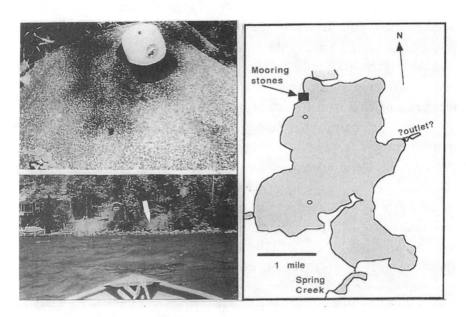

FIGURE 11: The massacre site on Big Cormorant Lake. The mooring stone is one of two adjacent boulders with holes, now on private property. It is half hidden in the bushes at the tip of the white pointer. Johnson photos, 1996.

It was a good opportunity to rest and replenish their supplies of smoked fish for the next long leg of their journey. The next morning ten of the party remained in camp repairing gear and smoking fish caught the afternoon before, while Knutson and nineteen other men took the boats out fishing. They found the best fishing in a large bay on the far side of the lake out of sight from the camp. Their catch was excellent, and they noted a small stream flowing southward out of the bay.

Late in the day, the sun was low and the wind was calm when

the men in the boats rowed the four miles back across the lake to the camp. As they approached the mooring stone, now in the shadow of the hill, there was no usual cheery greeting from the men on shore. In the eerie silence a terrible foreboding gripped the men in the boats. When the first boat hit the stony shore, the man at the bow jumped off and ran up the hill to the camp. With a shout of horror and a curse he announced that all ten of their comrades were dead. All the men, in shock, gathered around the bloody corpses. Clearly there had been a battle and the outnumbered Norsemen had lost. What weapons they had were now gone, together with the smoked fish and the equipment for the camp that had been unloaded from the boats.

For a short time they stood, stunned by the gruesome deaths of their friends. Then as the twilight deepened, Knutson decided that they should spend the night in the boats on the lake. The Indians could not be far away, and, with no boat visible at the camp, the Indians probably knew that they had not killed all the Norse on the lake that day. Although a night attack was not likely, the moon was full and an attack was a possibility. So they retreated to the boats and anchored on the glassy lake offshore.

No one slept that night, and there was much discussion as to what should be done next. They were still in danger from a force of hostile Indians, somewhere to the west of the lake. They all had their own weapons in the boats, but had no suitable tools to enable them to bury the dead men. Even if they had proper tools, burial would have been time consuming and would have left them exposed to another attack when daylight returned. Yet, to leave their dead exposed and untended was unthinkable. A burial in the lake was the only practical thing to do.

When the night was over and the long dawn of summer made it possible to see what needed to be done, they salvaged what they could from the camp, wrapped each dead man in his cloak, and added a few stones to make sure his body stayed down in the lake. It was all a painful and heartbreaking process, and when the corpses were being loaded into the boats, a firesteel fell out of a pocket of one of the dead men and fell unnoticed between the mooring stone and an adjacent boulder. They rowed the funeral boats out well away from shore, and as each dead man was lowered into the water and disappeared beneath the surface, their priest uttered a prayer for his soul. No one spoke as they took to the oars again. As the sun lifted above the eastern horizon, they slipped out of the lake by way of the little stream flowing out of the big bay where they had fished the day before.

Every man on the expedition carried his own firesteel. Hardly any other aspect of life in the wilderness was more important than being able to start a fire. But no one would have been starting a fire between two boulders at the water's edge, and the probability of losing a firesteel when starting a fire is also extremely small. The loss of the dead man's firesteel is the only reasonable explanation for its presence between the two boulders. As documented by Holand,[46] young ten-year-old E.O. Estenson found that firesteel when fishing from the rocks in 1870. He and his family were traveling through in a wagon, looking for land on which to settle, and there were no settlers living anywhere in the area at that time. The firesteel is now in the Runestone Museum in Alexandria, Minnesota, and it confirms Hjalmar Holand's identification of Big Cormorant Lake in Chapter 11 as the site of the massacre described on the Kensington runestone.

---

46.   Ibid., 139.

CHAPTER 9

PAUL KNUTSON AND THE KENSINGTON RUNESTONE

It would not be fair to say that Knutson was lost. He was, however, frustrated and confused. After struggling with the two boats up Hay Creek, and now leaving Big Cormorant Lake by way of such a small stream, he knew they were not on a route frequently taken by traders through the wilderness. His goal was to travel southward and eastward to reach the large river, the Mississippi, shown on his simplistic map. We would not expect any major departure from those two directions. On the cover of his 1946 book, *America, 1355–1364*, Holand proposed a route that departed from the lake on its east side. This questionable route reached the Kensington area after many irregular changes in direction, one of which persisted toward the west.

Big Cormorant Lake in 2011 is separated from Holand's proposed pond outlet on the east side by a wide tree-covered ridge with summer cabins on it. That possible exit point would not have been obvious to Knutson. He may not have known about it, and there is a simpler route that the Norsemen probably took. They had fished all day in the

87

bay at the south end the day before, and Knutson would have been looking for an outlet and would surely have seen the creek flowing out of the lake at that time. His hope now was that he might have crossed the drainage divide, and that this small creek, Spring Creek in Figure 11, might lead them to an eastward-or southeastward-flowing river, a tributary to the major river on his map, the Mississippi.

So Knutson and his men slid the boats down Spring Creek for three miles to Pelican Lake, Figures 10 and 11. They toured around the shore for six miles and found a substantial outlet stream known today as Pelican River. After a southward mile of easy downstream rowing, they were on Lake Lizzie. The Pelican River flows west one mile from Lizzie to Prairie Lake where it again flows southward. From that point they enjoyed a twenty-seven-mile downstream float due southward to where the Pelican joined the Ottertail River, which came in from the east, Figure 12. The Ottertail continued another five miles to the south before its course turned decisively westward as far as the scouts could see from the best high points they could find—a disappointment for everyone.

Knutson's disappointment in the Ottertail's westward turn was lessened when the scouts reported that, at the turning point, they looked eastward and could see an almost continuous array of small lakes with short portage connections. These lakes stretched eastward for five miles to the larger Swan Lake. Knutson was reluctant to abandon the easy river route, but there was no other choice, and eastward was the direction he wanted to go.

A day later they were on Swan Lake with a nice camp on high ground. Swan Lake lies in a trough, and connects easily by small lakes to Mineral Lake two miles to the south. Two more portages, each a stone's throw wide, and they reached the interconnected Ten Mile Lakes. Knutson did not know it, but the outlet to the southeast was the head of the Pomme de Terre River, small but quite floatable.

Five more easy miles, a little to the east but mostly to the south, and they were in Pomme de Terre Lake, which stretches another four miles southward. The Pomme de Terre then resumed and they made good time with the current for another five miles southward to Barrett

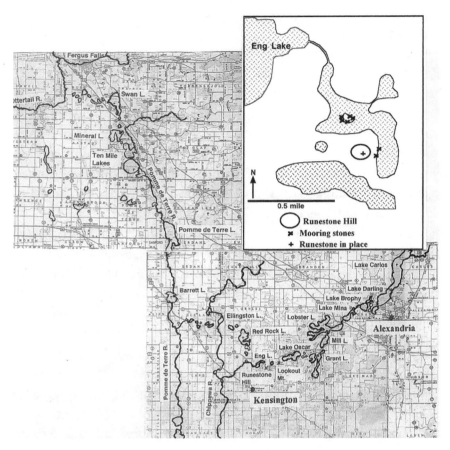

FIGURE 12: Knutson's route from the Ottertail River to the Kensington area and beyond. Inset shows Runestone Hill and vicinity with small lakes as of 1362.

Lake. There Knutson was surprised to find the same tribe of Indians they had encountered just a few weeks earlier during their search for the vanished Norse residents. He instantly realized that following this stream farther southward was useless. The tribe was well acquainted with the region, however, and they told him that if he wanted to find a stream flowing to the east, he would have to travel through the lakes to the east for at least ten days, beginning at a point a short distance to the south. They did not linger at Barrett Lake. Three miles to the south, the scouts hiked a mile up a tributary creek and reported a scattered array of lakes extending farther eastward, and Knutson then ordered an eastward course.

After five miles of intermittent portaging between small lakes they arrived at Ellingston Lake. Ellingston is only a mile wide, and a substantial river, the Chippewa, enters from the north and leaves to the south. But Knutson's course was eastward as well as southward, so he rejected the Chippewa River, putting all his bets on eastward travel by lakes. Again he sent out the scouts. After three miles and two long unwelcome portages the boats were in Red Rock Lake. They seemed to have found a good place to camp because 600 years later a shoreline rock was reported there with the runic date of 1362 carved on it. Rowing their way through a jigsaw pattern of bays and points, they reached the southern end of the lake.

They found no easy exit. The scouts reported that two half-mile portages would put them on a small creek that flowed out of a modest lake to the east. Half-mile portages were not welcome either, but they had to be done. The men pulled the boats up the creek over beaver ponds and dams to mile-long Eng Lake. Its map outline is a coiled rattlesnake in the act of striking eastward. An easy sail to the nose of the snake, followed by a short portage up and over a broad ridge, and they were in a small narrow lake where in the distance at the south end they could see a bare grassy hill, another high elevation from which to survey the surrounding countryside. And in their view just in front of the hill was a small tree-covered island, untouched by prairie fires and offering the promise of a campsite with welcome shade from the hot summer sun.

The first boat pulled up to the island shore at a likely mooring spot, and the bowman gave a great shout. He had found a mooring stone already in place. That was a pleasant surprise. Although they had usually moored both boats at the same mooring stone, this time, the bowman in the second boat joked that he might as well find another one for himself, so the second boat moved on and suddenly, he too shouted that they had indeed found another one. This novel development excited them all, and they disembarked and set up a camp with great enthusiasm. Knutson detached himself from the camping activity, and made a systematic search around the edge of the three-acre island. He found three more mooring stones. In the remaining daylight, men in one of the boats decided to do a little fishing. They had hardly started trolling along the shore when again the shout was heard—they had found another mooring stone, at the base of the hill.

The men were excited, and Knutson was overjoyed. All those mooring stones could only mean that they were now on a main route used by the old itinerant traders who had traveled across the country-side, and that somewhere not far to the east there would be a good river route to join the streams shown on their trader's map. Knutson's optimism was contagious, and the men could now hope for an end to the wearisome portaging. That evening, Knutson decided they would lay over on the island long enough to catch and smoke enough fish to last for a few weeks of rapid and uninterrupted travel. He knew that they would have to winter somewhere in the Great Lake area, and it was important to quickly find some of the old Norse traders still living on Lake Superior to host him and his nineteen men before the winter put an end to travel.

The following day while the men were fishing, Knutson made a closer inspection of all parts of the island. Seldom had he seen so many boulders in one location. Knutson had in mind a runestone memorial for their ten massacred comrades, but not just any stone would do. At last he found the kind of stone he was looking for. Among the bushes in a jumble of boulders at the east side of the island, there were two that had smooth surfaces within which the crystalline quartz contained grains of fine sand, so small that only the young men with good eyes could see them. They were graywacke stones, stones so hard that only the most carefully fire-hardened chisels could be used to inscribe the runes. But once inscribed, the runes would last forever.

Although Knutson briefly considered the possibility of putting the runic memorial inscription on one of the two stones and leaving it in place on the island, he quickly rejected that idea, because there the runestone would become hidden amid other rocks and bushes. The high hill to the south was the only place for the stone, because he could see that the hill was covered by grass, having been kept cleared of trees and bushes by occasional prairie fires, and travelers would not fail to climb the hill to look around the countryside.

FIGURE 13: The Kensington Runestone as displayed in the museum at Alexandria, Minnesota. The rigorous translation is discussed in Appendix E. Photo by L. J. Westin.

Knutson, always the wise commander, had made sure that among the chosen men with him was a man whose trade had been a stone mason and runesmith, and that man carried with him the tools of his old trade, the best chisels that the blacksmith's skill could produce. Knutson put him to work on the boulder. The runesmith saw that the stone seemed to have natural cleavage planes. He went to work, first carefully testing the stone with his chisel, and then trying to cleave the stone. He was successful in cleaving away much of one side of the

TRANSLATION OF THE RUNESTONE INSCRIPTION

1: 8 Gøtlanders (Swedes) and 22 Northmen on

2: [this] back-taking journey from

3: [?] Vinland extreme west [West Vinland]. We

4: hove to anchorages by 2 skerries one

5: days journey north from this stone.

6: We were also fishing one day. After

7: we came home found 10 men reddened

8: with blood, and dead. AV[e] M[aria]

9: Salvation from evil fate.

10: [A] troop [of] 10 men have a large winter-house to look

11: after our ship 14 days journey

12: from beyond this island. Year 1362.

boulder, creating a large flat face. The runesmith then chiseled away some of the lower third of the stone, making the stone less heavy and easier to be erected with the lower third set into the ground.

Knutson approved the stone and after telling his man what information he wanted on the stone, he sat down and dictated it a few words at a time. The runesmith then slowly and carefully inscribed the lines of words in runes across the stone. The first nine lines he placed on the broad face; the last three on the side. The runesmith was indeed an expert, for he did not bother to cut horizontal guidelines for each neat row of runes, as was often done. Knutson wanted to tell a short story on the stone in which the main event was the deaths of his ten men back on the lake with two islands. He assumed that the future readers of the inscription would be the Graenaveldi Norse traveling or trading in the area.

No person is named in this inscription. If the commander had been one of the victims, he surely would have been named, which is consistent with our plausible assumption that the Norwegian, Paul Knutson, was in fact leading this foray through central Minnesota. He did not personally carve the inscription, but he was surely its author. It was indeed a fine memorial stone. In twelve lines of the inscription, Knutson piously honored the lost men. He alluded to the purpose of their journey (taking back, or regaining the trade), and stated the trade empire context: the West Vinland origin of the expedition and the location where they left their ship over the winter on Hudson Bay. We give a complete line-by-line and word-for-word transliteration and translation in Appendix E.

Knutson planned to erect the memorial stone on the hilltop, and in line twelve the direction indicated for the journey (from beyond this island) was on a line northward from the hilltop. Any Norse fur trader who read the inscription in the years that followed would have known that the author of the inscription had left his ship on Hudson Bay, far to the north. The following day they ferried the runestone around the hill almost to the south end of the little lake, and two of the stoutest men carried it up to the top. They set it into the ground facing southward on a slight slope just south of the crest of the hill.[47] It was the logical place where a traveler would certainly see it as he climbed the hill to look around the countryside after he moored his boat to one of the stones on the southeast side. Knutson could not have known that, as the centuries slowly passed by, frost heaving of the soil on the slope would tilt the stone over on its face and leave it buried beneath a tree where farmer Olof Ohman found it in 1898.

All good things come to an end. After a few lazy days on the island with full stomachs every night, Knutson's band of survivors reloaded the boats to prepare for the next portage. Less than a mile to the northeast of Runestone Hill, the scouts had visited a still higher hill,

---

47. This hillside location south of the crest of the hill is consistent with a remark made on page 97 of Holand's 1940 book, *Westward to Vinland*, in which he says that digging was done at the site "on the hillside." It is also consistent with an old newspaper picture and one other from the Ohman family file. It is not consistent with another family file picture, probably in the 1940s, showing a site on flat ground, where a brass plaque is located a few hundred feet to the west of the hilltop.

now called Lookout Mountain, the second small "x" in Figure 12. From that hilltop they could see a wide pattern of lakes to the east, and somewhere among those lakes there would be the start of an eastward-flowing river. Where the next portage took them is difficult to say—possibly by way of Solem Lake and then a portage around Lookout Mountain to Lake Oscar.

After an easy sail of almost three miles eastward on Oscar, they had three very short portages into Blackwell Lake, then Grant Lake, and through the site of the modern-day Holmes City northeastward into Mill Lake. From Mill Lake it was a carry of about 200 yards into Lobster Lake. From Lobster, an outlet stream flows into Lake Mina and on into Lake Brophy, and their long ordeal of portages was done. From there the stream flows through small lakes and into Lake Darling and the larger Lake Carlos, near Alexandria, Minnesota.

Hjalmar Holand suggested that they might have left the Alexandria neighborhood by way of Geneva Lake and upstream to Jessie Lake where there is a mooring stone.[48] From Jessie there is an eastward route with long portages to the Sauk River and the Mississippi. However, by the time Knutson reached the Lake Carlos outlet, it would have been obvious that they had found a substantial stream, the Long Prairie River. They would have followed it downstream to the east, and it is unlikely that they were ever aware of the upstream Geneva-Jessie route and its many portages. The Long Prairie River runs generally eastward for thirty miles with increasing flow before turning northward to join the Crow Wing River, which again flows eastward to its confluence with the broad Mississippi. At last they were on the main river shown on the old trader's map, and Knutson must have heaved a sigh of relief as they floated rapidly southward.

In a few easy days they would have encountered the St. Anthony Falls in what became the city of Minneapolis. Shortly afterward on their left was the unmistakable broad mouth of the St. Croix River, shown on their map. Then it was up the broad, lazy St. Croix to Taylors Falls, and a short portage past the monster potholes, ground out thousands of years ago during the ice age by boulders spinning in the

---

48.   H. Holand. *Westward from Vinland*, 212.

current in holes in the bedrock. Then back on the water, rowing upstream on the now faster-moving river. After several more days they would have been at the headwater portage into the Brule River, followed by a short run downstream to the great Lake Superior where sails could again be used.

There on Lake Superior our story of Paul Knutson ends. Perhaps they did reach Lake Superior before winter set in, and they might have found a small outpost of old Norsemen with whom they spent the winter. Perhaps they did not, for they had a late start on their eastward journey and were delayed between Hawley and Kensington while trying to get over the drainage divide to an eastward-flowing river. But the last firm evidence of Knutson's daring traverse across half the continent is the Kensington Runestone, dated 1362 and found on the hill three miles northeast of Kensington, Minnesota, in 1898. There is no other evidence to show that Knutson passed that way. After the 1354 proclamation by King Magnus, the few Scandinavian historical documents that survive do not mention him. He may never have returned to Norway.

The tragedy told on the Kensington stone might be the last documented evidence of this highly competent Norseman who, at King Magnus's request, left a comfortable life in Norway to command the first major European expedition that ever attempted to establish a beachhead of European commerce and culture in North America. Was his epic trek back across the continent to Norombega ever completed? We do not know. We can only hope that somewhere in the fourteenth century wilderness of the trade empire, Knutson might have inscribed another runestone, yet to be discovered, that would tell us something of his fate.

CHAPTER 10

KING HAAKON AND THE SPIRIT POND RUNESTONE

The saga of the Last Kings is nearly told. Although the fate of Knutson is unknown, Haakon's fate is not unknown, and it will be easy to follow him back from the trading post at the mouth of the Nelson River on Hudson Bay to his royal place in Norwegian history. The bargaining at the York Factory village would be Haakon's last trading occasion, and it occurred as the frosts of the final days of the arctic summer cleared the air of the black flies and mosquitoes and made life on shore more pleasant. He welcomed the half-social, half-business activity as the furs were brought in. It took his mind away from the loss of his friends. The trading brought in many fox furs and a few of the great white bearskins that were highly desired in Norway, and it capped a successful series of trading visits at ports on the journey from Norombega that summer of 1361.

But the days were now becoming shorter, and to make port in Norombega before the storms of early winter, Haakon could not delay his return. After finishing the trading and restocking their provisions, he and Knutson said their goodbyes, and on a cool, frosty morning the crew raised sail on the cog ship and Haakon set their course eastward. They did not enter James Bay this time, and only occasional short pauses along the coasts were made to get fresh water and break the monotony of the voyage. The wind and weather were favorable as they sailed the great arc around Whitemansland and finally turned southwestward along the Vinland coasts and around the Cape Cod hook to their headquarters on Narragansett Bay.

Little had changed at Norombega since they had sailed away in the spring. Regular masses were now being held in the new church for those of the Norse who were inclined to accept the ministrations of the priests. Many who were not so inclined preferred the independent life that had been one of the motives for their migration to the Western Lands. Haakon himself was also of an independent mind, although he was a natural diplomat and never thoughtlessly exposed his views. Having enjoyed, or endured, four winters at the Norombega head-quarters, he decided to spend his last winter in the Western Lands elsewhere with his crew and some of the men who had spent three years constructing the church and would now be returning to Norway. The men, too, favored a change to a location where the hunting and fishing might be better than around the populated village on Narra-gansett Bay.

Haakon's choice was a small inlet on the coast of southern Maine where he had hove to once on his first exploratory voyage. It was a "hop," as the Norse called it. At high tide, his ship could be sailed to the head of the inlet and anchored safely in a small, deep lake that had a navigable connection to the sea only near high tide. It would be a perfect shelter from the storms of winter, and was two sailing days closer to Norway than the village of Norombega. There were no nearby tribes of Indians and consequently the hunting would be good. Best of all, the salmon were plentiful in the neighboring river flowing down from the north, and smoked salmon was the preferred fare for the long voyage back to Norway. We know the little lake as Spirit Pond.

Some of the goodbyes of the women of the Norombega village were tearful when they pushed away from shore and the breeze filled their sail. They then pointed their ship eastward and rounded the hook of Cape Cod for the last time. On reaching the rugged coastline of Maine, they found the little inlet, and at high tide they towed the cogship carefully into the pond. Building a house on the shore near the ship occupied them for a short time before settling in for the winter, and the men enjoyed their last chance to hunt and fish in the Western Lands. It was an opportunity particularly appreciated by those who had spent all their time constructing the church. As the commander, Haakon hunted or fished only occasionally for pleasure, while the men did the winter tasks and the serious fishing to supply the smoked salmon for the coming return voyage. That autumn the fragrant smoke from their smokehouse often hung in the air over Spirit Pond.

Haakon did a lot of thinking that winter—the loss of his retinue of friends and their crew was seldom far from his mind. Hanging out with his chosen retinue would have helped to pass the time, but now those young fellows were gone. His skald, the poet, was his only remaining close companion. The poet was a man who had served in Magnus's court, and, earlier, in the English courts. Haakon had thought that he and Knutson should have someone to note their accomplishments in the great adventure. So, in 1355 Haakon had chosen the poet after he chose the companions in his retinue, and throughout the expedition the poet was always near at hand.

And now the time had come for the poet to do his thing. Haakon knew that he would have to tell the kinsmen of his lost companions about that tragic event of the great storm, and he would relive the pain of their loss each time it was told. After much thought, he decided that recounting the story would be limited to one occasion. He would hold a memorial service for the lost men after he arrived in Bergen, and on that occasion with all the kinsmen present he would tell his story with the help of the poet. They would compose a chivalric poem in honor of the lost men, and, as part of the memorial Haakon himself would perform the recitation of the poem as his personal tribute to them and their families.

Haakon and his poet friend spent many evenings by the fire, discussing the events of the expedition and its climax in the fury of the great storm on that July day of 1361. The discussion with the poet helped somewhat to relieve his feelings of loss. The skald felt that Haakon's accomplishments should be the focus of the poem, but for Haakon the poem was not an ego trip. A brief mention of Haakon, the explorer, would be enough. The emphasis would be on the loss of the retinue of gallant young men in the storm. The daghrise coordinates of the location of the great storm relative to the Spirit Pond hop would tell the audience the great extent of Haakon's travels.

But as the poem took shape, expressing the dates of events appeared to be a problem. Haakon was uncertain as to how he should tell the tragic date of the storm. Normally, the event would be told as occurring in a year of the king's reign. But which king? If he used the year of his own reign, it would be a public insult to his father who was still a king, though now with his powers reduced by the rivalry of both his sons. And if the year of his father's reign were used, it would not speak well of Haakon's own position as the king succeeding his father. Haakon spoke freely to the poet of his misgivings, and the skald proposed that Haakon's age would be a good way to express the year numbers without raising questions about anyone's reign. Everyone in the court knew Haakon's age, and his skald said it would be much easier to fold his age into the couplet rhythm of the poem than to use either reign. Thus it was that the skald's choice of Haakon's age for the year numbers in the Spirit Pond inscription gives us precise and unique dates of 1361 and 1362 for the loss of Haakon's retinue and his last winter at Spirit Pond in the Western Lands.

To make it possible for Haakon to memorize the poem and to refresh his memory before he recited it a few months later in Norway, the poet obtained a small stone from the ship's ballast and cleaved it to form two flat sides on which the runes of the poem were to be inscribed. The space for the inscription was small, so he abbreviated half the words, sometimes indicating the absence of letters by a short bar over the words, as can be seen in the runic patterns of Figure 14.

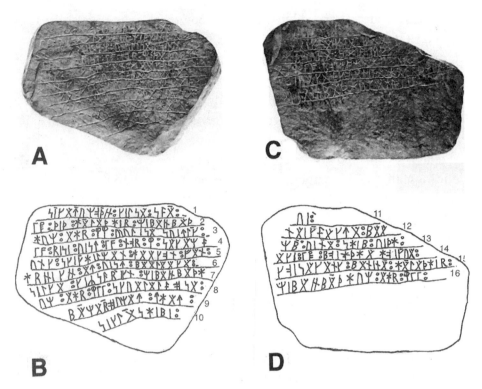

FIGURE 14: A: Side #1 of the Spirit Pond inscription runestone. From the Collections of the Maine State Museum, mainestate-museum.org. B: The runes from Side #1. C: Side #2 of the Spirit Pond inscription stone. From the Collections of the Maine State Museum, mainestatemuseum.org. D: The runes from Side #2. The "overbars" above words indicate an absence of letters in abbreviations. See Figures 37 and 38 for greater detail.

In the memorial recitation these abbreviations would have been no problem for Haakon and the skald who were already familiar with the content of the poem. However, more than six centuries later the prevalence of those abbreviations prevented the Harvard professor, Einar Haugen, from making a translation. Haugen viewed the inscription as a hoax by some unknown person, but we viewed it as a puzzle to be solved by restoring the abbreviated words and paying careful attention to the grammar and the historical context.

The restoration of these short word forms has not been easy, and is discussed in detail, word by word, in Appendix F. Here we show the poem in its transliterated form with Roman letters and the Old Norse language, followed by the English translation. All the abbreviated words have been restored from their shortened forms. Some short compound words such as "GELSA" and "SELGA" remain for poetic reasons. We give a discussion of the runic numbers in Appendix G. The poem has a couplet rhythm, and every other sylable is emphasized, with an apostrophe to show minor emphasis on some word endings. The "R" is a trilled "r" in most cases, as in the Scottish dialect, and the "Wepaing Baedhum," translated as "Weeping Fountains," is the poet's metaphor for the mourning families of the lost men.

SIG-INN-AET-TUM O-DREN-GI-R'
GEL-SA SLE-AE' SJAU-TAN DE-D'.
HAEL-Á-DHE-R' WE-PAING-BAE-DHUM.
AH-R' TI-GR' TI-GR'
WE-U-LES-A SVEIT-LAG TOL-F'
RI-SE' VEST EIN TVEIR NOR TI-GR'.
SAG-AM JUNG FOL-KUN-G'.
SKEGG-HIL-MA-N' HAA-KON FA-N'
H-RING –Í-GENG AT VEST BAA-LAA-GA
SEL-GA KEY-SAR-REG-N'.
WE-PAING-BAE-DHUM,
AH-R' .. TI-GR'.. EIN-N'EIN-N'.
SK-VAL-Á-LJOO-SA! BE-A-TAE-MA-RI-A!
OO! U-MAT THAT SIGI-LLA SHIP-I VE.
NÁ-EGG-JA AKT-A', BAA UM-B' VINN-A',
SHI-P' VID-H A-GI .
SJAU-TAN BOI-H-DHA HOEG-G-VA,
KOI-SA-SÁ-GANG, BA-NI-NÁ-M'.
HAEL-Á-DHE-R' WE-PAING-BAE-DHUM.
AH-R'.. TI-GR'.. EIN-N'EIN-N'.

Here again is the English translation:

> Fallen kinsmen, ever valiant fellows. A roaring sea struck
> seventeen dead.
> Hail to you, Weeping Fountains!
> Year 20, we lost the company of twelve companions
> 12 daghrise westward (900 miles), 10 daghrise northward
> (750 miles).
> The saga of a young Folkung.
> Bearded chief-man Haakon discovered a circle by being able
> to sail toward the west on the lakes ("laaga") of the
> trade empire.
> Weeping Fountains! Year 21.
> A shout into the burning lights! Blessed Maria! Alas!
> Powerless those on the Seal-ship to proceed
> to obtain an edge to devote attention in regard
> to win the ship against the terrible storm.
> Seventeen presage their inevitable battle stroke, accept the
> sinking,
> the bane of their approaching death.
> Hail to you, Weeping Fountains! Year 21.

Perhaps the most remarkable aspect of this remarkable runic document is the set of coordinates relative to Spirit Pond, which tells us
that the men were lost off the southern coast of Hudson Bay. That
knowledge has enabled us to reconstruct the voyage that brought
Commander Knutson from New England to the mouth of the Nelson
River on Hudson Bay, and from there by afterboat to the Graenaveldi,
and later to the site of the Kensington runestone northeast of Kensington, Minnesota. The Kensington inscription tells of their ship
being guarded over the winter at the port, and Commander Knutson
would have kept his Sealship there for his return to Norombega.
Therefore, the loss of Haakon's twelve companions in the storm that
warm summer day occurred on the way out to the Nelson River
trading post because the poem says that those on the Sealship were

powerless to aid the men on the sinking ship. Haakon would have taken the other cog ship back to New England after the hot summer days of 1361 had passed.

There is one tantalizing question about the Spirit Pond runestone that will remain unanswered. Why was the inscribed stone abandoned at the edge of Spirit Pond? Perhaps Haakon had committed the poem to memory and felt he no longer needed the stone as a reminder. Or perhaps the skald extended the length of the poem and needed a larger stone to contain the longer inscription. One thing is certain: That miniature runestone was not left half buried at that remote and unattractive location as a stone to be read and admired by future Norsemen living in the Western Lands. It was surely a "notebook" tool, with its inscription intended for future recitation in Norway.

After the winter at Spirit Pond in 1362, Haakon and his men set sail for Norway. Shortly after midsummer they arrived at Bergen to a somewhat subdued welcome. The memorial service was a sad occasion for those who had lost sons when their ship went down. Haakon's recitation of the memorial poem at the service honoring the lost men established a shared sense of loss because of a cruel twist of fate, and none of the bereaved members of the court blamed Haakon for the tragedy.

Haakon's return to Norway in 1362[49] is a historic fact because the records say that he was acclaimed king of Sweden in 1362 to replace his dead brother, Erik XII. He honored his betrothal to Margrethe of Denmark by marrying her in the spring of 1363. She was ten at the time, and was brought to Norway to be secluded and educated in the royal customs until she became Haakon's mature queen at age sixteen.

As far as we know, Haakon never returned to the Western Lands. Whether or not the matter of trade with the Norsemen there was pursued, we do not know. Certainly the loss of the young men of his retinue, the best youth of the Norwegian court, would have

49. In most medieval countries the new year began on 25 March, not on 1 January (M. Ragnow, personal communication). The year dates for events of the summer sailing seasons would remain unchanged with this custom and Haakon's return to Norway and his acclamation as king of Sweden probably occurred in late summer or early fall, soon after his return and well before the depths of winter on 1 January of our 1363.

undermined the support of the nobles for the venture. Then the dispute over the coveted province of Skaane erupted again despite Haakon's marriage to Margrethe. Her father, Valdemar, took Skaane by force soon after the wedding. Of course, this angered the Swedish nobles, and they deposed Haakon, bringing in Albrecht of Mecklenburg as their king.

Magnus refused to accept this action. He put together a small army of Norwegians and foolishly invaded Sweden to try to regain the crown for the Folkung clan. But he was defeated and captured, and held for ransom for six years until Haakon could raise a large sum of money to free him. The Swedes were not happy with the German, Albrecht, who was then deposed, and Magnus was allowed to rule a small part of southwest Sweden. He died as a result of a shipwreck in 1374. Haakon remained king of Norway, "much loved by his subjects," until his death in 1380. Queen Margrethe's life was marked by tragedy, for she lost her husband, Haakon, at the age of forty, and their son also died at a very young age. But she was a talented woman with great diplomatic skill. In later life she greatly reduced the influence of German traders in Sweden, and she united Denmark, Sweden, and Norway in the famous Kalmar Union.

Magnus's ego was certainly a factor in sending out the expedition to restore the trade. How ironic it would be if his headstrong character also destroyed his chances of successfully maintaining that trade when the expedition ended, for his ego certainly led to the unwise invasion of Sweden, resulting in his capture and imprisonment and making necessary the large ransom that drained Haakon's limited resources. Those resources might otherwise have been used to successfully reestablish trade with the Norsemen in the Western Lands, thus regaining Norway's trade empire and, possibly, changing the course of history. Ah . . . what might have been!

EPILOGUE I

A list of North American invasions by peoples of Europe would extend back into the last ice age. Twenty thousand years ago the Solutreans traveled from Spain and France to North America in skin boats along the edge of the North Atlantic ice pack when sea levels were more than 300 feet below the level in 2011. On the way, they lived by hunting seals on the ice using spears tipped with the beautifully fluted Solutrean points found in Europe.[50] In America their fluted spear points

---

50. Dennis Stanford of the Smithsonian National Museum of Natural History delivered a lecture at the 44th annual Nobel Conference at Gustavus Adolphus College, St. Peter, Minnesota, on 8 October 2008. His talk was titled "The Ice-age Discovery of the Americas: Constructing an Iberian Solution." He described the Solutrean hypothesis of European migration to America by way of the fringe of the heavy sea ice at the Ice Age maximum when world sea levels were quite low. The migration has a modern analog in which Eskimo families live in their boats while hunting seals on the ice over many days or weeks at sea. His convincing evidence for the Ice Age movement of people between Europe and North America included the measured carbon 14 age of 22,760 years (personal communication, 2011) for a mastodon bone accompanied by a stone knife. The knife and bone were brought up from deep water by fishermen who were dredging for halibut, fourteen miles off the New Jersey coast and near the edge of the continental shelf. In another example a Solutrean "leaf" point was recovered with submerged material on the shelf, and was dated to an age of 18,000 years. The similarity of the knife and points to those found in Europe provide a convincing link between Ice Age peoples living along the coasts of France and Spain and the peoples of North America. Although Stanford makes a good argument supported by reliable facts, members of the archeological community often ignore facts not in agreement with other preferred theories, as we have found in the case of the American runestones. A. Lawler briefly summarizes the opinions of workers favoring the first appearance of the Clovis people at a later time, about 12,800 years ago (*Science*, 234, 302, 2011).

are what we call Clovis points, which have been found throughout the United States at ancient campsites that were dated after 20,000 years ago. But no campsites with fluted points are found that are younger than about 11,000 years ago. About that time another group of people of Asiatic origin arrived in North America by way of the Beringia land bridge before the rising sea level separated Alaska from Siberia. These people, who were the ancestors of the American Indians we know, were the first invaders to be armed with bows and arrows. The Clovis/ Solutrean men and their fluted spear points then vanished from the North American record.

The Solutreans had lived for generations by hunting seals on the ice just off the cold coasts of Europe. At air holes in the ice, a seal could be taken with a well-thrown spear attached to a rawhide cord, and the seal's carcass and spear would be recovered. But if an arrow were used, the wounded seal would vanish down the hole and the arrow, too, would be lost. It was a case of "use it or lose it." The Solutreans lived by the spear and had lost the technique of bow and arrow. On the other hand, the invaders from Siberia had hunted their way over the land bridge with both spears and arrows. When conflict occurred, it would have been an unequal contest. The highly successful hunters from Siberia had better weapons, and would have absorbed any Solutreans not felled by arrows.

The many half-buried stone structures in the rocky woodlands of New England hint at later and more sophisticated Europeans who may also have arrived in skin boats, but melted away into the Indian populations of North America. Certainly the sod houses of Celtic style on Greenland that predate the first Norse occupation suggest that Irish peoples had preceded the Norse to Greenland and probably also to the Western Lands. If not arriving in skin boats, then perhaps they came in primitive wooden ships.[51]

Then a thousand years ago the Norse arrived and maintained a thin foothold on the continent by means of trade. For nearly three hundred years prior to 1340, trade goods flowed between the Norse part of the

---

51.   F. Mowat. *West Viking, The ancient Norse in Greenland and North America* (Toronto: McClelland and Stewart Ltd., 1965), 48–55.

continent and Norway by way of Greenland. Yet, when the Greenland colonies were abandoned and the trade link failed, the Norse identity on the continent could not be sustained. Their culture disappeared and the surviving Norsemen were also absorbed by the Indian people.

This period of Norse trade was not without its historical consequences, however. It was less than a hundred years after the Greenland colonies were abandoned that the young sailor, Christopher Columbus, is thought to have sailed to Iceland. Inevitably, the Icelanders would have told him about the past trading in the lands beyond Greenland and the resulting wealth that had flowed to Norway. Columbus brought this information home, and, in an effort to obtain funds for his expedition, he would have told Queen Isabella of Spain the story of the trade in the Western Lands. Although she was favorably inclined, she refused him for lack of money in the royal coffers, it was said. But some influential people of the Spanish court did not abandon his proposal. How could they have been persuaded to act in the face of the queen's negative decision? The story of the traders' wealth that had flowed to Norway from the Western Lands must have convinced them, and they did a little "creative accounting" to convince the queen to recall Columbus and fund his expedition.[52] So it was that King Magnus's dream of a lucrative trade was kept alive in other minds.

It was in the century of Columbus that firearms came into extensive use, Johannes Gutenberg invented the printing press with moveable letters, and European society enjoyed an amazing technological and cultural advance. A hundred years after Columbus died, European settlers again sailed to the Western Lands, settling in Quebec in 1604 and in Jamestown, Virginia, in April 1607. They brought with them new weapons, new knowledge, and a tradition of literacy that glued their people tightly together. The last European invasion of the Western Lands had begun.

---

52. David Satava. "Columbus's First Voyage: Profit or Loss from a Historical Accountant's Perspective," *Journal of Applied Business Research* Vol. 23, Fourth Quarter, 2007. Some men in the Spanish government other than the Royals had become sold on Columbus's proposal. After the Queen refused Columbus "for the last time," they identified both funds and ships and renewed the favorable arguments to the Queen, who then recalled Columbus and began the final contract negotiations to enable his expedition.

PART B

·DISCOVERIES
ON THE GRAENAVELDI

CHAPTER 11

DISCOVERIES OF THE KENSINGTON RUNESTONE AND "THIS ISLAND"

Harvest time, 1898. Late in the summer, Olof Ohman, a Swedish immigrant, was pulling up stumps of trees with a winch to clear land on the farm three miles northeast of Kensington, Minnesota, where he had settled a few years earlier, Figure 15. He was working on the stumps near the top of a forty-foot-high hill, nearly surrounded by low-lying pasture and cultivated land, when he pulled up a stump with a large rectangular stone clasped tightly in its roots. Olof's ten-year-old son, Edward, called his father's attention to strange markings on the stone. Olof carefully chopped away the roots to free the stone, and his neighbor, Nils Flaaten, and Willie Sarsland[53], who was harvesting

---

53. R. Nielsen and S.F. Wolter, *The Kensington Rune Stone, Compelling New Evidence* (Duluth, MN: Lake Superior Agate Publishing, 2006), 2, 379–384. The following quote from Edward Ohman regarding his role in the discovery in 1898 was obtained from Edward in a 1949 interview with the Minnesota Historical Society: "I was ten years old and going to school at the time. As a rule we (Olof Jr. and Edward) came home from school and brought lunch out to Dad. We also helped him until he quit for the evening. This happened when we pulled this stump, an aspen, or we called it a poplar tree. It

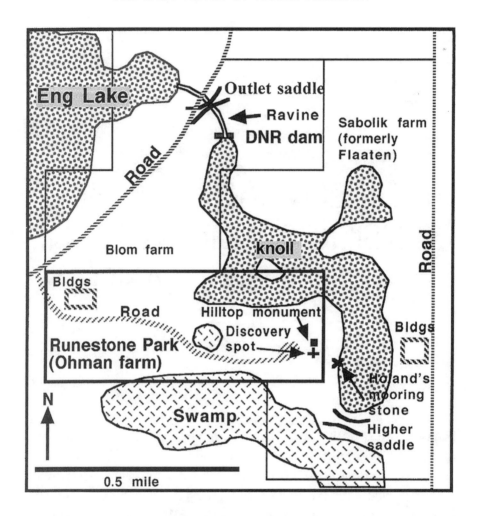

FIGURE 15: The Kensington runestone discovery site on the hill in Runestone Park, Douglas County, Minnesota. Heavy rectangular outline is now a park that was the farm of Olof Ohman in 1898. The farm to the east was occupied by Nils Flaaten in 1898 and in 2011 is owned by the Sabolik family. The lake at the foot of the discovery hill was created in recent years by a dam built across the drainage channel by the Minnesota Department of Natural Resources.

in an adjacent field, helped him to clean the dirt out of the runic inscription, Figure 13. The runes were inscribed only on the upper two-thirds of the face and one side of the stone to enable the erection of the stone with the lower third set into the ground, as was often done for such memorial stones in Scandinavia.

Although the evidence of Olof Ohman's honest discovery was documented in detail and attested to in the years that followed, the authenticity of the stone and its discovery became the subject of a bitter 100-year-long controversy.[54] Linguistic authorities said it was a

---

was eight to ten inches in diameter and growing on top of the stone. Our neighbor, Flaaten, came over as he was grubbing across the section line—the line between my dad's place and his. He was also quitting. Dad was disgusted about the stump, hard work, and also stones. Just before we went home, Dad drove his grub hoe to see how deep it went into the ground. And as it happened it was flat under and we sluffed it up. Here I sat down on it and started to dig in the dirt with my hands as kids usually do and I suggested to Dad that we take it home and use it for a doorstep. The story goes that it was used for a doorstep, but it never was. When I was sitting on the stone I told Dad that we ought to take that home and put it in front of a door. Just then I discovered the carving on it. I told Dad that something was written on it."
See Appendix H: Benedict Carey's test for an honest story, which, when applied to Edward's interview, makes his story an unquestionably honest one.

The exact spot of the runestone discovery is uncertain. The spot close to and south of the crest of the hill shown in Figure 15 is consistent with a later photo that depicted the site as being on a slope. Al Lieffort, Douglas County Park superintendent, supplied the photo, courtesy of Darwin Ohman, that shows a man, Cliff Roiland, standing by a long embedded pole marking the site on a slope below the hillcrest with the trees along the Flaaten fence line in the background. Other pictures, taken probably in the 1940s, suggest that the site was west of the hillcrest on a flat surface along the present approach road to the hilltop. A bronze plaque now marks the spot on the flat.

54. Books by H.J. Holand, *America 1355–1364*, 1946, and *Westward from Vinland* (New York: Duell Sloan and Pearce, 1940) summarize the initial arguments for authenticity of the Kensington stone. Barry Hanson (*A Defense of Olof Ohman–the Accused Forger*, Archaeology ITM, 3194 S. Smith Creek Road, Maple, WI 54854) has made a systematic study of the errors and falsehoods that have been used by the stone's opponents. R. Nielsen and S.F. Wolter's 2006 book *The Kensington Rune Stone, Compelling New Evidence* (Duluth, MN: Lake Superior Agate Publishing, 2006) documents much new material supporting the stone's authenticity. R.A. Hall, *The Kensington Rune-Stone: authentic and Important* (Bluff, IL: Jupiter Press, 1994) provides scholarly support for the stone's linguistics and critically analyses E. Wahlgren's book, *The Kensington stone: a mystery solved* (Madison, WI: University of Wisconsin Press, 1958), which condemns the stone as a fraud. T.C. Blegen's book, *The Kensington Rune-Stone: New Light on an Old Riddle* (St. Paul, MN: Minnesota Historical Society, 1968) is an authoritative study that concluded that the Kensington stone was a hoax. A more complete list of the literature on the stone can be found on the Internet. As of this writing, the proponents of the stone accept the physical arguments and the later linguistic findings, while the opponents rely on the old linguistic arguments, half-truths, and old unfounded rumors, and ignore the documented physical factors.

hoax because some of the runes did not conform to any known runic writings, and many people simply could not believe the evidence that medieval Norsemen had been visiting the interior of the continent. The news of the discovery was published in the area newspaper and the story excited much local interest. The inscription was soon roughly translated, and the stone was displayed in the window of the Kensington bank. But when Professor Breda, a linguist at the University of Minnesota, looked at the inscription, he did not view it as authentic because it was contrary to his knowledge of the Vinland Voyages of the Norse that occurred shortly after AD 1000.

The stone was subsequently shipped to Northwestern University at Evanston, Illinois, where it was carefully examined by Professor George Curme. Curme noted the weathered condition of the runic surfaces, and that this was consistent with a long exposure to the weather after being inscribed. He also sent photographs of the inscription to scholars in Scandinavia. Their verdict was that a pre-Columbian expedition by Norsemen into the central part of North America was ridiculous, and they labeled the stone a "clumsy fraud." So the stone was returned to Olof Ohman who leaned it against the wall of his granary and went about his business.

There it might have remained but for a scholar from Wisconsin, Hjalmar Holand, who visited the Kensington area nine years later when doing research for an article on Norwegian immigration. Everyone he talked to remembered the excitement of the runestone discovery and its demotion from authenticity to fraud. Holand was quite familiar with runes himself, and with "eager expectancy" he went out to the Ohman farm and gave the stone a short examination. Its inscription so impressed him that he got permission to take the stone home with him to make a detailed study. This he did, and he concluded that those who condemned the stone as a fraud because it contained some words that were not Old Norse were wrong, because evolutionary changes in the language had occurred prior to the 1362 date carved on the stone.

Holand published the results of his study in *Skandinavaen*, a Scandinavian newspaper in America in 1908. In his article he summarized the discovery and the evidence that it had been in the ground for many years as shown by the clasp of the roots around the stone and the weathered appearance of the runic surfaces. Holand's article reignited interest in the stone, and was the first of many articles and books he wrote during the remainder of his life as he intensively studied every aspect of the runestone.

To explain the stone, he developed a hypothesis of the Paul Knutson expedition as an exploratory religious mission. His detective work, using the runic account of the men who "fished a day in a lake with two islands one day's journey northwards from this stone," eventually enabled him to identify the site of the massacre of the ten Norsemen as Big Cormorant Lake, a few miles southwest of the town of Detroit Lakes, Minnesota.[55] There are two and only two small rocky islands in Big Cormorant Lake, and on the northwestern shore, not far from one of them, a local farmer directed Holand to boulders having mooring stone holes where the Norsemen had moored their boats on the day of the massacre in 1362.

The stone and the circumstances of its discovery were thoroughly examined over a period of two years by a committee of the Minnesota Historical Society headed by N.H. Winchell, a noted geologist. In the committee's report of 1912, they concluded that Ohman's discovery was an honest one, and that all the physical evidence favored the authenticity of the stone and its inscription, but they deferred to the linguists for a final judgment. Most of the linguists were not convinced, although a few over the years have come to the stone's defense. Robert Hall, for example, went into great detail in his later 1994 book, *The Kensington Rune-Stone: Authentic and Important*. And in one rare example, anthropologist Alice Kehoe has discussed the Kensington runestone in a favorable light.[56]

The Kensington runestone enjoyed a measure of respect in America for a brief time, and in 1946 it was placed on exhibit at the Smithsonian Institution. This so enraged some of the American linguists who

---

55.   Holand. *Westward from Vinland*, 187–197.

56.   Alice Kehoe. *The Kensington Rune Stone, approaching a research question holistically*, (Long Grove, IL: Waveland Press, 2005), 65.

had ignored the physical evidence that they campaigned against the acceptance of the stone and turned the news media opinion against it to the extent that news stories about the stone now usually have a contemptuous tone. One of the linguists, Professor Johan Holvik, was so aggressive in his attempts to discredit the runestone and the Ohmans associated with its discovery that he attempted to get Arhur Ohman to sign a false statement regarding the holestones on the Ohman farm.[57]

The stone was returned to Minnesota where it is now on exhibit at the Runestone Museum in Alexandria. Since that time the so-called linguistic questions that argued against the stone have been largely answered by research into the medieval literature. The arguments for authenticity have, however, been plagued by a wide variety of rumors and half-truths that have made the responses of the stone's opponents more like political screeds than honest debate. The propagation of these untruths has continued into the present time, and has so poisoned the well that most authorities refuse to consider any new evidence.

Nevertheless, a few amateur scholars have continued to try to collect evidence of the stone's authenticity. Barry Hanson, a chemist, initiated an effort to get a physical measurement of the age of the runic surfaces by making weathering studies, a laudable effort, but one that was not likely to be successful because of the unknown variable weathering rates during the history of the stone. For this effort he involved Scott Wolter, the manager of a St. Paul laboratory, for testing concrete materials. Wolter made a high-resolution photographic inventory of all the runes of the inscription. Hanson also wanted to engage University of Minnesota academics in the effort and so contacted Professor Paul Weiblen and author Johnson. Professor Weiblen later made the first recorded observation of the bleached pattern left by the tree roots that had enclosed the runestone at the time of its discovery—a modern-day confirmation of Olof Ohman's description of his 1898 discovery, and another item supporting the stone's authenticity.

---

57.   R. Nielsen and S. Wolter, *The Kensington Rune Stone, Compelling New Evidence,* 463.

No professional stone letter-carver had ever examined the Kensington stone. Author Westin is both a professional sculptor and letter carver, and Hanson contacted her and arranged for a detailed microscopic examination of the inscription at the museum in Alexandria.

On 27 January 2001 the authors met with Hanson, museum director Lu Ann Patton, and staff members at the Runestone Museum in Alexandria to perform a three-hour examination of all surfaces of the runestone. At the close of the afternoon, Westin gave a short report of the findings. Her conclusions were that the 204-pound runestone had been shaped from a somewhat larger graywacke rock. The front surface on which most of the runes were inscribed had been formed by cleaving away a large slab from one side of the original stone, as indicated by chisel marks on the top front edge. Graywacke is a hard, fine-grained rock, well suited for carving the fine details of runes. The precisely carved rows of runes and the shaping of the stone, in her opinion, had been done by a stone carver with substantial experience, experience not possessed by Olof Ohman, the farmer who discovered the stone.

A decisive result of the examination was the observation of surface roughness differences that were brought about by different weathering rates of the various rock crystals in the stone. We compared four surfaces under the microscope: the uncut surface exposed to the weather for thousands of years, the cleaved surface on which the runes were inscribed, small surface areas exposed when the cleaved surface broke away during the inscribing process, and a "fresh" surface exposed in a cut when geologist N. H. Winchell chipped off a "flake" for microscopic examination in 1910, leaving an area of surface that had never been exposed to the weather. We observed that the surface where the flake had been removed was microscopically smooth. The cleaved surface containing runes and the areas exposed during the carving of the inscription were distinctly rougher, and the ancient surface, which had been exposed to the weather for thousands of years since a glacier had carried it to the Kensington area, was the roughest of all. The inescapable conclusion, similar to that reached by several investigators a hundred years ago, was that the cleaved front surface and the side cuts of the runes themselves had experienced much weathering relative to Winchell's "fresh" surface, and therefore the inscription on the cleaved surface was made long before the stone was found on the hill in 1898, a conclusion quite consistent with the inscription date of 1362.

Westin also had the intriguing thought that the slab that had been cleaved off to form the front face of the stone might still be found at or near the Norse camp at the site of the runestone's discovery. After hundreds of years, this would seem unlikely, but we decided to go to the site the following spring and evaluate that possibility.

On a cold day, 28 April 2001, Westin, my wife Betty Johnson, and I drove from Minneapolis to the former Ohman farm. The farm is now a Douglas County park. It is also known as the Runestone Park, and the discovery is commemorated by a monument on the hilltop, located on the map of Figure 15. The hill is said to have been free of trees because of prairie fires when the first of the modern settlers saw it. The hill is also somewhat isolated, but is connected to elevated land to the southeast by a saddle fifteen feet above the base of the hill.

In 1898 the hill overlooked a large area of low-lying farmland to the northwest, north, and east. This land had been a grassy marsh before the first immigrant settlers arrived. Before Olof Ohman arrived in the neighborhood to settle on his farm in 1891, the first settlers had already ditched and drained the marsh area into Eng Lake to the north to permit cultivation of the low land. Ohman never saw that land as anything but a low area of field and pasture. Author Johnson had visited the park years earlier when the low land east and northwest of the hill consisted of two large cow pastures.

When we arrived at the park that day we found that the view had changed. Except for a small knoll topped by a few visible rocks and some young trees, a shallow lake now covered all of the low-lying land. This lake was formed by a dam, which had been built across the drainage channel by the Minnesota Department of Natural Resources to create a wildlife area. To the north from the hilltop the new lake stretches for half a mile over to the DNR dam and the outlet drainage to Eng Lake. But a hundred years before, the discovery hill was nearly surrounded by cultivated land and pasture with no island in sight. The unexplained absence of the enigmatic "island" of the inscription, when coupled with unfounded rumors that Ohman himself had carved the inscription, reinforced the skeptical opinions maintained by the opponents of the stone's authenticity. Of all the objections raised by the opponents of the runestone's authenticity, only the question of the missing "island" remained unanswered. But in the skeptic's mind, that question alone was enough to keep the runestone labeled as a hoax.

To address the "island" question, Hjalmar Holand, the leading twentieth century proponent of the stone's authenticity, made the assumption that past water levels had been at least fifteen feet higher and had covered the connecting saddle to make the hill "this island" of the inscription. The skeptics scoffed at this, and even those favoring the stone were not at all comfortable with that explanation. Holand proposed that the lake of those times would have been part of a chain of waterways that the Norsemen had followed to reach the Kensington site. He strengthened this idea by collecting reports of stones found at the edges of waterways in western Minnesota, and which contained holes like those in Figure 16. He assumed that the stones had been used to moor boats in past times. The cylindrical holes chiseled into them are analogous to ancient holes in rocks along waterways in Scandinavia, which are known to have been used to moor boats.[58] He was delighted to find one of these mooring stones standing near other rocks near the base of the discovery hill in the former marsh on the Flaaten farm.

Nils Flaaten was Ohman's neighbor to the east, and the north/south fence line bounding their properties lies halfway up the side of the hill. That mooring stone and another large granite boulder with a similar hole were later hauled up to the hilltop from the edge of the old Flaaten pasture on the east side of the hill, and they now stand by the monument commemorating Ohman's discovery.

---

58. Holand. *Westward from Vinland*, 203–204. In the mooring process, a line attached to the bow of the boat has a metal or wooden pin attached to the other end. The pin is inserted into the hole in the top of the stone, which is above the level of the bow, leaving the line stretched horizontally across the stone to the anchored boat.

FIGURE 16: Two typical holes each chiseled into a granite boulder like the many dozens of others found in western Minnesota and eastern South Dakota. Some are found at the edges of lakes or streams and many are found well away from streams and sometimes on distant hilltops. The one-inch diameter holes, three to eight inches deep, have a slightly triangular shape that develops naturally when hammering a broad-blade chisel.

We had read Holand's account of his investigations and had found his island hypothesis difficult to accept. Author Johnson had visited the park years earlier, and had observed that the land surface at the drainage outlet from the low area into Eng Lake did not appear to be high enough to have formed a natural dam needed to raise the water level as much as fifteen feet. That was subsequently confirmed using a government topographic map in which the land at the outlet was about ten feet below the saddle southeast of the hill[59]. But that day in 2001, Westin and I became convinced that Holand's assumption of high water levels was clearly wrong. One would expect to find evidence of beach erosion high on the hillside if water level had once been high enough to make the hill an island. But our careful examination of the hill found not the slightest trace of any such beach erosion.

Lacking any better idea, we naively began our search at the base of the hill on the east side, looking for the discarded runestone slab or any other trace of an ancient Norse campsite. The ground there was covered with the closely grazed grass of the cow pasture, and was within a good stone's throw of where Holand had found the mooring stone eighty-odd years ago. This was the logical place where travelers of long ago would have moored their boats or canoes when they climbed up the hill to look over the surrounding country.

Holand had proposed that his mooring stone had "rolled down the hillside" and across the grassy strip to its original location at the edge of the marsh. As we combed the strip of land between the base of the hill and the edge of the lake, that idea also seemed extremely unlikely. Boulders embedded in glacial till might slump downward when exposed, but rolling down on the slope of the hill that we saw there was not realistic. Although it seemed quite improbable, we speculated that perhaps the runestone had been carved on an island in some neighboring lake and had been carried up the discovery hill from a camp down by the mooring stone. But our meticulous examination of the pasture at the base of the hill revealed no trace of any camp.

After a two-hour search in the cold wind, we climbed back up to the warm car, parked by the monument on the hilltop, and once again considered the puzzle of the Kensington runestone and the two mooring stones now on exhibit, but which had once stood in Nils Flaaten's pasture at the base of the hill's east side. Westin wanted one last look for other mooring stones at the shoreline, this time on the

---

59.   USGS Kensington, Minnesota, N4545-W9537.5/7.5, 1966.

north side of the hill, so we made our way down the slope and out to the water's edge where our discussion continued.

Fueled by the frustration of our fruitless search, our conversation became an animated exchange of ideas and speculation. Most of the runestone story was simple and clear, but it ended in a riddle. The Norsemen were on a journey, literally a "back-taking journey," that is, a "taking back journey," and had previously camped at a lake one "dags rise" to the north. They had been out fishing all day, and had come home to that camp to find ten of their comrades "reddened with blood, and dead." Then the inscription says they had left a troop of ten men guarding their ship over the winter "14 days journey from beyond this island." The nautical "fourteen-days' journey" plausibly puts their ship on the coast of Hudson Bay at the mouth of the Hays and Nelson rivers at the site of the future eighteenth-century York Factory trading post. Everything in the inscription seemed plausible, except "this island." If not the discovery hill, then . . . what island?

Suddenly, in a flash of mutual inspiration, our riddle was solved! We realized that the little seven-foot-high knoll, Figure 17, now surrounded by water in full view two hundred yards to the north, must have held the island campsite we had been looking for. It would have been an island in a lake in 1362 also, but shallow lakes disappear over hundreds of years as they slowly become filled with mud and cattail debris, and the first modern settlers never saw the ancient lake—only a low, soggy area to be drained and cultivated. In 1362 the Norsemen would have found the graywacke boulder among the many rocks that we could now see on the three-acre island knoll. It would have been shaped and inscribed at the island camp, ferried across the water to the hill and carried up almost to the top where it was erected as a memorial for future Norsemen to see and read. Then, like grave-stones on hillsides do as the centuries pass, the stone slowly tilted over and sank beneath the grassy debris of the hill, to be at last brought to light by farmer Olof Ohman in 1898.

FIGURE 17: "This island" of the Kensington inscription as seen from the top of Runestone Hill on 27 May 2001. Before the Minnesota Department of Natural Resources flooded this low-lying area, the area consisted of pasture and cultivated fields. In 1362 the original shallow lake would have resembled this photo by L.J. Westin.

All of our frustration melted away, and we could hardly contain our excitement as we drove back to Minneapolis. The next day the weather was still cold, but we returned with Westin's kayak and paddled out to the little island, unknowingly violating the law, as a police officer told us, because boats were not allowed in the park. The island is now divided in half by a fence line. It had not been pastured in recent years, and was now partly covered by trees, a thick growth of last year's grass and weeds, and some thickets of thorny bushes. The south half was part of the Runestone Park and the north half was property of the Sabolik family who own the farm occupied by Nils Flaaten in 1898.

Unsurprisingly, our search among the bushes and accumulated

dead growth again failed to reveal a campsite. We did find three more mooring stones, and after getting permission from the Saboliks to search further we saw two others buried and nearly concealed in the muck near the island shoreline. There are still others said to be now below the surface of the lake. We also found another graywacke boulder of a general size and shape similar to the runestone. The rune-carver of 1362 had a choice of boulders on which to carve his inscription.

These holestones at the edge of the old marsh have been known to the local people for some time. The skeptics say, with more than a little scorn, that the holes were all made to permit blasting to obtain stone fragments for building foundations. Indeed, there is documented evidence that Arthur Ohman, one of Olof's sons, did use that technique.[60] We have seen the remains of several well-exposed and blasted stones on a hillside not far from the Ohman farm buildings. These were likely the stones blasted by Arthur. But chiseling typical six-inch-deep holes requires much effort, and no farmer would go to the trouble to chisel many more holes than needed in rocks sunk in the muck at distant locations if he had easily accessible rocks close to his farmstead. And certainly Arthur Ohman would not have been blasting Nils Flaaten's rocks on the far side of Runestone Hill, half a mile or more from his own barn.

Thus, a common-sense analysis says that the holestones around Runestone Hill and the little island were chiseled for the purpose of mooring boats, as was the Norse custom. The Flaaten (now Sabolik) farm sits on the height of land that separates drainage westward to the Minnesota River from eastward flow to the Mississippi. The presence of five holestones that we have seen on the island, the two now on exhibit at the top of the hill, and others that have been reported, tell us that the shallow medieval lake at Runestone Hill was often used by Norsemen when traveling between the headwaters of the

---

60. In *The Kensington Runestone, Compelling New Evidence*, 463. This handwritten and witnessed statement made in 1963 is evidence of the acrimonious conflict with Professor Holvick, an opponent of the runestone's authenticity, who was attempting to entrap Arthur Ohman by having him sign a false statement concerning the holestones on his farm, in some of which he had carved holes to blast for building stones.

Minnesota or Red River and the Mississippi River to the east.

Finally, for a skeptic to believe that Olof Ohman or any of his contemporaries forged the inscription on the runestone, the skeptic would have to believe that the forger had knowledge of the rocky knoll as an island in a lake despite the fact that the earliest settlers saw only a marsh. Olof Ohman himself arrived years after the marsh was ditched, and he never saw it as anything but a knoll surrounded by low-lying pasture and cultivated land. The Kensington runestone is authentic beyond any reasonable doubt, and the linguists who pit their fixed negative opinions against the physical evidence will lose the game.

CHAPTER 12

HOLESTONES AND SETTLEMENTS ON THE GRAENAVELDI

Our validation of the Kensington runestone inscription by the recognition of "this island," only a short rifle shot north of the discovery site, certainly makes the holes in the stones along the old Runestone Hill waterway even more believable as mooring stones. Similar holestones are frequently found on waterways throughout western Minnesota where Norse fur traders may have moored their boats, as Holand had proposed. Holand had also received reports of holestones located on hills high above the water level. He suggested that these had been chiseled out by young settlers of modern times who would fill them with black powder to blast the stones for Fourth of July fun. This idea should not be dismissed too quickly because in settlement days black powder was commonly used for blasting logs when making firewood for the rural stoves of that time. But pounding a typical six-inch-deep hole with a chisel requires a lot of hard work as we have found when doing it ourselves. This makes Holand's explanation for the unblasted holestones on hills more difficult to accept.

At that point in our investigation we were convinced that Norse traders had once traveled widely in western Minnesota collecting furs to supply the historically documented Greenland-Norwegian fur trade. Except for occasional white polar bear skins, the furs did not come from Greenland—they came from North America. The most efficient way to harvest those furs was to use Norse middlemen who would have lived at trading posts or who traveled on the continent and collected the furs from the Indians living there. This would have been quite similar to the seventeenth-century French traders who traveled the wilderness trading for furs from the Indians. Some local people on the plains thought that the Norse also had long ago lived as more numerous settlers in the region. We had seen no evidence for this and thought that idea was probably not correct. But we had more to learn.

Our recognition of the island knoll in Runestone Park as "this island" of the inscription became widely known in the Kensington locality. We were invited to present our findings to the Kensington Heritage Society at the Society's meeting hall and museum in Kensington. On that occasion the talk was well attended. In the audience was Judi Rudebusch, a local authority on holestones. She lives with husband Larry on a farm sixty miles to the west in eastern South Dakota. After the meeting Judi invited us to come over to South Dakota and look at some of the many holestones that she has catalogued, and which, she said, were too far from and too high above the streams to be used as mooring stones in 2004.

The local opinion in South Dakota was that hundreds of years ago when the Norse were there, the water levels were much higher in those days, and thus could have enabled the stones to be used as mooring stones. Having just eliminated the hypothesis of high water levels at Runestone Hill, we were skeptical of that explanation for the wide separation of the South Dakota holestones from the streams. But curiosity is a powerful motive, and we decided to accept Judi's invitation to come and inspect the South Dakota stones.

On 18 September 2004 we drove to the town of Milbank on the

ancient prairie of eastern South Dakota, and from there out to the Rudebusch house near the village of Corona. The Rudebusch farm is on the Whetstone River, about twenty-seven miles upstream from the mouth of the Whetstone where it empties into the head of the Minnesota River at the south end of Big Stone Lake. The wide distribution of mapped holestone sites in the Whetstone River area and in Pope County, Minnesota, is shown in Figures 18A and B. These sites are located on the headwaters of two great mid-continent river systems. The Minnesota River from its head flows far to the southeast, eventually twisting around to join the Mississippi in the Minneapolis area, and then flowing southward to the Gulf of Mexico. Big Stone is a long, narrow lake, a remnant of mighty River Warren that drained the rapidly melting ice sheet in glacial times. At the north end of Big Stone a short portage leads to Lake Traverse, the head of the Red River of the North. The Red River water flows northward into Lake Winnipeg and from there into the Nelson River, which flows northeastward and enters Hudson Bay near the site of the eighteenth century York Factory trading post, about 900 miles north of the Whetstone as the crow flies.

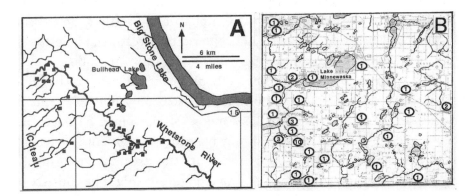

FIGURE 18: Holestone sites on the Graenaveldi. A: Whetstone area, Roberts County, SD, Judi Rudebusch and Bruce Kunze. B: Pope County, MN, Leland Pederson. Pope County is located about sixty miles to the east of the Whetstone River area. Circled numbers are the number of holestones at each site. Faint squares are mile sections.

That September day was warm and bright when we arrived at the Rudebusch farm. Judi Rudebusch is well known for her work in tabulating the locations of holestones in that region, and she had obtained permission from the landowners to give us a tour of the holestone sites. Also on the tour were Cal and Celia Courneya of Alexandria, Minnesota, who have a strong interest in the holestones of western Minnesota. Our first stop on the tour was at the Settje house in the village of Corona. There at the doorstep was a small holestone found by Jim Settje in a pile of stones cleared from fields south of Bullhead Lake, Figure 18A. At the time of the discovery, the hole in this stone was nearly full of fine iron rust, the residue of an iron rod that had long ago stood in the hole and slowly rusted away.

Our next stop was at the "A" site, in a pasture at the top of a steep slope about twenty feet above the Whetstone River. Nearly concealed in the grass and almost buried in the glacial till at the edge of the slope, we found ten holestones within a length of about 120 feet, Figure 19. The holes were well centered on all the stones. Four of these stones had been damaged by blasting—two of them to a minor extent and one quite shattered, with all of the large fragments still in place. The blasted stones were perhaps examples of the settlers' Fourth of July celebrations that Holand had proposed to explain the holestones that were elevated high above the water levels in Minnesota.

But again the question immediately came up: Why would the celebrants have chiseled out ten holes and blasted only four of them? It makes better sense to assume that medieval Norsemen chiseled the holes, and the modern settlers simply blasted a convenient few where they were found. The ten stones high above the stream were certainly never used for mooring stones. A single holestone might be consistent with flagpole use at a trading post, but ten holestones in a ragged row at the edge of the slope high above the river are not. Their true purpose was then a perplexing mystery.

FIGURE 19: The "A" site on the Whetstone River, looking eastward in May 2005. The nine holestones are marked by white flags on poles, and the tenth is being excavated. Left to right: Hughes, Rudebusch, Mills, Westin. Photo by Johnson.

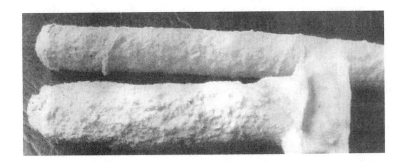

FIGURE 20: Silicone rubber castings of two holes in the stones showing negative images of extreme roughness caused by long-term weathering effects. The casting in front is five inches long. Castings by Cal and Celia Courneya, photo by Judi Rudebusch.

FIGURE 21: A life-sized carved image of a medieval drinking horn at site B. Most of the lichens have been removed to obtain a clean image. Note the highly unusual symmetry of the boulder. The skilled carver of the drinking horn may have also used his chisel to shape and enhance the symmetry of the stone. L. J. Westin photo.

For several years, Cal Courneya has been gathering evidence of long-term weathering that increases the roughness of the inside surfaces of these cylindrical holes in boulders found in Minnesota. He developed an effective technique to document the weathering effects by making silicone rubber castings of the holes. This technique shows that in deep holes the weathering process or the repeated freezing of standing rainwater can have extreme effects. In rare cases the bottom of the hole has been enlarged by slowly removing bits of the rock, thus making the casting look like a penis.

On that September afternoon, we observed Cal and Celia as they made a casting of hole #3, as numbered from the closest holestone flagged in Figure 19. Using a small water pump, they first flushed out the debris that had accumulated in the hole. In addition to dust and bits of weathered rock, the hole contained a large amount of iron rust and a remnant of the original iron as determined by a magnetic test. This holestone, like the Settje stone, had once held an iron object, probably an iron rod. With the hole cleaned out, the two liquid components of the rubber were then mixed and poured into the hole. After allowing many hours for the rubber to solidify, the flexible casting was carefully withdrawn from the hole the next day. The far image in Figure 20 shows the casting from that hole, with all the pits and flat hollows due to weathering now visible in negative form on the surface of the rubber.

FIGURE 22: Close-up view of the drinking horn image. It is eleven inches from lip to tip. The handle is a feature not seen on other surviving medieval drinking horns. R. G. Johnson photo.

After the #3 hole had been filled with the liquid rubber, we all drove on to the next site, the "B" site. Here we opened a pasture gate and viewed a well-grazed grassy slope down to a nearly dry creek. The slope was covered with a scattered array of granite boulders. Without comment, Judi led us halfway down the slope to one of the larger and well-exposed stones, a boulder of gray granite. We had been amazed at the ten holestones earlier that afternoon, but here we were shocked. On the surface of the boulder, sharply illuminated by the afternoon sun, was a deeply carved and life-sized image of a medieval drinking horn, Figures 21 and 22. The Norseman who did the carving probably used his own drinking horn for a model. These photos show that a handle had been carved at its left side, and we could see that the original sharp edges had been somewhat eroded by weathering.

About a hundred feet from this "horn rock" was another smaller boulder with a carved image of a sharply pointed knife, Figure 23. This is an image of a table knife. In medieval times the sharp point was used like we use a fork to eat meat. Forks only came into common use in Europe about AD 1600.[61] The horn rock and the knifestone had been found by Judi Rudebusch's grandfather when he claimed the land as a homestead in the latter part of the 1800s. They were said to have been similarly weathered and lichen covered at that time.

FIGURE 23: Carved image of a medieval table or kitchen knife used to cut and impale meat before forks came into use about AD 1600 in Europe. Bottom: Restored outline, after compensating for weathering losses of stone at the edges. L J. Westin photo.

These carvings evoked a torrent of speculation, and our questions came tumbling out. Why were they carved? Could they have been gravestones? Where was the possible Norse house? Why were there no

---

61.   P. Hardwick. *Discovering Horn* (Guilford: Lutterworth Press, 1981).

holestones at this site? These questions remained open for a year before we could begin to answer them. Our tour continued as the afternoon waned. We visited several more sites, always with the holestones located not far from a stream, but never close enough to the water to have been used as mooring stones—and many of the small streams would not have floated a canoe except when flooded. At one site we found a group of four holestones high above the creek and the length of a football field from the water. At each of two other sites there were two holestones separated by a hundred or more feet.

At one of those sites, the holestone more distant from the creek had been discovered by a farmer in the 1950s. He struck it with his plow when turning over the prairie pasture sod for the first time. The hole at the top of the stone was half a foot below the surface of the sod. He dug the stone up and moved it to the side of the field where we found it with other stones that had been cleared from the field. The buried condition of this holestone when it was discovered is not a reliable measure of its age, but nevertheless, it is consistent with an age of hundreds of years, and the unique unearthing of the stone had excited considerable local comment.

These stones were usually found far from the nearest farmstead, and their proximity to streams, large or small, seemed to be their main shared characteristic. The purpose of the stones was a mystery, and two days later we drove home, discussing our observations all the way back to Minneapolis. One question came up again: Could the carved stones and the scattered holestones be grave markers? If so, it might be possible to collect datable materials by excavating around the stones. Bone can be preserved for long intervals if the soil is not too acidic, and the presence of many glacially deposited fragments of limestone suggested a soil of low acidity. Urged on by such thoughts, we made plans to dig around some of the stones the following spring.

On Friday, 13 May 2005, we returned to the Whetstone area and spent three days working with Judi Rudebusch and a few of her friends on the holestone problem. We were joined this time by Westin's husband, Charlie Hughes, and Dr. Lawrence Mills, a retired professor with an interest in early people of the Americas and related archeology. Our team mapped the "A" site and made an excavation where the grass was thin at the #2 holestone as measured from the west end of the array. No disturbance of the glacial till layers or any indications of a grave were found. We also mapped the horn rock area, the "B" site. We then excavated deeply on the uphill side of the horn rock, keeping in mind the Greenlander's custom of burying their dead with head to the west. Here the only disturbance of the old glacial till appeared to be the result of animal burrows. With a strong wind and a 45°F temperature, our enthusiasm for further digging was limited to a small, shallow pit on the downhill side of the horn rock. That hole yielded a fist-sized rectangular block of granite that appeared to have had a possible application as a hammer or some type of primitive cooking tool.

During lunches and dinner with our hosts we pooled our ideas and enjoyed serious discussions of the Norse artifacts that we had seen, and their puzzling locations relative to the streams. The holestones on the Whetstone River were certainly not mooring stones, and we added the idea of Norse settlements to the idea of the itinerant Norse traders. No itinerant trader passing through would have taken the time to do the meticulous carving of the drinking horn and then done the image of the kitchen knife on another stone a hundred feet away. Those works of art surely tell us that a Norseman was living at that site not far from the stones. Although we excavated across one somewhat flat spot sheltered from winter winds by a nearby hillside, we found no indication of a floor or hearthstone. The spot may have been a natural slump on the hillside. But the long weekend came to an end, and on Monday we filled in all the excavations and returned to Minneapolis.

After considering everything that we had seen, we were able to eliminate several possible uses for the holes in the stones. (1) Land surveyors needed only shallow holes to mark a surveyed position. These holes were deep and therefore were not made by surveyors. (2) The holes were too plentiful to have been made to hold flagpoles for trading posts. (3) They had not been made to obtain rock pieces for building foundations. (4) They had not been made for blasting to facilitate clearing rocks from the fields because most of them were partly buried in place at edges of the fields, just where the last glacier left them thousands of years ago. They were not grave headstones.

Other conclusions followed. These carvings were old. The drinking horn image in the granite boulder showed considerable loss of stone material around its edges due to weathering, which implies a medieval time when drinking horns were in common use and had a significant social and symbolic importance. The age of the knifestone image was probably greater than 400 years, based on the style of the knife. On the other hand, we had not been able to identify any dwelling site, and despite much speculation we still did not have a good working hypothesis to explain the purpose of the holestones and the enigmatic carvings of the knife and drinking horn. Nevertheless, the evidence clearly pointed to a medieval occupation of the area along the Whetstone River by Norsemen.

On 14 September 2005, we returned again with Professor Mills to the Whetstone neighborhood for another three days of investigation. We got to work and enlarged the excavation on the west side of the horn rock, carefully working down to a depth of 2.5 feet. Here we found that the downward sequence of prairie sod, limey clay, and limey pea gravel left by the last glacier was undisturbed even by animals. Test pits to the north and south were no different, and again we concluded that the horn rock was not a grave marker. However, the enlarged excavation did produce an artifact, a simple round scraper with a knapped edge. It lay buried in the sod hardly more than two feet from the rectangular granite "hammer" that we had found in May. The peculiar shape of the hammer and its close association with the scraper leave little doubt that they were used as tools sometime long ago. But were they Indian or Norse? Why were they abandoned within four feet of the horn rock? Frustrating questions, indeed.

Judi Rudebusch gave us another tour, and this time we saw many typical holestones high on hills and far from any stream. Who would have chiseled them, and why? Surely not for flag poles at later traders' rendezvous sites, because water was not easily available.

Again we engaged in much discussion with Judi after days of digging, and now we were able to argue a plausible picture of Norse settlement in the area. The Norse took up all the useable land on Greenland before AD 1000 and the two colonies there would soon have become overpopulated. But the Greenlanders were a seafaring people and the landless younger sons would have been active in their small ships exploring the continental lands to the west. Many would have become traders with the Indians to supply the lucrative Greenland-Norwegian fur trade. That trade resulted in the annexation of Greenland by Norway under the reign of King Haakon IV in AD 1261, before a cooling climate caused the demise of the Greenland colonies. Doubtless the Greenlanders found the mouth of the Nelson River on Hudson Bay early in their voyages and traded there.

The name York Factory, given by the first seventeenth-century traders to the trading post settlement at the mouths of the Nelson and Hays rivers, may have been handed down from the times of Norse trading, when "jorvik" was the Norse word for a trading village on a stream. As we know from the bishop's voyage (see Appendix C) and other old maps, in later medieval times there was a period when trading sites on streams inland from the sea were often designated as "yorks."

Eventually, the restless young Greenlanders would have followed the rivers southward to the treeless plains of South Dakota where they settled and collected furs that were obtained both by trading with the Indians and by their own devices. The streams feeding the Whetstone River would have teemed with fur-bearing animals, and the open country was not unlike treeless Greenland. In many respects a lifestyle there may have been more interesting than in crowded farms on the Greenland coast. And trading furs annually with Greenland merchant ships at the York Factory site would have kept the Norse settlers supplied with items to maintain the trade with the Indians, plus iron tools, knives, whetstones, kitchen utensils, drinking horns, and other things that made life easier for the Norse themselves. However, this picture of Norse settlement still lacked an explanation for the holes and the drinking horn and knife images on the stones. A medieval Norse artist might have done the knife and drinking horn for his own pleasure, but we have found by experience that the deep holes are difficult and time-consuming to chisel out and would not have been done for pleasure.

This third visit to the Whetstone River sites that September did not add very much to our evidence for Norse settlement, but the answer to the holestone question was closer than we knew. Thanks to Internet communications and information technology, Judi Rudebusch has been engaged in a never-ending search for sources of information on Norse history and culture. She had developed a correspondence with Valdimar Samuelsson of Reykjavik, Iceland, an engineer who has a strong interest in early Icelandic history and Norse explorations. She had told him about our investigations and our evidence for Norse residence in the Whetstone River area, and the holestone mystery that had yet to be solved.

Valdimar became interested in our work because similar holestones are found on Iceland. With the help of the long days of the far north that summer of 2005, he looked into some of the ancient property boundary lines near Reykjavik and found that they were still marked by holestones like those we saw in South Dakota, and this was surely the answer to the holestone puzzle. Like similar stones on Iceland, the isolated single holestones at the edges of fields and not far from the South Dakota streams had been the end-point markers for ancient property boundary lines, defined by holestones when the Norse farmer-traders occupied the area in medieval times. But South Dakota farmers have now cleared nearly all such stones off their fields and the old widely spaced stones in rows are gone. Even holestones up on hilltops were probably end-point markers, for on Iceland the marked boundaries extended also to the hilltops, as shown on updated maps of the old properties, Figure 24.

An example of an Icelandic boundary marker is shown in Figure 25. In an open pasture Valdimar found an ancient boundary, Figure 26, which is marked by widely spaced volcanic boulders containing nearly cylindrical holes that were typically made with a broad-blade chisel. This line of stones may date from as early as the thirteenth century when the Church began to acquire many of the small farms. After consultation with Sesselja Gudmundsdottir, an author, on the history of this area, he reported:

In Iceland on Kelines on the SW coast there is an uninvestigated line of stones, where the line starts on a known coastal boundary between two farms. Those boundary stones are believed to be from before 1400 AD, and formed a piece of land where the monastery at Videy Island got grazing rights for cattle. Grazing at the sea coast was all year grazing due to an abundance of seaweed.

From the earliest times, the settlers in Iceland used poles to mark the land boundaries. Valdimar reported an example from the *Landnámabók*, Chapter 73:

When settlers (about 900 AD) could not mark their land with natural marks like in most cases (hills, rivers, and so on) they would use wooden poles. Example: The early settler Gardar Svavarsson gave his slave, Nattfari, land on the northeast of Iceland. He marked his land with wooden poles.

Permanent markers for the boundaries were needed and the use of holes in stones to hold the poles in position is understood. The use of holes in stones for marking boundaries may have evolved from the earlier custom of mooring boats to stones on the shore near the owner's dwelling. In the English translation of the second volume of the old Icelandic law book *Gragas Konungsbók II*,[62] Judi Rudebusch found instructions for handling land disputes:

If you have trouble with your neighbor over the boundary stones, you are to call your warranty man and you are to meet at the 'mooring stakes' (to resolve the dispute).

---

62. V. Finsen, ed. *Gragas: Konungsbok*, 2 vols. Copenhagen, 1852, Old Icelandic normalized with Danish footnotes and comment, reprinted in 1974.

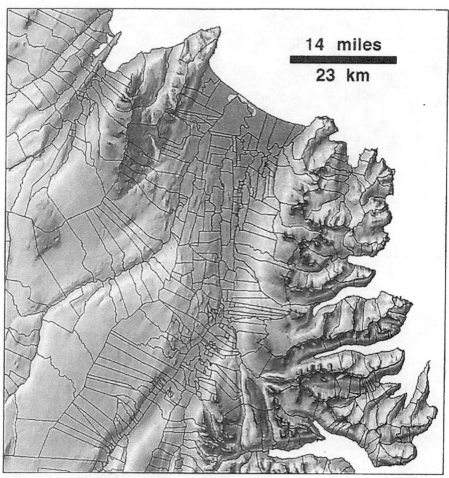

3. mynd Landamerki á Norðausturlandi.

FIGURE 24: Plan view of an area in northeastern Iceland showing how the ancient property boundaries were established using streams and high ridge lines as well as cairns and marking stones. We have seen such stones (holestones) on a high ridge crest of the coteau in eastern South Dakota. From: www.nytjaland.is.pdf

FIGURE 25: A boundary marker hole in bedrock on Iceland. A steel rod rebar has been set into the rock next to the hole to ensure that its location could be easily found. Photos by Valdimar Samuelsson, used with permission.

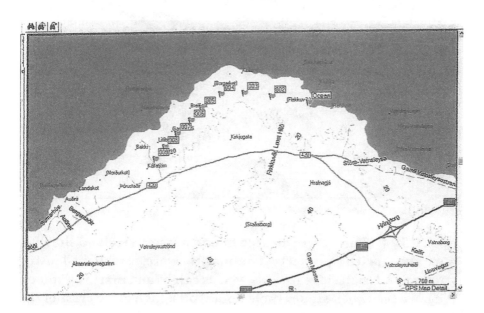

FIGURE 26: A line of holestones marked in this illustration by flags on an ancient pasture boundary on the coast of Iceland near Reykjavik. Courtesy of Valdimar Samuelsson.

FIGURE 27: A relief carving from the Island of Gotland that depicts the transfer of land (top) and the custom of walking the land boundaries when establishing a new boundary or when annually re-affirming an old one (below). State Historical Museum, Stockholm.

The "mooring stakes," the "festar haell,"[63] is a legal term. "Haell" has the meaning of a peg, a pin, or a stake in the context of marking property boundaries. "Festar" means "to stick fast" and "to settle, to stipulate." The term "festar haell" is the legal stipulation for an agreed-upon property boundary marker, that is, the stake fastened firmly into a hole chiseled into the rock. So, the *Gragas* tells us that marking boundaries with holestones was a venerable legal practice in Iceland, and the custom would have been carried forward with the Norse wherever they settled. However, we found no lines of stones in the Whetstone area on the scale of those observed on Iceland. In Iceland

---

63. See "festar" (Zoëga, 136) and "haell" (Zoëga, 222). The keys to the repetitive references in all our translations are summarized at the beginning of Appendix D.

the land has remained pastured, and the holestones are still in place. But settlers of the late nineteenth century in South Dakota and Minnesota cleared away all the stones on their fields to permit cultivation. Consequently, the remaining holestones that we observed were at the edge of the cultivated land, in pastures, or in some cases in piles of rock that have been cleared from the fields, and a few at the top of high points where cultivation was never attempted.

Valdimar also noted that on Iceland it had been the custom to "walk the landmarks" of the farms (email communication of 21 March 2006), a widespread custom in Scandanavia, Figure 27. Walking was done on Rogation Day by people of the neighborhood to revalidate the land boundaries. In one old document,[64] the land-walking committee tells the new owner "to set and cover two more mark stones with witness stones."

The witness stones were used to make sure the mark stones (the holestones) were visible and could be located in the future when the land walking was done again. This implies that not all the boundary stones in Iceland had poles inserted into holes, particularly in later times when all the trees had been cut down and poles were not readily available. Wooden stakes eventually decay and disappear, but in South Dakota the iron rods that once stood in the Settje stone and in the No. 3 stone at the "A" site would have lasted a few centuries before they rusted away, and while they remained no witness stone would have been needed. But iron rods would have been precious, and most hole-stones would not have had one.

The hornstone and knifestone at the "B" site would have needed witness stones. Perhaps the hammer-sized block of granite was at one time just such a witness stone sitting on top of the hornrock to aid in locating the marker rock on the boundary in the tall prairie grass of medieval times. The neighbors were then "walking the property boundaries" of an artistic Norseman who chose to carve a drinking horn image instead of chiseling a simple cylindrical hole to mark the

---

64. *Reykholar 1572: Stofnum Arna Magnussonar*, Reykjavik. The ritual of walking the boundary is also depicted in a relief carving from Gotland as shown on page 248 in *The Norsemen*, by Eric Oxenstierna, translated and edited by C. Hutter (New York: New York Graphic Society, 1965).

boundary near his house at the edge of the stream.

It is a safe conclusion that in the Whetstone area there were medieval Norse properties with boundaries that were defined by hole-stones, properties that were spaced along even the smallest streams at intervals much like those of the ancient farms on Iceland, Figure 24. Did the Dakota Norse have livestock like their ancestors on Greenland and Iceland? Sheep and cattle could have been transported to the Whetstone area in the small boats used by the Norse, although trans-porting livestock in boats upstream and over portages the 900 or more miles from Hudson Bay would require considerable effort.

But the Norsemen on the Graenaveldi had to pay for their drinking horns, knives, cooking utensils, hammers and chisels, iron rods, ropes, and other necessities of life, such as, perhaps, wool clothing. For payment, they would have traded furs. Fur was the most valuable commodity of those times, and the property boundaries would most likely have defined areas along the streams and away on the prairies, areas in which pelts could be harvested every year in addition to the furs obtained in trade from the neighboring Indians. That trade may have been necessary to maintain peaceful relations with the Indian tribes. The streams would have harbored beaver, mink, and muskrat, and the prairie terrain would have supplied ferrets, ermine, and badger, and occasionally a wandering black bear. The furs not used at home for protection against the bitter cold winters would have been carried in small boats northward down the rivers to the trading post on Hudson Bay, Figure 9. There the trade bargains would have been struck annu-ally with the West Greenland sea merchants who took the furs back to Greenland for eventual shipment to Norway and the European markets. The downstream trip during the spring flood could have been done in little more than seven weeks.[65]

The concept of fur trade with the people of North America is well founded. Helge Ingstad[66] provides details in support of the trade,

---

65. Seven weeks was the time required when Minnesota students Scott Miller, Todd Foster, and Matt Lutz traveled by canoe from Big Stone Lake to Hudson Bay in the spring high water period in 2005, as reported when interviewed by author Johnson.

66. H. Ingstad in *Westward to Vinland*.

which was taxed when the goods arrived at the port of Bergen:

> In 1516 the Norwegian Archbishop Erik Valkendorf
> planned an expedition to Greenland, and for that
> purpose he took steps to collect information about
> conditions in that faraway land. In his notes we are told
> that there were black bear and marten in that country.
> A similar and quite independent piece of information
> appears in a work by Absalon Pedersen Beyer in 1567.
> He relates that in Greenland there were sable, marten,
> deer, and huge forests; but none of these are, in fact,
> found in Greenland. Both Valkendorf and Absalon
> Beyer lived in Bergen, the centre for the Greenland
> trade. In that city there must have been available lists of
> products that originated in Greenland, not least because
> both King and Church collected taxes on them. For that
> reason it seems likely that some of the information
> cited by Valkendorf and Beyer was based on such lists of
> imports—but these lists on the other hand, would not
> specify whether certain commodities, such as sables and
> the furs of black bears, had come from Greenland or
> from North America via Greenland.

Although the Whetstone River area has not yet yielded archeological evidence for the Norse other than the holes in stones and the
two carved images, there is significant evidence for Norse river travel
northward. There would have been many campsites along the Red and
Nelson Rivers that were repeatedly used during their annual trading
voyages to the port on Hudson Bay. In 1871 one of these campsites was
found by a settler, Ole Jevning, on his newly claimed farm about four-
and-one-half miles north of the town of Climax, Minnesota. The site
is on a dry knoll adjacent to a bayou of the Red River. Documents that
describe this discovery were published by Hjalmar Holand[67] and
Jevning's letter is reproduced here.

---

67. Holand. *Westward from Vinland*, 215–217.

Climax, Minn. June 8, 1914

I have your letter concerning the firesteel which I found. I settled here in June, 1871, and we were the first to take land around here. A short time after I settled here I was boring holes with a six-inch post-hole auger. When I got about two feet down I heard something scrape against the auger and I pulled it up thinking I had struck a stone. The dirt clung to the auger and I examined it looking for the stone and found a little firesteel. It was much rusted and there was also some charcoal and ashes. It must have been there a long time because the place where the hole was bored was on a dry elevation. The firesteel is just the same size and form as my grandmother used 65 or 66 years ago. And now I will tell you how it is used . . .

[Signed] Ole Jevning

Some years later A.O. Stortroen, who was Jevning's son-in-law, made a notarized affidavit relating these facts of Jevning's discovery. This document was added to Holand's collection, and the firesteel now rests in the Kensington Runestone museum in Alexandria, Minnesota. The notarized affidavit is important because it shows in a legal sense that the firesteel was not brought into the country by a modern-day settler. The denial of authenticity of this firesteel by Wallace and Fitzhugh[68] is a denial of documented fact, apparently made to defend their opinion that no medieval Norse settlement on the continent occurred. The best explanation for this firesteel is that it was lost by a medieval Norseman when making his annual trip to Hudson Bay to trade his furs.

---

68. B. Wallace and W. Fitzhugh. "Stumbles and pitfalls in the search for Viking America." *Vikings: The North Atlantic Saga* (Washington: Smithsonian Institution Press, 2000), 374–384. Wallace and Fitzhugh present an astounding array of unsupported and distorted "facts" in condemning American runestones and all the artifacts of European origin that support medieval presence of Norse on the continent.

The holestones imply ownership of defined property along the streams, and it is legitimate to speculate that a simple system of government prevailed, much as in the Iceland homeland, where the annual governing meeting was called the "Althing." We have yet to precisely identify any site where such a regional meeting might have been held. But a possibility would be the current Hartford Beach Park on the south shore of Big Stone Lake where a creek comes down from the prairie above, just off Highway 15, Figure 18A. This location would have been a pleasant place that was accessible by rivers from both Dakota and western Minnesota.

The "A" site with its ten holestones in a ragged row above the Whetstone River might have been the site of a local meeting place, known in Iceland as a "Thing." Within two miles of that site there are nine holestone locations. If a Norse extended family occupied a "farm" corresponding to each of these locations, every time the head of the household went to a local meeting and took his dog along, he could have used a wood pole or iron rod in one of the ten holestones to tie up his dog during the meeting. And the Norse, like the Indians, most certainly had dogs. So it appears that the Norse had at least three uses for the holestones: mooring boats, marking property lines, and tethering animals. If flags or banners were used on the Graenaveldi in those times, they could also have been attached to poles set into the holes.

The absence of any visible remains of a house at the "A" site is not surprising. In the intervening 600 years or more the wood of the house would have totally decayed, and on the flat surface of the bluff back of the holestones the remaining stone hearth and postholes would have been covered deeply with dust brought by the winds from the more arid plains to the west. A careful excavation would be necessary to reveal the ancient hearthstone and postholes of the building.

To summarize the picture of the Greenlanders' widespread trading activity in North America, we conclude that an important part of the fur trade in the twelfth, thirteenth, and early fourteenth centuries involved a Norse colony on the prairie veldt of South Dakota and western Minnesota. An equally important part was the trade with the

Norsemen living along the coasts of Vinland and Whitemansland.

In Appendix C we describe evidence for a bishop's visit to Vinland on a trading ship in AD 1117 and 1118. Furthermore, we know the Greenland trade in goods from the continent was taxed by Norway. Here is an account from the early Icelandic records that contain the discussion by Sturla Thordarson, a thirteenth-century Icelander, on the taxation of the Greenlanders by the king of Norway. Valdimar Samuelsson's translation from Jon Duason,[69] a modern scholar in Iceland, describes the formal arrangement at the time of Greenland's annexation in 1261:

> He (Duason) refers to the writings of Sturla about when the King of Norway wanted tax from people of Greenland in 1257 to 1261. Sturla said: "This fall those men (tax men) came from Greenland: Ivar Enggla-son, Oddur from Sjoltum, Pall Magnusson and Knarrar-leif. They had been four years out and got a promise from people that they would pay the King's tax. The promise was from all people, all the way to the polar-star, Leidarstjornu. Then Jon Duason said: "When the King sent tax men to Iceland there was never more than one man, but to Greenland the King sent four. This shows they must have gone over all Whiteman land, Vinland, and farther, including Graenaveldi . . ."

The "veld" is a cognate of the Old English "feld," a field or, specifically, a grassland with few trees. This usage of the word "Graenaveldi" therefore distinguishes the open plains of North America from the better-known woodlands of the Vinland part of the trade empire. From the writings of the Icelandic historian Jon Duason, we know that King Haakon IV of Norway could rightly be called the first king of Norse America, because he made an honest effort to make sure that all the Norsemen in the trade empire were informed of his tax on the

---

69. J. Duason. *Landkonnun og Landbam Islendinga I vestur Heimi* (Exploring and settling of Iceland in the western world), Reykjavik, 1941.

trade when Iceland and the Greenland trade empire were annexed in 1261.

Finally, we can thank Judi Rudebusch and our friends in Iceland for solving the mystery of the many, many single, isolated holestones that are scattered over the Dakotas and Minnesota. They were used as mooring stones or boundary markers for the properties of the Norse farmer-traders. Without the fur trade with the Indians, it is not likely that the Norse could have lived peacefully on those relatively isolated "farms" during medieval times. When Greenland became colder and the trade ceased, not all the tribes would have continued to tolerate the Norse. Hostilities doubtless occurred, and the Norse way of life on the plains disappeared, leaving behind only carvings of a drinking horn, a knife, and the holestone boundary markers. To survive, the Norsemen merged with a friendly tribe and became known to the regional Indians as the large tribe of white Indians, the Mandans, when Pierre Verendrye found them living in five villages on the upper Missouri River in 1738.[70]

---

70.   Holand. *Westward from Vinland*, 264–267. The evidence that we describe linking the
Mandan Indians to their ancestral Norse is quite strong, but this link is not new.
Eminent geologist and scholar N.H. Winchell suggested that the Mandans' culture
was derived from the Norse of medieval times. See N.H. Winchell, *The Aborigines of
Minnesota*, 1911, 574. Cited in Holand, 1946, 237. H. Holand. *Westward from Vinland*, 265.
Holand also cites Pierre la Verendrye's *Journal (1738)*, in *South Dakota Historical Collections*,
VII, 340 ff. Verendrye's impression when he encountered the first of five Mandan
villages was that the description of "white Indians" was a gross exaggeration, but upon
visiting the other villages, he found that indeed there were large numbers of people
with blond characteristics. This is made clear in the following translation from the
Journal by Brymner, *Report on Canadian Archives*, Ottawa 1889, 1890, 3, ff:
      M. de la Marque and I walked about to observe the size of their fort and their
fortifications. I decided to have the huts counted. It was found that there were 130 of
them. All the streets, squares and huts resembled each other. Several of our Frenchmen
wandered about, they found the streets and squares very clean, the ramparts very
level and broad; the palisades supported on cross-pieces mortised into posts of fifteen
feet to twice twenty feet. There are green skins which are put for sheathing where
required, fastened only above in the places needed, as in the bastion there are four at
each curtain well flanked. The fort is built on a height in the open prairie with a ditch
upwards of fifteen feet deep by fifteen or eighteen feet wide. Their fort can only be
gained by steps or posts, which can be removed when threatened by an enemy. If all
their forts are alike, they may be called impregnable to Indians. *Their fortifications are
not Indian. This nation is mixed white and black. The women are fairly good-looking, especially
the white, many with blond and fair hair.* Both men and women of this nation are very
laborious; their huts are large and spacious, separated into several apartments by thick
planks; nothing is left lying about; all their baggage is in large bags hung on posts;

And that is how our story ends. The descendants of the medieval Norsemen who chose to leave Greenland and live in the Western Lands are with us still. Many have blended completely into the population, but not all. We have a nation of the Iroquois who, according to Arlington Mallery,[71] are more Norse than Indian and now live along the St. Lawrence River. And the descendants of the medieval Mandans now share the larger Graenaveldi with earlier immigrants from Siberia and with their cousins who arrived more recently from Scandinavia and northern Europe.

---

their beds made like tombs surrounded by skins . . . Their fort is full of caves (caches) in which are stored such articles as grain, food, fat, dressed robes, bear skins. They are well supplied with these; it is the money of the country . . . The men are stout and tall, generally very active, fairly good looking, with a good physiognomy. *The women have not the Indian physiognomy.* The men indulge in a sort of ball play on the squares and ramparts. [Emphasis is ours.]

Although it has been suggested that the blond characteristics of these people originated from contacts with European fur traders of the eighteenth century, similar trader contacts with other Indian tribes did not result in a significant change in the tribal appearance there. George Catlin (*North American Indians*, P. Matthiessen, ed., (New York: Penguin Books, 1989), 87–97, suggested that the tribe originated as an amalgam with a blond race, possibly the Welch. He lived with the Mandans for many months in 1836, and wrote extensively describing their unique traditions, culture, and physical characteristics at a time when the tribe still numbered a few thousand people. He wrote:

I have been struck with the peculiar ease and elegance of these people, together with the diversity of complexions, the various colours of their hair and eyes; the singularity of their language, and their peculiar and unaccountable customs . . . There are a great many of these people whose complexions appear as light as half breeds; and amongst the women particularly there are many whose skins are almost white, with the most pleasing symmetry and proportion of features, with hazel, with grey and with blue eyes . . . Since that time (of Lewis and Clarke) there have been but very few visits from white men to this place, and surely not enough to have changed the complexions and the customs of a nation.

The almost fifty holestone sites identified in Figure 18 could have represented a population of 250 Norse if at least five individuals lived near each site. The large number of unmapped holestones elsewhere on the Graenaveldi could have doubled or tripled that number to give an estimated population of ~750 Norse that merged with a friendly tribe. If that tribe had been of comparable size, the blond imprint of the Norse on subsequent generations would easily have resulted in the "white" tribe of about 10,000 Mandans found by Verendrye in 1738 on the Missouri River.

71.   A. Mallery and M.R. Harrison, *The rediscovery of Lost America*, 53, 54.

EPILOGUE II

Every explorer, upon returning from far away unknown lands, writes a report. His sponsor requires it and his ego demands it, for why discover new things unless their story can be told? Authors Johnson and Westin are no exception, and the story of our discoveries had to be told. Hence the book.

The book began as a report of our investigations in western Minnesota and South Dakota featuring our recognition of "this island" of the Kensington runestone inscription and the identification of holestones as Norse property boundary markers. Our hypothesis of a fur trade context to sustain the Norse settlers on the plains was and is a core explanation for the Norse settlements. We also expected to propose a link between our findings on the central plains of North America and other Norse trade activity and settlement on the eastern coasts.

That plan seemed to be inadequate after we contacted Sue Carlson of the *New England Antiquities Research Association* to find out if we should be concerned about the Spirit Pond runestone, about which we knew very little. Her generous response was to send us the entire history of the Spirit Pond stone, consisting of the reports and most of the literature on the stone written since its discovery in 1971. We quickly abandoned our first idea for the book because the Spirit Pond inscription contained the name "Haakon" and his lost "companions twelve," which we thought could be a key to the history of the rune-stone. Indeed it was, and that made the Spirit Pond stone even more significant than the familiar Kensington runestone. We quickly identified "Haakon" as fourteenth-century Haakon VI of Norway, the un-named "you" in King Magnus's enigmatic 1354 proclamation. There were other Haakons in Norwegian dynastic history, but only Haakon VI fits precisely together with all the other pieces of this historical jigsaw puzzle. It was a puzzle for which our solution was made possible by two key contributors, historian Marguerite Ragnow of the University of Minnesota, who coached us on the requirements for accurate translation of the Old Norse runes, and Sue Carlson, who has had a sustained interest in the Spirit Pond runestones for many years.

In her own translation, Sue Carlson was the first to recognize that the Spirit Pond inscription was a poem. She had also flagged many points where the meaning of the poetic inscription was quite uncertain, and much more needed to be done to find its unknown context and to make good sense of what the inscription said. On a first examination of the runic inscription, one of author Westin's observations was that in many cases the runic word was marked by a short bar (called an overbar) above the word to show that the word was an abbreviation, a common practice that she had already encountered in many medieval Latin manuscripts. She remarked that if the abbreviated words and other poetically shortened words could be restored, she could probably translate the inscription herself.

So Westin began the difficult task of word restoration, which required nearly three years of our joint effort in which we restored every shortened word to its grammatically correct ending and its probable intended meaning. Context was crucial to an accurate translation. Author Johnson dug into the history of events in Scandinavia leading up to the acclamation and the empowerment of Haakon VI as king of Norway. The context for the inscription then slowly became clear. Rather than just a simple report describing our discoveries, our focus broadened to include King Magnus's six-year expedition to the

Western Lands. Finally, the pieces of the puzzle came together to provide a complete explanation for the existence of these two controversial American runestones. But controversies do not often end quickly, and the authoritative acceptance of our story remains to be seen.

APPENDICES

APPENDIX A:

NORSE ON THE CONTINENT: L'ANSE AUX MEADOWS AND CARBON 14 DATING

Although technically not on the continent, the thoroughly investigated Norse settlement at L'Anse aux Meadows at the tip of the long northern promontory of Newfoundland, Figure 28, implies trade in the Vinland area in the years following the Vinland Voyages of discovery that ended about AD 1017. There is abundant evidence that this site was a ship repair site where trading ships probably wintered. The site is located on small Black Duck Brook that empties into Epaves Bay (Shipwreck Bay). It faces the open sea, though protected somewhat from "northeaster" storms by a small peninsula. The published carbon 14 age of this settlement brackets the known interval of the Vinland Voyages. Because of that, Wallace has identified the site as the location of Leif Eriksson's houses.[72] She argues that such a prominent

---

72. B.L. Wallace. "The Viking Settlement at L'anse aux Meadows," in *Vikings, the North Atlantic Saga*, 215. Also "An archeologist's interpretation of the Vinland Sagas," ibid., 227. Likewise: S.E. Morrison insists that Leif's wintering site was L'anse aux Meadows, see: *The European Discovery of America* (New York: Oxford University Press, 1971), 47. Neither Wallace nor Morrison cite their source for the translations of the description of Leif's approach to his "hop." On the other hand, Keneva Kunz's compendium of all the Icelandic sagas is quite authoritative, and there the details of Leif's approach to his first wintering site are quite clear, as shown in Figure 28. That site is Carpon Cove, not L'anse aux Meadows.

settlement at the time of the Vinland Voyages would surely have been noted in the sagas if it were a site other than the one occupied by Leif, subsequently by his brother Thorvald, and still later by the expedition of Thorfinn Karlsefni, who had Leif's permission to use the houses as his base in the new land.

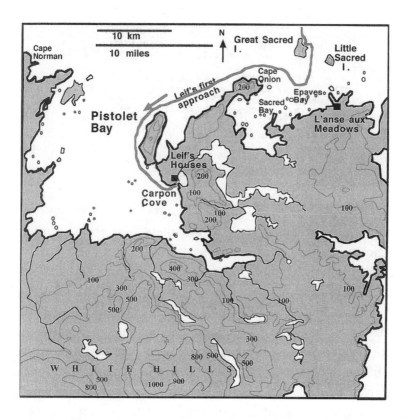

FIGURE 28: The Pistolet Bay neighborhood on the tip of the northern peninsula of Newfoundland. The L'anse aux Meadows site is seventeen miles northeast of the probable site of Leif Eriksson's houses, as shown at Carpon Cove. The water in the "hop" would have been somewhat salty, and Leif's houses may have been built at the mouth of the river half a mile to the northeast of the black square where fresh water would have been available. The Carpon Cove site is uniquely consistent with the description of Leif's first approach in the saga of the Vinland Voyages. Elevations in feet.

Nevertheless, contrary to the site description in Leif's saga, the L'Anse aux Meadows site is fully exposed to the open sea to the north-west and it is not on a "hop," Leif's lake that was connected to the sea by tidal flow. In *The Saga of Greenlanders* the description of Leif's discovery[73] precisely matches his approach shown in Figure 28. The saga says:

> ... They sailed towards it (the land) and came to an island (Great Sacred Island), which lay to the north of the land, where they went ashore. In the fine weather they found dew on the grass that they collected in their hands and drank, and thought they had never tasted anything as sweet. Afterwards they returned to their ship and sailed into the sound, which lay between the island and the headland that stretched out northwards from the land. They rounded the headland and steered westward. Here there were extensive shallows at low tide and their ship was soon stranded, and the sea looked far away to those aboard ship. Their curiosity to see the land was so great that they could not be bothered to wait for the tide to come in and float their stranded ship, and they ran aground (with the afterboat) where a river flowed into the sea from a lake. When the incoming tide floated the ship again, they took the boat and rowed to the ship and moved it up into the river and from there into the lake, where they cast anchor ...

Carpon Cove in Pistolet Bay is "far from the open sea" and a river flows into the cove out of a lake through a narrow neck. Leif's ship ran aground in Carpon Cove before high tide on the day he arrived, so the eager Norsemen took their small afterboat and rowed it into the lake without waiting for the tide to rise to enable them to tow the ship into the lake. For ships, the L'Anse aux Meadows site is safer than

---

73. Kunz. *The Sagas of Icelanders*, 639.

Leif's site because it has fewer shoals and has deep water up to the shoreline. The L'Anse aux Meadows site was not where Leif landed and was not mentioned in the sagas of the Vinland Voyages. Therefore, the accepted age of the L'Anse aux Meadows settlement that falls within the interval of the Vinland Voyages is wrong.

Reidar Nydal of the Norwegian Institute of Technology published an authoritative review of the age measurements of the wood and the peat in 1989.[74] The currently accepted age measurement for the site is within the statistical range of AD 986–1022, and was obtained from carbon 14 measurements of sixteen wood pieces found within the collapsed walls of peat in one of the dwellings where extensive ship repair had occurred. The age range of thirty-six years deceptively brackets the age of the Vinland Voyages that began a few years after AD 1000 and ended about 1017, as known from historical records.

Figure 29 shows the calibration plot used to convert raw carbon 14 ages to calendar ages over the last thousand years. It shows that wood, which grew at the time of the Vinland Voyages, would give an accurate calendar age, *if uncontaminated*, in contrast to wood grown more recently than about 1650, for which the calibration gives multiple ambiguous calendar year values. Nydal cautions that humic acid from decaying younger vegetation in the peat could have made the measured peat ages too young, and he says that no treatment was done to remove humic acid. But two of four peat ages listed by Nydal have ages in the range of 640 to 780 AD, which is 200–300 years older than the best of the measured ages of wood samples from within the houses.

We note that if humic acid from young vegetation might make the peat ages too young, then humic acid from decaying peat itself would have made the ages of the wood samples too old. The wood samples would have been contaminated by exposure to humic acid leached out from the older peat by centuries of rainwater soaking through the decaying collapsed walls, a fact not noted by Nydal. Therefore, the final age bracket published by Nydal is too old, and the true age of the L'Anse aux Meadows houses is younger, probably a few decades younger, than the Vinland Voyages. Consequently, we interpret the

---

74.   R. Nydal. *Radiocarbon 31*, 1989, 976–985.

settlement as a way station for the fur trade on the Vinland coasts that became important after the Vinland Voyage of Thorfinn Karlsefni about AD 1015, in which he showed how wealth could be easily gained by trading with the Indians for furs.

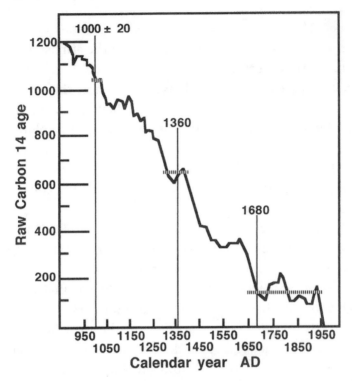

FIGURE 29: The calibration plot for converting raw carbon 14 ages of wood to calendar ages. See Stuiver et al., *Radiocarbon 40*, 1998, 1041–1083. This plot could be used, with minor adjustments, for any organic material in this age range that grew in equilibrium with the carbon dioxide of the atmosphere. Hatched crossbars indicate the range of uncertainty (excluding small random statistical variations) in calendar age for three respective raw carbon 14 ages.

It is appropriate to note here that the calendar ages of wood, or any other organic material formed by extracting carbon from the atmosphere, cannot be measured with any reliability if the material is younger than about AD 1650 because several widely spaced younger calendar year values in the calibration plot correspond to any one raw carbon 14 measurement. In the case of attempts to date the mortar of the Newport Tower by carbon 14 methods, rainwater containing carbon dioxide will have penetrated into the mortar of the Newport Tower over the centuries. Rainwater is slightly acidic and will have contaminated the mortar by carbonic acid reactions and by carbon atom exchange with younger carbon 14 from the atmosphere.[75]

Because of this effect, mortar used in 1360 for church construction would not be dated reliably with carbon 14, and the error effect of younger carbon from the atmosphere could have given the age of 1680 that has been claimed to support the hypothesis of a colonial age for the tower (see J. Hale, et al. "Dating ancient mortar," *American Scientist 91*, 2003, 130–137). But this age is ambiguous because of the multiple values of the calibration plot, Figure 29, and it is erroneous because of contamination by younger carbon.

The historical record of Verrazzano's voyage of 1524, discussed earlier, contains observations of the tower. Verrazzano was the source of the 1569 Mercator map rendition of the tower, Figure 4, published half a century before European settlement began in New England. Although Giovanni himself did not mention the tower in his report, his brother, Gerolamo, who was also on the expedition, certainly observed and examined it, because he put the tower in the correct area of the coast on his simplistic map. Gerolamo called it a "tolovilla." "Tolo" is derived from the Greek "tholos," a "centralized building of circular plan," an apt description of the Newport Tower.[76]

---

75. An excellent summary of the problems involved in the carbon 14 dating of the mortar in the Newport Tower is found in a paper by Rob Carter, "Radiocarbon Dating of the Newport Tower" (Edgecomb, ME: *NEARA Journal*, vol. 41 Number 2, winter 2007, 35–41).

76. C.F. Waidmann. "Who built the Newport Tower?" In *The Newport Tower: Arnold to Zeno.* J. Dranchak, ed. (Edgecomb, ME: NEARA Publications, 2006).

APPENDIX B:

NORSE ON THE CONTINENT: WHITEMANSLAND AND THE FUR TRADE

Place names handed down over the centuries indicate Norse habitation on the coasts of Labrador and northern Quebec, commonly known to the Norse as "Whitemansland," Figure 3, from the natives' custom of wearing their fur clothing skin-side out. Place names on current detailed Canadian maps[77] of the Labrador and Quebec coasts often end in the suffix "vik," the Norse word-ending that indicates a man's residence or a village, which was usually named after the original Norse settler. Eight of these Canadian names are the phonetic equivalent of Norse names still in use on Iceland, and forty-two others have the "vik" suffix attached to a non-Norse name or word in the contemporary Indian dialect, usually applied to locations on the coasts that were probably occupied by the mixed-blood descendents of the original Norse. The eight examples are displayed in Table 1.

---

77. Coastal maps in Index #1, *Maps of the National topographic system of Canada*, Natural Resources Canada, Ottawa, Canada, K1A OE9.

TABLE 1

Canadian place name	Icelandic place name or name*
Adlavik	Adlaivik or Adalvik
Aivirsiuvik	Iversson* + vik
Arvavik	Alvik
Aulassivik	Olauss* + vik
Aulatsivik	Olafsvik
Kovik	Kollavik
Makkovik	Markvik
Savik	Selvik

There is documented evidence of one Icelander who lived in Whitemansland soon after the Vinland Voyages. The *Landnámabók*, the Icelandic *Book of Settlements*, tells us that Ari, son of Már of Hólum, was a trader who was well known in Ireland. The *Landnámabók* provides a genealogical record of prominent Icelanders from the time of settlement through the twelfth century, and the translated narrative[78] tells of Ari's residence in Whitemansland with other Norsemen:

Már of Hólum married Thorkotlu, the daughter of Hergils; their son was Ari. He (Ari) was driven off course to Whitemansland; that some people call Ireland the great; that lies west of the ocean near Vinland the good; that is said to be six (sixteen?) daegra (twenty-four-hour days) of sailing westward from Ireland. Thence Ari was not able to go away and was baptized there. These things were said first by Raven the Lymreksfarer who for a long time had business at

---

78. In chapter 43 of the *Landnámabók*, *Sturlubók* version, Eiriki Rognvaldssyni, ed., posted on the Internet December 1998. A complete copy is on the Wikipedia site (accessed March 2011).

Lymrek in Ireland. The poet asked Thorkell Gellisson to tell men of Iceland that he had heard from a conversation with Thorfinn, Earl of the Orkneys, that Ari had claims (of land) to hold in Whitemansland, and could not get away, and he was well-respected there.[79]

Ari's lineage makes possible an estimate of the approximate date when he lived in Whitemansland. The *Landnámabók*, Chapter 30, says that Ari's great grandfather, Ulfur the talkative, came to Iceland with Steinholf the tall, probably in the AD 930–950 interval. Ulfur married Björgu, daughter of Eyvindar "austmanns" who was an earlier emigrant from Norway. Ulfur's son was Atli the red. Atli married Thorbjörgu and their son was Már of Hólum. He married Thorkötlu, and their son was Ari. As in the well-known example of Thorfinn Karlsefni who came to Greenland from Iceland with his ship and forty men and then married Gudrid, a Greenlander, it appears that men of means on Iceland usually spent some time accumulating wealth before marriage. Consequently, the span of time between Ulfur's arrival and marriage in Iceland and his great grandson Ari's trading voyages could easily have been ninety to one hundred years. This would place the time of Ari's trading and his residence and baptism on Labrador around AD 1030 or 1040, perhaps twenty years after the Vinland Voyages.

In an excellent summary of evidence for pre-Columbian trading by Greenland Norse in North America[80], Richard Nielsen presents evidence for Norse trading activity in Whitemansland as far north as Ungava Bay. Most of his discussion concerns other parts of the continent where rivers provided trading routes for the Indian populations and the resident Norse. The emphasis is on the Red and Nelson River route, which is known to have been used by the Mandans to carry furs to the trading post (the factory) on Hudson Bay in the 1670s.

There is abundant evidence for the furs that were collected in

---

79. Arlington Mallery, in *The Rediscovery of Lost America*, 79, puts Ari's residence somewhere along the St. Lawrence River rather than in Labrador.

80. R. Nielsen. "About the West: Early Scandinavian Incursions into the Western States," *Journal of the West*, January 2000, Vol. 39, No. 1, 72–86.

medieval North America and were delivered to the port of Bergen in Norway. Nielsen cites Prytz (1991), who noted that the imports from Greenland included marmot, otter, beaver, wolverine, lynx, sable, and black bear furs, all of continental North American origin. Prytz (1991) also reported a 1369 statement by Philippe de Meziéres who said:

> The King of Norway had an enormous kingdom. And parts of it were an island in the ocean so far from Norway and beyond Godeland (Greenland?) that some ships sent to collect tax for him from his subjects took three years on the voyage back and forth.

This is probably a reference to the voyages around 1261 in which King Haakon IV sent out men to arrange the formal annexation of Greenland and Iceland, and in which he made known to all the Norsemen involved in the trade that the trade would be (or would continue to be) taxed. Nielsen also cited Thompson (1996), who stated that in 1567 Absalon Beyer of Bergen wrote that "Greenland is a country rich in wild game, white bears, sable and marten; there are marble, crystal, fish, wadmal, butter, mighty forests."

Although a minor part of the trade, consisting of polar bears and walrus hides and tusks, did come from the arctic regions associated with Greenland, the sable, marten, and other highly prized furs surely came from North American areas to the south, not Greenland. This abundance of furs that were taxed when delivered to Norway represented a source of wealth to both the government and the merchants of Norway who received and marketed the furs. It is easy to see how the possible restoration of the trade would have motivated King Magnus to organize his 1356 expedition to the Western Lands.

Nielsen offers a measured discussion of critics who refuse to even consider the evidence for the medieval Norse trade in North America. This obstinance may to some degree be the result of the critics' long-standing opposition to the authenticity of the Kensington runestone, for to accept the possibility of Norse fur trade on the Graenaveldi would imply possible acceptance of the runestone's authenticity. Such professional opposition tends to generate thoughtless opposition also to any related evidence.

Another interesting citation by Nielsen is Bowers (1950), who reported a Mandan myth of creation in which their founding father was a white man whose cattle were "too weak to survive and went back across the ocean." Myths are not evidence, but Sherz (1991) reported a horse skeleton found in a pre-Columbian mound in Aztalan, Wisconsin (Thompson, 1992), and Bailey (1991) reported horse skulls from other old mounds in Michigan (Cyr, 1991). It would appear that the Norsemen living on the Graenaveldi may have had cattle and horses that were no longer bred in the years after the trade ceased and hostilities occurred.

Appendix C:

Norse on the Continent: The Bishop's Voyage

For over 200 years widespread trade with the Norse people in the Western Lands continued and became so important that it resulted in the annexation of Greenland by Norway in AD 1261 during the reign of King Haakon IV. Its importance in the twelfth century is suggested by the voyage of Bishop Eirik Gnupsson to Vinland, a voyage with fascinating implications. His voyage is mentioned in one of the inscriptions on the document containing the controversial Vinland Map. George Painter endorsed the validity of this inscription and gives the following translation in complete ecclesiastical phrasing.[81]

> Eirik [Henricus], legate of the Apostolic See and Bishop
> of Greenland and the neighboring regions arrived in this
> truly vast and very rich land, in the name of Almighty
> God, in the last year of our most blessed father [Pope]
> Pascal [II], remained a long time in both summer and
> winter, and later returned northeastward towards
> Greenland and then proceeded [home to Europe?] in
> most humble obedience to the will of his superiors.

---

81.   G. Painter. *The Tartar Relation and the Vinland Map*, in *The Vinland Map and the Tartar Relation* (New Haven, CT: Yale University Press, 1965), 255.

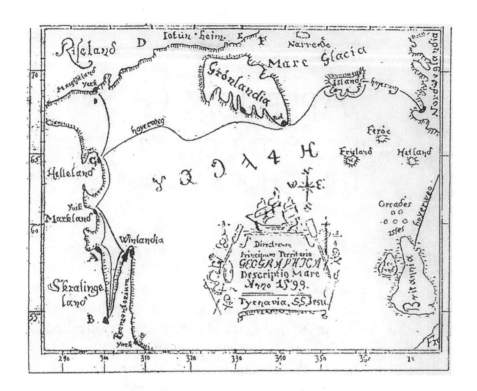

FIGURE 30: A Jesuit map of 1599 from a church archive in Hungary. Most of the information on this map was quite probably copied from a map (now lost) that was drawn by Bishop Eirik Gnupsson, who is known to have visited Vinland in 1117 and 1118 when the medieval climate was quite warm. The darkening effects on the paper caused by aging have been removed in this image. From *Westward to Vinland* by Helge Ingstad.

Pope Pascal II died in AD 1118, and Gnupsson's visit to Vinland that year implies a dutiful assessment of the neighboring regions of the Greenland domain. As a legate of the pope, Gnupsson would have written a report describing what he saw in the lands beyond Greenland, and this report would have been entered into the Church records. That document is not yet known, although it may be sequestered deep in the Vatican archives. There is, however, an AD 1599 Jesuit map[82] from a Hungarian Church archive that depicts precisely the kind of voyage that Gnupsson would have made. The features and information on this map, Figure 30, were apparently obtained by copying a much older map, as was often done. The older map source is implied by the marked sites of the two Greenland colonies, both of which had been abandoned long before 1599, and by the depiction of Greenland as an island, consistent with the mild high latitude climate of the twelfth century. Greenland shown as an island tells us that the Norse had circumnavigated Greenland. In contrast, most maps of explorers drawn in the Jesuit's later time show Greenland connected to the continent because the climate had become colder, and they could not penetrate the thick sea ice that joined Greenland to the continent. The 1570 Skalholt map, Figure 31, drawn in Iceland by Stephansson,[83] is just such a map. Gnupsson is the only bishop known to have visited Vinland. We shall assume that the features and place names on the Hungarian map were obtained by the Jesuit cartographer from a map in Gnupsson's older twelfth-century report. The Jesuit cartographer must have had both Stephansson's map and the bishop's map on his desk when he drew the map of Figure 30 because the notation letters on Stephansson's map also appear on the 1599 map. The Jesuit cartographer gave preference to the features on the bishop's original map, possibly because he was preserving the information on the bishop's older and physically deteriorating document. The routes shown are clearly traders' routes, and the bishop apparently sailed with one of the twelfth-century merchants who carried on the Greenland trade.

From this copy of the bishop's map we can directly infer Norse settlements on the continent, and we can learn interesting things by retracing his voyage. We assume that he joined a merchant captain at

---

82. Ingstad in *Westward to Vinland: The discovery of pre-Columbian Norse house-sites in North America* (New York: St. Martins Press, 1969). An image of the original unrestored map is found on page 120 of *The Viking Discovery of America* by H. Ingstad and A.S. Ingstad (Checkmark Books, 2001). Some authorities assert that this map is not an authentic 1599 map. We strongly disagree, for reasons given in our discussion of "The Bishop's Voyage," Appendix C.

83. This version of the Skalholt map with the Latin notes is found in: *The Vinland Map and the Tartar Relation*, plate XVII.

Bergen on the southwest coast of Norway, and departed from there in the spring of AD 1117. Following the "hoyerweg," the main route, they traded at four ports in well-populated Iceland. Then sailing against the prevailing winds, they stopped at the East Greenland settlement, probably at Brattahlid, located at the head of a long fjord about fifty kilometers from the open sea, where Erik the Red had settled in AD 986.[84] There the bishop no doubt attended to his affairs with the local Church officials. Note that this site is designated as a york, a name derived from "jorvik," the old Norse name for a trading village on a stream somewhat in from the sea.

Leaving Brattahlid, they sailed first northwestward with the West Greenland Current then northward and again westward on a course to counter the effects of the cold Canadian Current flowing southward, thus bringing them to a trading site in Helleland on the northern end of Labrador, marked as "C." This was probably in the sheltered Eclipse Channel behind North Autlatsivik Island. At this time it would have been late in the sailing season, and their next port of call, the york in Markland, was probably where they spent the winter. This site is about sixty miles southeast of the modern village of Nain, at the south end of a large bight filled with islands. In this bight the only location that meets the definition of a york is Flowers Bay, a sheltered inlet about fourteen miles long with a river entering at its west end, Figure 32. For natives and Norsemen alike it was an ideal location to spend the winter, with high ground for houses adjacent to deep water mooring sites, and with nearby brooks to supply fresh water. Their trading there was probably quite rewarding.

---

84. J. Haywood in *Historical Atlas of the Vikings* (New York: Penguin Books, 1995), 96.

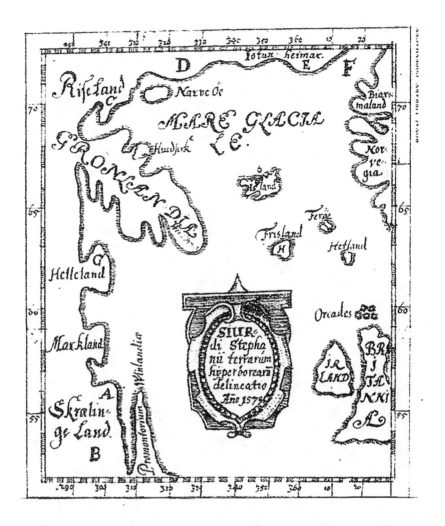

FIGURE 31: The Skalholt map of AD 1579, drawn in Iceland after the Greenland colonies had been abandoned because of the cooling climate. From the *Vinland Map and the Tartar Relation*, Plate XVII, Originally from the Royal Library, Copenhagen.

They would have left the Flowers Bay york as early as possible in the spring of 1118, and sailed southward to the site marked "A," Figure 30, clearly identifiable as the modern-day Sandwich Bay. From there they crossed the Strait of Belle Isle and hugged the Newfoundland coast southward to site "B" on Port au Port Bay near the modern city of Stephenville. The bay here is enclosed by a large "L"-shaped island, which is connected to the coast by a causeway. The outer western arm of the "L" extends about twenty-five miles to the north, and this may explain the absence of the Gulf of St. Lawrence on the map. Spring weather on Newfoundland is often foggy and rainy. If the bishop saw the long western arm of the "L" disappearing into the misty distance to the north, he could have made the mistaken assumption that the coastline from Sandwich Bay extended south to the western arm of the "L" at Port au Port bay.

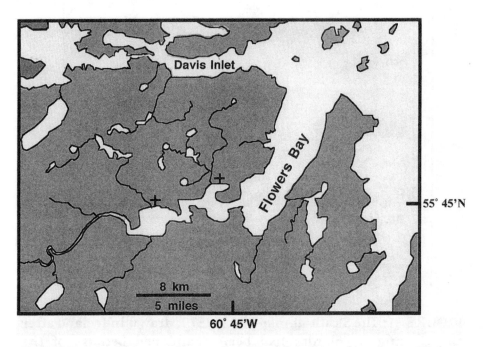

FIGURE 32: Flowers Bay, the Markland york where Bishop Gnupsson probably wintered over in AD 1117. The crosses mark sites where ships could be moored close to shore. The extreme tides and mud flats shown on the original Canadian map would have made it difficult to anchor elsewhere.

With completion of trading at the "B" site, they sailed northward along the coast to visit briefly at one of the two settlements at the northern end of the Winlandia promontory. They touched again at the

Flowers Bay york, and made a last trading stop to pick up the winter's harvest of furs at North Aulatsivik Island, the "C" site. Their next stop was the york on the Meta Incognita peninsula on Baffin island, labeled Riseland on his map. The bishop seems to have attached a name of his own to this port, because it is also shown as a "Mocgtjaland," or a "Mosquitoland" when translated phonetically with a soft "c" and soft "j." They would have arrived early in the summer when the mosquitoes and black flies were at their worst. These insect pests would have greatly impressed a visiting European man of the cloth who had never before experienced an arctic summer.

Beyond that mosquito-plagued site, however, the reconstruction of their route becomes a real puzzle. One would have expected them to take an often-traveled trading route directly back to southern Greenland, but they did not because that route is not shown on the map, Figure 30. Instead, it is likely that they sailed northward around Greenland. No such route is shown on the map, but that way would not have been a common trade route, and the Bishop was faithfully depicting only the common routes. Perhaps the captain hoped to trade for walrus tusks at points along his northward course, and, although the bishop was duty-bound to return to Rome, he had no obligation to return immediately to Brattahlid. We know that other Norsemen had also been at least as far northward as Skraeling Island in the Kane Basin at the northwest corner of Greenland, latitude 79°N, Figure 33. Archeologists have recovered abandoned Norse artifacts there that included iron wedges, a carpenter's plane, fragments of chain mail, and woolen cloth that was carbon 14 dated to AD 1190.[85] But from the Jesuit's copy of the bishop's map, we know the bishop did sail that way because he left another unique name, "Iotun heim," at the top of the map, Figures 30 and 33.

---

85. P. Schledermann in *Vikings: The North Atlantic Saga*, 250.

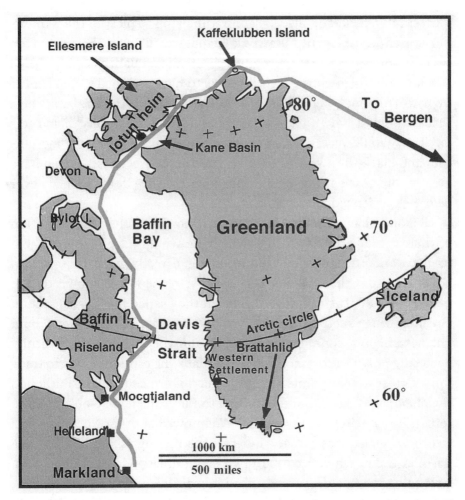

FIGURE 33: The Bishop's circumnavigation of Greenland, inferred from the "Ioten heim" name on the Ellesmere Island area, as discussed in the text.

From the southern end of Baffin Island, they sailed northward along its east coast to Cape Dyer, then northwestward past the spectacular Baffin fjords to Bylot Island, and northward past Devon Island to the Kane Basin, a total distance of 1,300 miles. The Kane Basin is halfway up the 500-mile length of Ellesmere Island, where we find the name: "Iotun heim." On the Skalholt map, however, Stephansson named the area farther to the north "Iotun heiman," which is an old plural form, ending with "an." With an interchanged "I" and "J," this resembles the modern Jotun heimen, a plural name that translates as "Homes of the Giants," and was attached to well-known mountains in Western Norway by poet Asmund Olavsson Vinje in 1862 (Wikipedia source, June 2009). Stephansson placed his label, the plural "Iotun heiman," far beyond Greenland at the northernmost and coldest imaginary part on his map. This location is consistent with Norse mythology in which "Jotunheim" translates as "Giantland," a cold and mountainous region given to the giants by the gods after the creation of the world. The Jesuit cartographer, however, followed the bishop's earlier map and placed his label "Iotun heim" on the area we know as Ellesmere Island at the northwest corner of Greenland.

But why did the bishop use a singular form of the name, and why did Stephansson use the old plural form? This difference is meaningful because the singular form implies that the bishop is speaking of a large population in the singular usage of the name. "Iotun heim" is "Home of the Iotun," just as "Skraelinge Land" is "Land of the Skraelinge," or in modern terms, "Land of the native American." But who were the Iotuns?

Recall that our traveling bishop was a well-educated man, and would have known something of Greek mythology as well as Norse. In one Greek myth, Io was a beautiful maiden in a love triangle with the god Zeus and his wife Hera. To protect Io from Hera's jealous machinations, Zeus transformed her into a heifer (a young cow). As a heifer she wandered all over the world, eventually returning to Egypt where she was transformed back to her womanly form. The many long-haired arctic muskoxen that lived along the coasts of Baffin and Ellesmere Island could have been observed by the bishop. The muskoxen greatly impressed the early explorers, and were known as "giant cattle" that were very "difficult to take," according to the Latin note, "C," on Stephansson's map. Somewhere in the vicinity of the mountainous area on Ellesmere Island in AD 1118, the bishop probably had firsthand contact with herds of muskoxen, and he named the area "Home of the Iotun" after the mythical heifer, Io.

In that most ancient of English literature, *Beowulf*, where Old

English and Old Norse words find common roots,[86] the word for "giant" is "eoten." Its pronunciation was probably little different from "Iotun." Long afterward, Norsemen like Stephansson, the author of the Skalholt map of about 1570 AD, would not have been acquainted with Greek mythology, and would not have known of the beautiful Io and her mythical connection to the muskoxen, and Stephansson probably never saw the bishop's map. The Norse rune for "I" was often used for both "I" and "E" and the word "giant" was written "Ioten." Judging from the Latin note "E" on Stephansson's map, reproduced in *The Vinland Map and the Tartar Relation*, Plate XVII, he viewed that far northern coast as the home of two giants: "Geruthi and Gudmund-ifus," not a large population.[87] Therefore Stephansson used the old plural form "Iotun heiman" specifically for two giants.

---

86. C.L. Wrenn, ed., *Beowulf, with the Finnesburg Fragment*, 1973 revised edition by Bolton Harap Limited, Pub. 829 3 B45.

87. *The Vinland Map and the Tartar relation*, map XVII, Latin note E.

APPENDIX D:

TRANSLATION OF MAGNUS'S 1354 PROCLAMATION, FROM THE DANISH

The keys to page numbers within references used here and in all our translations, when not otherwise designated, are:

(G) = Eric V. Gordon, *An Introduction to Old Norse*, A. R. Taylor, ed., second edition (New York: Oxford University Press, 1957);

(Z) = Geir T. Zoëga, *A Concise Dictionary of Old Icelandic* (Toronto: University of Toronto Press, 2004);

(MS) = Anthony L. Mayhew and Walter W. Skeat, *A Concise Dictionary of Middle English from AD 1150 to 1580* (1888);

(DO) = *Engelsk-Dansk Ordbog* by Johannes Magnussen, Otto Madsen, and Hermann Vinterberg (Copenhagen: Golden Valley Bookseller-Nordisk, 5th edition, 1937) (Oxford: Clarendon Press, 1888);

(N) = Richard Nielsen and Scott Wolter, *The Kensington Rune Stone, Compelling New Evidence* (Lake Superior Agate Publishing, 2006);

(BT) = Joseph Bosworth, *An Anglo Saxon Dictionary*, T. Northcote Toller, ed. (Oxford: Clarendon Press, 1989). See also the online version.

In past attempts to translate Magnus's 1354 proclamation, historians could not benefit from the scholarship found in twenty-first century dictionaries, and they lacked the clue of the name "Haakon" found in the Spirit Pond runestone. Consequently, the peculiarities of the grammar that make good sense only in the context of "Haakon" were glossed over or ignored. The part between the double asterisks includes the part that has been misunderstood previously. For the "edh" symbol, we use "dh."

As cited in the footnote in the earlier discussion of the 1354 proclamation, Magnus's words in one of the two surviving copies in nineteenth century Danish are given here. Some of the rigor may be lost in our translation because of the need to bridge from the Old Norse to the Danish of the 1600s and then to the modern forms. The word-by-word translation of the part between the double asterisks deals with the part in which historians have incorrectly assumed that the "you" referred to Paul Knutson, or "Powell knudszen" in the Danish:

> Magnus med gudz naade Norgisz Suerigis oc Skone
> Konning Sender Alle mend som dette breff See eller
> høre gudsz hellsze oc sind. **Wi ville Att i Wide Att i
> haffuer tagett alle de mend som i *kaaren Ville fare aff
> Alle huad heller de ere neffnde eller ey neffnde, mine
> handgange mend eller Andre mendsz Suendt och Aff
> andre mendtz der j faa till osz att førre der med som
> Powell knudszen som høffuitzmand skall Vere paa
> *kaaren, fuld befalling Att neffne de mend i *kaaren
> som hannom tycker best thillfallden Vere, baade thill
> Mestermend og Suenne.** Bede wi att de Annamme
> denne Vor befalling *rett god willie for Sagen, att Wi
> giøre dett i heder thill gud Och for Vor Siells och
> forelldre skyld Som Vdi grønland haffuer Christendom
> och Ophold thill denne dag oc Vill end ey lade
> nederfalle om Vore dage, Wider det i Sandingen, Att
> huilchen som denne Vor befaling bryder, skall faa Vor
> sande Wblyhed, oc der paa Suare os fuld breffue brodt.
> Giordt y Bergen Maendagen effter Simonis och ludae
> dag paa Siette Aar och XXX Wor Regis herrer her

Omer Østernis wor drottsetter Vdi Norge Jnseylende.

**Vi = We = The royal "We," the king is speaking.

Ville = desire (Z 490).

Att = at = that (Z 22).

i = you (DO 37).

"Wide" = "vide" in the Runeberg text is derived from the Old
Norse "vedhi" (Z 477) = "to pledge," and is declined here
simply as the verb "pledge." The king is asking for a formal
commitment from Haakon. Later he says, "We ask for the
acceptance of this our command . . . ," referring to the
"you," not to Knutson.

Att i = that you.

haffuer = hálfur (Z 187) = on your part. The "lf" had apparently
been interpreted as "ff," an easy mistake to make if the
crossbar were too long in the original.

tagett = take, take in command, "take" in the sense of posses-
sion, hold (DO 312), taka = forceful taking (Z 430, 432).

alle = all (Z 10).

de = those (DO-51).

mend = Men (DO 187).

som = who (DO 288).

i kaaren = in the choosing, from "kaare" = to choose (DO 148).

ville = desire (Z 490).

fare = to journey, to sail (Z 127), (DO 71).

aff = af = with (Z 1).

alle = all (Z 10), altogether, the whole group, the retinue. In an
equally likely alternative, the phrase may end with "af"
and an understood "you," thus reading: " . . . desire to
journey with (you), all from . . . "

huad = hvadan = from wheresoever (Z 216).

heller = either (DO 121).

de = they (DO 51).

ere = be (DO 68).

naffende = navnte = named (DO 205) or titled.

eller = or else (DO 65).

ey = ei = not (DO 63).

navnte = named (DO 205).

mine = minn = (from) my (Z 297).

handgangne maend = retainers (Z 183), (DO 187) the king's
personal attendants.

eller = or else (DO 65).

Andre = other (DO 14).

Mendtz = maends = men's (DO 187).

Suendt = svenne = sveinn = young attendants (Z 420).

Och = oc = ok = also (G 374).

Aff = af = of (DO 4).

andre maend = other men (DO 14, 187).

der = who (DO 53).

"i faae til os" = "would be acceptable to us," or "would be useful
to us" (G 342), probable subjunctive mood with "e = i."

Att = at = upon (Z 20), denoting presence.

förre = för = (the) trading voyage (Z 157).

dermed = "With that" (DO 53), "So saying," or "That being said."

som = from "sómi" = honour, (the) honourable (Z 396), (the)
Hon. Paul Knutson.

som høffuitzmand = som Hovidsmand = (the) Hon.
Commandant.

skall = shall (DO 272, 278).

Vere = vaere = be (DO 358).

paa = upon (DO 230).

Kaaren = Kaaring = choosing (DO 148), being chosen?

fuld = (in) complete (DO 96).

befalling = command (DO 20).

Att = at = to (DO 29).

naevne = name (DO 205).

de = those (DO 51).

mend = Maend = men (DO 187).

som = who (DO 288).

hannom = (for) him (G 294), dative.

tycker = tykkes = pl. of tyk (DO 329) = stout, hence "stouts" =
   stout or strong men.

bedst = bezt = best (G 335).

thilfallden = from "tilfelliligr," suitable (Z 436).

vaere = vaeri = would be (G 308) subj. pl.

baade = both (DO 21).

thill = til = for (DO 21).

Mestermend = masters, officers (DO 193).

Og = oc = and (G-374).

Suenne = svende = journeymen, crew (DO 306).

**

Appendix E:
WORD-BY-WORD TRANSLATION OF THE KENSINGTON INSCRIPTION

Figures 34, 35, and 36 display the transliterated letters and the translation into the equivalent English words. The key to cited dictionary and textbook references is found at the beginning of Appendix D. Here we rely on the Old Norse textbook of Gordon and the Old Icelandic dictionary of Zoëga, which is an Old West Norse equivalent. To make the most accurate translation, knowledge of the context is required. The author's cultural background and the circumstances under which the inscription was composed could leave their marks on the runes of the inscription, but here strict interpretation is difficult. Because the expedition personnel consisted of both Swedes and Norwegians who had worked together for six years, a merging of dialects and a mixed usage of East and West Norse runes would be expected. The author is not named in the inscription, but we have assumed with good reason that the author was the commander of the "førre" to the Graenaveldi, Paul Knutson. He was a West Norwegian, and had been the Law Speaker for the Bergen Gulathing[88]. Yet the inscription has runes of likely East Norse origin; for example in the word VI or WI (G 394) = "we." Perhaps the runesmith who did the carving was one

---

88. *"The Thing"* Cited literature: Laurence M. Larson: *The Earliest Norwegian Laws* (New York: Columbia University Press, 1939). http://www.arild-hauge.com/elov.htm.

of the eight GØTER(UM) of the inscription and used some of his own East Norse rules. R.I. Page has a discussion of the different runic forms and practices over early medieval times.[89] Nielsen and Wolter suggest that the GØTER were from the Island of Gotland[90] (N 317), but this would not be consistent with the spelling of GØTER. Having said all this, we assert that the translation from the Old Norse, as detailed in this appendix with some caveats, is probably more justified than one made using only Old Swedish meanings.

Some of the differences between our interpretation and that of Nielsen and Wolter are respectively summarized in this list:

> OPDAGELSEFARD: "back-taking journey" vs. "up-taking journey"
> VINLAND OF WEST: "West Vinland" vs. "far to the west from Vinland"
> HAVDE LÄGER: "hove to anchorages" vs. "had camp"
> SKJAR: "skerries" vs. (not identified)
> OK FISKE: "also fishing" vs. "at fishing"
> HÄR: noun: "troop" vs. verb: "is, are"
> VÉ: noun: "large house" vs. preposition: "by"
> HAVET: noun: "high winter," or "winter" vs. noun: "inland sea"
> FROM: "from beyond" vs. "from"

As on the Spirit Pond inscription, the articles "a, an, the" are omitted, the runic "I" and "E" are sometimes interchanged, and the

---

89. Raymond I. Page. *Reading the Past: Runes* (Berkley, CA: University of California Press, 1993).

90. Nielsen and Wolter (2006) argue that the author was from the island of Gotland, and some words do suggest that. However, many of our interpretations, based on analysis of the grammar and the Old Norse meanings as detailed in Appendix E, are more consistent with a Norwegian author and a rune carver from Western Sweden in the context of the expedition. A "taking back journey" is consistent with regaining the trade, but an "uptaking journey" implies claiming land, which is not. "West Vinland" is grammatically more correct than "far to the west from Vinland." "Hove to anchorages" preserves the sound of the runic word and the "v" in the bindrune representing "vd," whereas "had camp" does not. "Have a large winter house" is based on a more accurate transliteration than "by the sea." "From beyond this island" conveys northward directional information, but "from this island" does not.

runic "B" and "P" are apparently identical. The rune for "V" is a dotted "M" rune. The "O" rune is used for both "O" and "Å." Two double dots above a rune indicate AE or OE. In a usage similar to the overbar in the Spirit Pond inscription, a dot is often used to represent one or more omitted letters, sometimes indicating a missing suffix giving the proper tense of the word. This usage occurs in "denna" and "nordr" in line 5, "varum" in line 6, and "fann" and "heim" in line 7. On the rougher surface of the side face, the dot is not easily visible in "denna" on line 12. The thorn rune at the beginning of a word or syllable is usually pronounced as "t," but if at the end or medial position, it is a voiced "d." In text we use "D" for the thorn and for the edh in discussions. In lines one through nine on the smooth cleaved face of the stone, even quite small dots can be distinguished in photos.

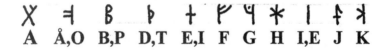

FIGURE 34: Runic letters used in the Kensington runestone inscription.

Here is the transliteration:

8 GØTER(UM) OK 22 NORRMENN PÅ
(DESSI) OPDAGELSEFARD FRO
VINLAND OF VEST VI
HAVDE LÄGER VED 2 SKJAR EN
DAGS RISE NORR FRO DENO STEN
VI VAR OK FISKE EN DAGH ÄPTIR
VI KOM HEM FAN 10 MAN RØDE
AF BLOD OG DED AVM

FRÄELSE AF ILL ŸE
HÄR 10 MANS VÉ HAVET AT SÉ
ÄPTIR VORE SKIP 14 DAGH RISE
FROM DENO ØH AHR 1362

Here again is the complete translation into English:

1: 8 west Gøtlanders (Swedes) and also 22 Northmen (Norwegians) on
2: [this] back-taking journey from
3: [?] Vinland extreme west [West Vinland]. We
4: hove to anchorages by 2 skerries one
5: days journey north from this stone.
6: We were also fishing one day. After
7: we came home found 10 men reddened
8: with blood, and dead. AV[e] M[aria]
9: Salvation from evil fate.
10: Troop 10 men (have) a large winter house to look
11: after our ship 14 days journey
12: from beyond this island. Year 1362.

Line 1

Runic 8 plus GØTER(UM) = Eight Swedes from the Väster Gøtland district of western Sweden (G 405). On the right leg of the "R" there is a very deep dot indicating an absence of the letters UM. This dot is the equivalent of the Latin abbreviation device of a slash across the leg of an "R" as described in Appendix I. On the stone, the double-struck "N" represents NN. GØTERUM is a Latinized word form translated as "West Gautlanders." In a similar usage, one of the medieval Danish annals is titled *Gesta Danorum* (G 165). Latinizing names was a practice often followed by people of importance, as in the example of the Gotland Island grave slab of Figure 42B. Note that the runic symbol for the Ø contains a nested rune, as was occasionally done also in Latin, as on the grave slab inscription. There, in the last letters for "in peace" = "ĪPACE," the "E" is nested within the "C." Because the author did not use the OG="and" that he used on line 8, it appears that his intent was to combine meanings (1) and (6) for OK:

> OK = "and also" (Z 320).
> 22, in runic positional notation.
> NORRMENN = Norwegians
> PÅ = "på" = "on" (G 311).

Line 2

Most of the first word in line 2 has been lost due to the breaking away of part of the top layer on the front of the runestone on which most of the words are inscribed, as can be seen in Figure 13. The missing word is probably "DESSI," the dative case of the demonstrative pronoun "this" (G 295), and the object of the preposition "on" in line 1.

OPDAGELSEFARD is a compound word. OP is from "opa" (Z 321), v. meaning "to go back," TAG (DAG) from TAKA = "to take" (Z 430), and FARD = FERD = "journey" (Z 135). "ELSE" is a suffix like "tion" in English. An awkward rendition would be "a back accretion journey," but a smoother "taking-back journey" (to restore the fur trade) will suffice. It is not an "uptaking journey" to claim land, in which case the word would have been spelled UPPDAGELSEFARD from "upptaka" = "taking up" or "seizure" (Z453). "Taking back" implies regaining something (the trade) that had been lost. Alice Kehoe has argued that trade was the likely motive for the Norse presence in Minnesota. An interesting note: the "L" in ELSE was initially misstruck with the flag at the top on the left side; then correctly restruck on the right side.

FRO = "frá" = "from" (Z 148).

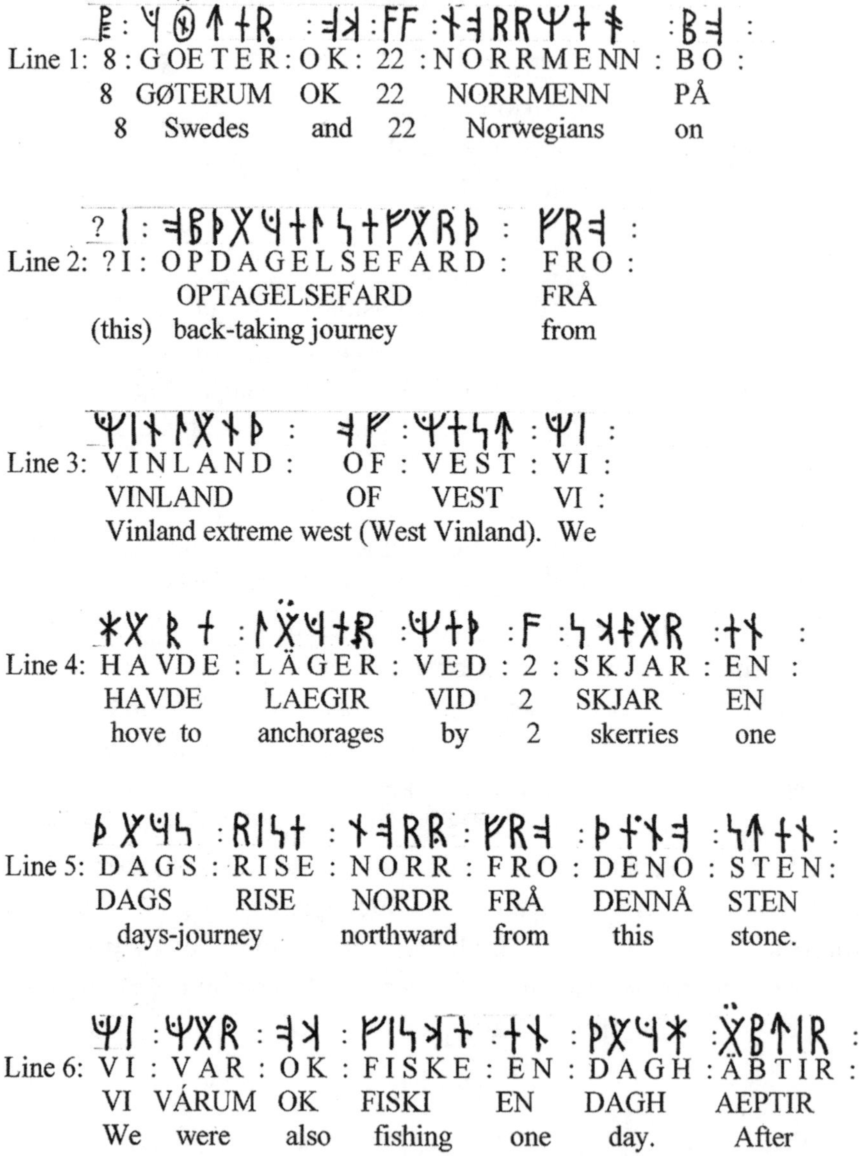

Line 1: 8 : GOETER : OK : 22 : NORRMENN : BO :
        8 GØTERUM   OK   22   NORRMENN   PÅ
        8 Swedes   and 22   Norwegians on

Line 2: ?I : OPDAGELSEFARD : FRO :
        OPTAGELSEFARD   FRÅ
        (this) back-taking journey   from

Line 3: VINLAND : OF : VEST : VI :
        VINLAND   OF   VEST   VI :
        Vinland extreme west (West Vinland). We

Line 4: HAVDE : LÄGER : VED : 2 : SKJAR : EN :
        HAVDE   LAEGIR   VID   2   SKJAR   EN
        hove to anchorages by 2 skerries one

Line 5: DAGS : RISE : NORR : FRO : DENO : STEN :
        DAGS   RISE   NORDR   FRÅ   DENNÅ   STEN
        days-journey northward from this stone.

Line 6: VI : VAR : OK : FISKE : EN : DAGH : ÄBTIR :
        VI   VÁRUM   OK   FISKI   EN   DAGH   AEPTIR
        We were   also fishing one day.   After

FIGURE 35: The Kensington runestone inscription, lines 1–6.

Line 3

VINLAND = the coastal area from Rhode Island to northern Newfoundland.

OF = an excess or extreme like "too, too much," or "far" (Z 318).

VEST, without a suffix, is usually used as an adjective to describe a specific location, e.g., "Vest-firdingar" = the West fjords in Iceland, "Vest-fyldir" = the Norse district of Vestfold (Z 486), and is therefore used here to designate a location, not a direction. On the contrary, with a suffix "r," "vestr" is a noun and designates the direction "west," with suffixes "vestry" = "from the west" (Z 486) and "vestan" = "west-wards" (G 395). If the phrase OF WEST modified journey, it would have followed OPDAGELSEFARD immediately. It does not. It follows and modifies VINLAND, and OF modifies WEST. WEST has no suffix and OF has the meaning of an extreme (Z 318). VINLAND OF WEST is therefore the extreme west part of Vinland; i.e., the expedition was from Norombega, Figure 3.

VI = "We," the East Norse dialect (G 394) as translated. It seems likely that, contrary to the example on (G 394), the pronunciation of "V" rune throughout this inscription is the "v" sound, not the "w" sound. The omission of the West Norse trilled "R" and the use of "I" instead of "E" was also done on line 3 of the Spirit Pond inscription, and we show from the grammar that the resulting bindrune there represents the royal "We" used when the King was speaking.

Line 4

The third rune in the first word is a bindrune in which a thorn has a short leg added to the staff below to make the letters VD, that is: HAVDE. Nielsen and Wolter (N 68, 69) equate this word to HAFDI = "had," with "F" replacing "U," and "D" replacing the thorn. But if HAVDE = "had," it would have ended with an "m" to agree grammatically with the preceding first person past tense "We" (Z 179). Instead, the leg on the staff is the Norwegian-style "U/V" representing the "v" sound, as in the tenth rune on the Kingigtorssuaq runestone inscription in the translated name: "Sigvatsson;" see Figure 48 in Appendix G. This leads phonetically to an idiomatic compound word: HAVDE =

"hove to," past tense, a quite appropriate nautical term in this context, meaning "to move the ship into a certain position or situation," or simply "to come to a halt" (*Online Etymology Dictionary*, © 2001 Douglas Harper). The present tense of the modern form is "heave to" with the origin of "heave" in the O.N. "hefja," the Goth. "hafjan," and in one cited usage in "hafa" (Z 180). An additional discussion of the Kingigtorssuaq inscription and its date is found in Appendix G.

LÄGER = LAEGIR, plural of "laegi" = "anchorage" (30 men in two boats) (Z 281, 536). The "R" was struck on the double dot to correct an erroneous dot placement.

VED = "vid" = "by" or "close to" (Z 487).

Runic 2 plus SKJAR = plural, "rocks in the sea," small rocky islands. Thus "We hove to anchorages by two rocky islands . . . " In (Z 372) "Sker," a rocky island, is singular, "skerja" is the plural. Here in SKJAR, the phonetic effect of the "J" has been moved forward and the "A" at the end is omitted.

EN = a short form of "einn" = "one" (G 292).

Line 5

DAGS RISE = Days journey (under sail) of 75 miles in twelve hours (Holand, 1940, 181).

NORR = "northward" (G 373, Z 315). The dot in the second "R" designates a missing suffix = "norrdr" = "northwards."

FRO = "frá" = "from" (Z 148), like "fro" = "from" (MS 95).

DENO = "denna" = acc. "this" (G 295).

STEN = "stein" = "stone, boulder" (Z 406).

Note: Here is another mistake that was corrected by the carver. Initially, he carved STN, realized he'd forgotten the "E," then overstruck the "N" as an "E," and continued to finish the word with the "N."

Line 6

VI = "we" (G 394).

VAR = "várum" = "were" (G 308). The dot within the "R" designates the missing "um."

OK = "also" (Z 321, meaning 6).

ᚢᛁ : ᚴᚯᛘ : ᚼᛁᛘ : ᚠᚭᚿ : � : ᛘᚭᚿ : ᚱᚯᚦᛁ :

Line 7: V I : K O M : H E M : F A N : 10 : M A N : R O E D E :
VE   KOM   HEIM   FANN   10   MAN   RODE
We   came   home   found   10   men   reddened

ᚭᚠ : ᛒᛚᚯᚦ : ᚯᚵ : ᚦᛁᚦ : ᛆᚢᛘ :

Line 8: A F : B L O D : O G : D E D : A V M :
AF   BLOD   OG   DED   AVM
with   blood   and   dead   Ave Maria

ᚠᚱᛅᛏᛚᛋᛏ : ᚭᚠ : ᛁᛚᛚ ᛦ :

Line 9: F R Ä E L S E : A F : I L L YE :
FRAE ELSE   AF   ILL YRDI
Salvation   from   evil   fate

ᚼᛅᚱ : 10 : ᛘᚭᚿᛋ : ᚢᛁ : ᚼᛆᚢᛁᛏ : ᚭᛏ : ᛋᛁ :

Line 10: H Ä R : 10 : M A N S : V E : H A V E T : A T : S E :
HAER   10   MANS   VÉ: HAVET :   AT   SÉ
Troop (of) 10 men (have a) large winter house to look

ᛅᛒᛏᛁᚱ : ᚢᛅᚱᛏ : ᛋᚴᛁᛒ : 14 : ᛑᛆᚵᚼ : ᚱᛁᛋᛏ :

Line 11: Ä B T I R : V O R E : S K I B : 14 : D A G H : R I S E :
AEPTIR   VARE   SKIP   14   DAGH   RISE
after   our   ship   14   days   journey

ᚠᚱᛅᛘ : ᚦᛏᚿᛅ : ᚯᚼ : ᚷᛆᚱ : ᛚᚠᚠᛚ :

Line 12: F R O M : D E N O : OE H : A H R : 1362 :
FRÅ UM   DENNA   ÖH   AHR   1362
from beyond this   island.   year   1362

FIGURE 36: The Kensington runestone inscription, lines 7–12.

FISKE = "fiski" = "fishing" (Z 137), part. pass. f., declined without the "n" (Z 542). However, "E" does not normally represent "I," and the author may have intended the runic "E" to be "É," pronounced as in English "let." This would be a difference in dialect from the Old Norse.

EN = "einn" = "one" (G 292).

DAGH = "day," acc. of "dagr" (Z 84).

ÄPTIR = AEPTIR = "eptir" = "after" (Z 115).

Line 7

VI = "we" (G 394).

KOM = "komum" = "came," past tense of "koma" (Z 245). There is no dot by the "M" to designate the missing "um." However, a microscopic examination shows a slash was cut across the OM, which probably indicates the missing UM, see Appendix I for some Latin examples of the use of the slash.

HEM = "heim," acc. of "home" (Z 536). A dot by the left side of the "M" indicates the absent "I."

FAN = FANN = "found," = pret. of "finna" = "to find" (Z 137).

The dot indicates the missing "N."

Runic 10 plus MAN = "men" (Z 284), Old Swedish plural (N 542).

RÖDE = (RAUD)v. "smeared (with blood)" or "reddened" (Z 341).

Line 8

AF = "with" (Z 1).

BLOD = "blood" (Z 59).

OG = "and," phonetically like "ok."

DED = the adjective "dead" (MS 59) if the author was using Middle English, "death" if using Swedish (N 542).

AVM = Ave Maria, an abbreviated prayer appeal continued on line 9. See Latin abbreviations for Ave Maria in Appendix I, Figure 59.

Line 9

FRÄELSE = FRAEELSE, is related to "frelsa" = "to save, to rescue" (G 346, Z 149), a second class strong verb (Z 542). Old Icelandic is "frjalsa," thus the "Ä" could indicate the former presence of the "j"

(MS 94). However, FRÄELSE ends in a runic "E" and none of the conjugated forms of "frelsa" ends in an "e." The ELSE part is the same as the ELSE part of OPDAGELSEFARD, which we have identified with the suffix "tion." We can therefore combine that suffix with "to save" and render FRÄELSE as "salvation."

AF = "from" (Z 1).

ILLŸE = ILL YRDE = ILL YRDI, from "illr" = "evil" (Z 227). The dotted "YE" bindrune has two dots. The single-dotted "Y" was apparently used in formal manuscript documents. It is found six times on page 42 of the "Västgötalagen blad 21.jpg" file from the Wikimedia Commons (11/19/2009). The second dot here indicates the absent RD. In (G 398) "yrdi" is referred to (G394) "verda" = "to happen." Thus: "Salvation from evil happening" or "salvation from an evil fate" was probably a common prayer for the souls of the dead.

On the side surface of the stone, a rougher surface, it is difficult to distinguish small dots in photographs of the remaining lines of the inscription, but see the 1899 photo (N 24).

Line 10

HÄR = HAER plus runic 10 plus MANS. There are two other points in the inscription where Ä = AE occurs, and HÄR should be interpreted in the same way. Hence: HAER = "herr" = army or troop (land or sea, Z 196, G 358). In Old High German "hari" is an army. A troop is a group of armed men, therefore in this context we have: a "troop (of) ten men."

MANS = "men's"(Z 284), the possessive form and is used here instead of the subjunctive "man eigu" = "men have"(G 306) to save space on the line. MANS is a possessive form for men serving under Knutson's command.

VÉ = "mansion" (Z 476), pronounced as in the English "let," and distinguished from the VI in line 7 by the crossbar on the staff making it an "É." The meaning here is a "large house."

HAVET = "hávetr" = "midwinter" (Z 188) or "high winter," i.e., VÉ HAVET = "large all-winter house." The "r," like other consonants, was frequently dropped from the word endpoint. See: Claiborne

Thompson, *Studies in Upplandic Runography*, Austin, TX, University of Texas Press, 1975, 65.

AT SÉ = "to see," "to look," SÉ is singular, present, subjunctive (Z 363, 543).

Line 11

ÄBTIR = AEPTIR = EPTIR (Z 115) = "after." In Zoega, AT SÉ (Z 363) is defined to include EPTIR. It may be that here the subjunctive case required the separate AEPTIR.

VORE = "vár" = "our" (G 293). The end letter "E" is probably the transitional form from the Old Norse to the modern form. In the contemporary Middle English "oure" = "our" (MS 165). "vore" = "our" in a 1937 Danish-English dictionary.

SKIP = "ship," acc. (Z 374). The Old Norse grammar does not tell us if there was one ship or two or more waiting to carry Knutson back to Norombega, but there was probably only one, because Haakon had taken at least one ship back to winter over in Vinland. If the thirty-man group had been able return to the Hudson Bay port in 1362, that number plus the troop of ten men guarding the remaining ship plus a crew of five to ten men would have totaled about fifty men. Any of the large cog ships of the Norwegian fleet would have been able to carry those men adequately.

"14" in pentadic form = "fourteen."

"DAGH RISE" = (nautical) "a day's sailing journey" of seventy-five miles in twelve hours.

Line 12

FROM = FRÅM = FRÅ (Z 148) + UM (Z 447, meanings 4, 11) = "from beyond." There might be a slash across the OM to indicate the missing "U" but it is not as certain as in KOM of line 7. The author anticipated the erection of the runestone on the top of Runestone Hill, because when looking from the hilltop out "beyond this island," one is looking northward in the direction of their ship on Hudson Bay, not toward Lake Superior, which lies eastward. Likewise, the use of "um" without the "U" in the compound word "SAGAMJUNG" is found in line 4 of the Spirit Pond inscription.

"DENO" = "denna" = "this" (G 295).

"ØH" = "island," common map usage.

"AHR" = "year."

Thus: "(a) troop of ten men have a large winter house to look after our ship fourteen days journey from beyond this island, year 1362." The subjunctive form "sé" was probably used because Knutson started his journey up the Nelson River before seeing that the men were in fact winter-housed.

APPENDIX F:

WORD-BY-WORD TRANSLATION OF THE SPIRIT POND INSCRIPTION

Here again is the complete transliteration:

SIG-INN-AET-TUM O-DREN-GI-R'
GEL-SA SLE-AE' SJAU-TAN DE-D'.
HAEL-Á-DHE-R' WE-PAING-BAE-DHUM.
AH-R' TI-GR' TI-GR'
WE-U-LES-A SVEIT-LAG TOL-F'
RI-SE' VEST EIN TVEIR NOR TI-GR'.
SAG-AM JUNG FOL-KUN-G'.
SKEGG-HIL-MA-N' HAA-KON FA-N'
H-RING –Í-GENG AT VEST BAA-LAA-GA
SEL-GA KEY-SAR-REG-N'.
WE-PAING-BAE-DHUM,
AH-R' .. TI-GR'.. EIN-N'EIN-N'.
SK-VAL-Á-LJOO-SA! BE-A-TAE-MA-RI-A!
OO! U-MAT THAT SIGI-LLA SHIP-I VE.
NÁ-EGG-JA AKT-A', BAA UM-B' VINN-A',
SHI-P' VID-H A-GI .
SJAU-TAN BOI-H-DHA HOEG-G-VA,
KOI-SA-SÁ-GANG, BA-NI-NÁ-M'.
HAEL-Á-DHE-R' WE-PAING-BAE-DHUM.
AH-R'.. TI-GR'.. EIN-N'EIN-N'.

Here again is the translation in English:

> Fallen kinsmen, ever valiant fellows. A roaring sea struck
> seventeen dead.
> Hail to you, Weeping Fountains!
> Year 20, we lost the company of twelve companions
> 12 daghrise westward (900 miles), 10 daghrise northward
> (750 miles).
> The saga of a young Folkung.
> Bearded chief-man Haakon discovered a circle by being able to
> sail toward the west on the lakes ("laaga") of the trade
> empire.
> Weeping Fountains! Year 21.
> A shout into the burning lights! Blessed Maria! Alas!
> Powerless those on the Seal-ship to proceed
> to obtain an edge to devote attention in regard
> to win the ship against the terrible storm.
> Seventeen presage their inevitable battle stroke,
> accept the sinking,
> the bane of their approaching death.
> Hail to you, Weeping Fountains! Year 21.

Figures 37 and 38 show views of both sides of the Spirit Pond inscription stone accompanied by the drawn runes with double dot word separators.

FIGURE 37: Above: the inscription on side #1 of the Spirit Pond runestone. From Collections of the Maine State Museum, mainestatemuseum.org. Below: the runes as drawn from side #1.

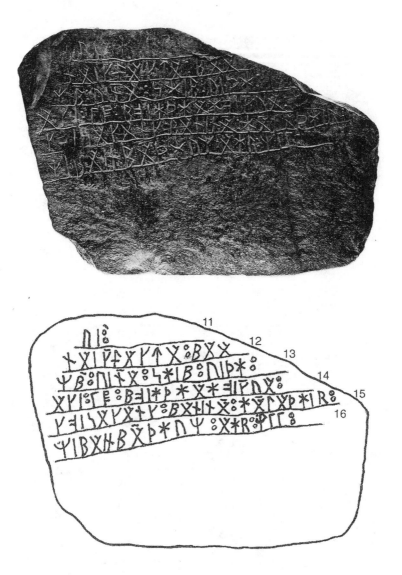

FIGURE 38: Above: the inscription on side #2 of the Spirit Pond runestone. From Collections of the Maine State Museum, mainestatemuseum.org. Below: the runes as drawn from side #2.

The author of this poem was a man broadly acquainted with northern European and Scandinavian literature because he goes beyond the Norse to occasionally use words from both Middle English and the older Anglo Saxon to achieve poetic meaning and the couplet meter.[91] At least five words are rooted in words found in the *Bosworth-Toller Anglo Saxon Dictionary*. It is not surprising that the king's skald would have this talent, but the use of non-Norse words tends to complicate the translation. These oddities are minor compared with the complications caused by the author's extensive use of abbreviations and other shortened word forms, a common medieval practice when space was limited on vellum or stone. For someone not familiar with this practice, these runic word forms have on occasion evoked the skeptical comment: "I see many words that are not known Old Norse words." But greatly abbreviated or shortened words were often used in medieval manuscripts, as in the examples given in Appendix H and I. A foremost American paleographer, Rutherford Aris, wrote in a discussion of the translation of common types of medieval manuscripts:

> One of the most difficult aspects of reading medieval manuscripts is the prevalence of abbreviations. In late cursive Gothic texts they can be formidable indeed and some technical passages are of a kind that "cometh not out save by prayer and fasting." [92]

This statement would apply equally well to the translation of the Spirit Pond inscription, which is on a small stone, with nearly half of the words shortened by the omission of letters. The translation of the

---

91. In the fourteenth century the cultural and trade links were quite strong between Norway and the British Isles, and this is consistent with a commonality of many words and the cognates in the languages of that time. An excellent discussion of this is found in *From Viking to Crusader: Scandinavia and Europe 800–1200*, E. Rosedahl and D.M. Wilson, eds. (New York: Rizzoli International Publications, 1992). On page 168, in the chapter "From Poetry to Literature," Author Preben Sorensen says: "The Scandinavian languages were closely related, but West Scandinavia had its closest contacts with the British Isles."

92. R. Aris. *Explicatio formarum litterarum: The unfolding of letterforms*. (St. Paul, MN: The Calligraphy Connection, 1990). www.vanstockum.nl. Author Westin's years of calligraphic study of medieval writings and her professional letter carving of classical inscriptions led us to the recognition of the various marks indicating the abbreviations early in our efforts on the translation.

Spirit Pond inscription is doubly challenging because it is a poem, and the author often used poetic license to achieve the couplet rhythm by shortening words or combining parts of words. One can hardly over-emphasize the importance of the recognition of these shortened word forms because, unless the words are restored to their complete forms, an accurate reading and translation would not be possible. Einar Haugen's effort to translate the Spirit Pond inscription[93] in 1972 failed because he apparently did not recognize that half the words were shortened. Our translation has been made using all the restored word forms.

In typical medieval manuscripts in Latin the shortened words can be indicated by a wide variety of superscripted letters, by double dots, and by small horizontal bars, called overbars. These overbars are placed above the words with the missing letters. One example of the super-scripted letter is shown in the grave slab rubbing in Figure 42 where the letters RLv are used for the Latin word "relevatus," meaning "relief from pain." In the two American runestones the indicators of short-ened words are single dots, double dots, and overbars of which there are twenty-two in the Spirit Pond inscription, although not all the shortened word forms are so indicated. In some cases the complete form can be inferred from the context. In one example on line 5, it was necessary to draw on the known history of that time to translate "UNG" as the short form of "Folkung," the clan name of Magnus and Haakon. Some words are compound words consisting of parts of other words. For example: "GELSA" combines parts of the word for "roaring" and "sea" to make "a roaring sea."

When making the translation, it was necessary to keep in mind the alternative possible phonetic values for some of the runes that the composer of the inscription could have used. These ambiguities in Old Norse inscriptions are discussed by Gordon (G 182). The articles "a, an, the" are understood in runic inscriptions, and to save space, adjacent words often shared a rune. Words are often separated by double dots. The key to the runes of the inscription is given in Figure 39, and the

---

93. E. Haugen. "The Runestones of Spirit Pond, Maine," *Man in the northeast*, Vol. 4, 1972, 62–79, 77.

key for the dictionary and grammar references is given at the beginning of Appendix D.

ᚠ ᚢ ᚦ ᚷ ᚱ ᚡ ᚼ ᛁ ᛂ ᚿ
F U,V D A A R K,G H I,E,EI E N

ᛋ ᛒ ᛘ ᚢ ᛏ ᚥ ᛚ ᛦ ᛃ LE OO,OH!
S B,P M W T O L Y J LE OO,OH!

ᚦᚼ ᚣ ᛏᚼ ᚾ
DH (voiced) EDH and TH (unvoiced) IN (ing, eng)

FIGURE 39: Runic forms relevant to the Spirit Pond inscription.

The rune written as an inverted "U" represents the phonetic value of either "V" or "U." Runes are sometimes dotted to indicate the choice of phonetic value, but the dots are small, if present, and are not easily distinguished on photos as they may still be filled with debris or have suffered some deterioration. In Norse inscriptions the single staff representing "I" was sometimes converted to "E" by a single dot or a short bar at the center of the staff. The two letters "IN" are ligatured (connected) in six of the eight times in which they occur. We infer that this ligatured bindrune form designates the sound of the letters "ing" or "eng," which is important for the grammar of some word endings and is similar to the usage given in Gordon (G 268). Another bindrune occurs in which a runic "L" and "E" are indicated by the half-crossed staff of the "L" combined to form a single rune. This is not to be confused with the "J" rune, which occurs three times in the inscription.

As discussed earlier, we date the inscription to the mid-fourteenth century, probably AD 1362. However, as the Norse language evolved during the thirteenth century, some changes occurred in Norway that did not follow the Icelandic dialect. Examples (G 319) are "Dat" for Norwegian "Det," and the retention of both "hr" in "hringa" and the retained "ae" indicated by the overbarred runic "A" in the Spirit Pond inscription. In the older Norse the thorn, "D" was used for both the voiced and unvoiced "TH." After AD 1225 in Norse, the thorn gradually came to be used only at the beginning of the word, and the interdental fricative, the edh, Figure 39, was used in other positions (G 268). The thorn was then used to represent only the voiceless sounds, while the edh represented the voiced "TH," as in "father." In the Spirit Pond inscription the author made the distinction between the voiced and unvoiced sound as was the custom after AD 1225, but he did not use the edh. Instead he used the thorn and "H" rune, "DH," for the voiced "TH" within words and the runic "TH" to express the unvoiced form at the beginning of a word on line 9. In our transliteration we allow the "DH" to remain to represent the later edh. The implication is that the primary dialect of the skald, who composed the inscription, was not west Norwegian. Neither was he an Icelander because the Icelandic runes for *a, p, d, t, s,* and *n,* were different from those on the inscription. Perhaps he was from a Swedish district, where the evolution of the language was somewhat different than in western Norway.

In Figures 40, 43, and 46 we display the line-by-line results of the translation. For each line of the inscription, we give the runic characters, followed by a transliteration to Roman letters, our choices of modern unabbreviated equivalents, and in the fourth line the literal English translation.

Line 1:

SIGATUM ODIN is a short phrase of three words with three over-bars that indicate nine missing letters. ATUM = "aettum," pl. dat., as in "family-folk" or "kinsmen" (Z 39, 525, 536). The "A" is not shared with SIG (Z 362, 542) because SIG (v. "siga") with the overbar is an adjective passive participle. The complete form of SIG is SIGINN = "fallen."

Next, we have a choice between two almost equally likely alternatives: O DRENGIR and ÓDDRINGIN. In Middle English "O" = "ever, always, aye," (MS 161) and "aye" in Old Norse is "ey" = "always, ever"

(Z 119). Our choice is the Norse word DRENGIR, pl. = "valiant fellows" (Z 93). This is an appropriate tribute to the lost men, and rhymes with HAEL-Á-DHER in line 2. The IN is the bindrune for "eng." However, the Anglo Saxon word ÓDDRINGIN = "taken away" by death (BT 771) also tells the poetic tragedy quite effectively, and has fewer missing letters in the abbreviation if the author intended the IN to be used twice.

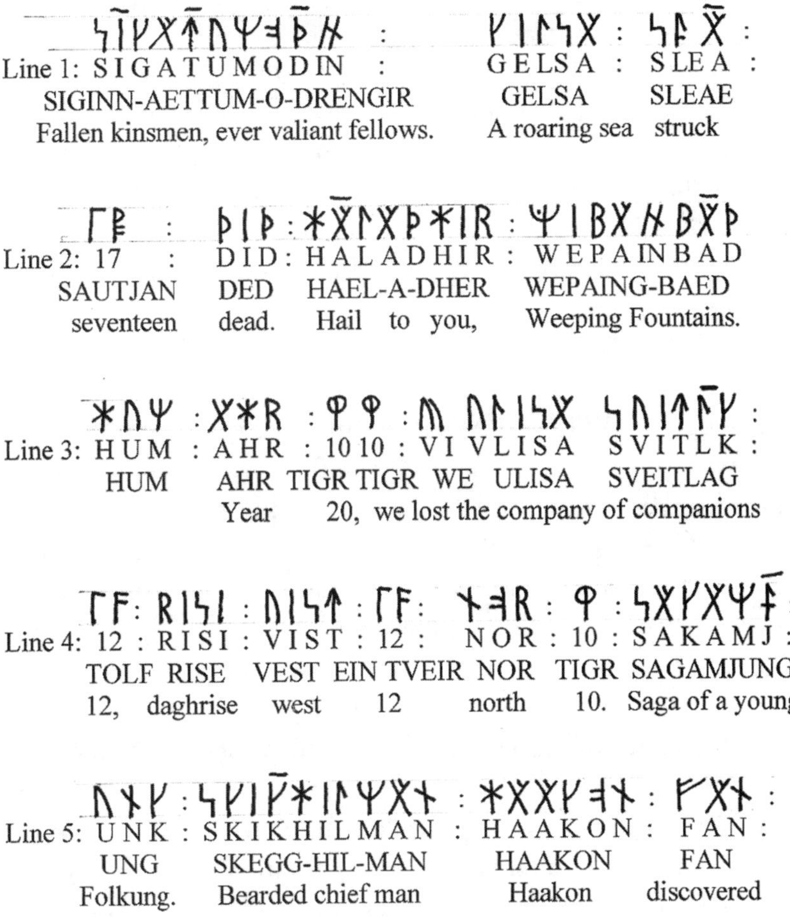

Line 1: SIGATUMODIN :
SIGINN-AETTUM-O-DRENGIR
Fallen kinsmen, ever valiant fellows.

GELSA : SLEA :
GELSA SLEAE
A roaring sea struck

Line 2: 17 : DID: HALADHIR : WEPAINBAD
SAUTJAN DED HAEL-A-DHER WEPAING-BAED
seventeen dead. Hail to you, Weeping Fountains.

Line 3: HUM : AHR : 10 10 : VI VLISA SVITLK :
HUM AHR TIGR TIGR WE ULISA SVEITLAG
Year 20, we lost the company of companions

Line 4: 12 : RISI : VIST : 12 : NOR : 10 : SAKAMJ :
TOLF RISE VEST EIN TVEIR NOR TIGR SAGAMJUNG
12, daghrise west 12 north 10. Saga of a young

Line 5: UNK : SKIKHILMAN : HAAKON : FAN :
UNG SKEGG-HIL-MAN HAAKON FAN
Folkung. Bearded chief man Haakon discovered

FIGURE 40: The Spirit Pond runestone inscription, lines 1–5.

To preserve the couplet rhythm the overbarred words were usually recited in their complete forms, while most of the compound words without overbars were recited as they are found in short form. GELSA without an overbar is a compound word with short forms: GEL and SA. GELLA = "to roar" (Z 163), and GEL is the short form of GELLANDI = "roaring" (Z 541), the active participle. SA is the short form for SAER or "sja," the nom. sing. of "sea" (Z 426). The rhythm of the poem is retained by recitation of the compound form as GEL-SA. In the last word on line 1, the half crossed "L" appears to be a bindrune for "LE." The overbarred "A" = AE, as in other words in the inscription. SLÁ is "to smite, to strike, to slay" (Z 386). But the transliteration is: SLEAE. "slae" is first pers. nom. of "kill" or "slay" and with the half-crossed "L" = LE we have a conversion to a preterite form: "slew" or "struck," like "slean" (MS 207). Continuing onward to line 2, the pentadic "17" is "sautjan" (G 292). DED = "déd,'" an alternative form of "dead" in Anglo Saxon (BT 198) and Middle English (MS 59). The complete sentences are: "Fallen kinsmen, ever valiant fellows. A roaring sea struck seventeen dead."

Line 2:

HÄLADHIR: WEPAINBÄDHUM, in which two "As" have overbars (shown by umlauts here). From the first two lines, translated as "Fallen kinsmen, ever valiant fellows, a roaring sea struck seventeen dead," we can assume that the poem is a funeral oration that was to have been delivered in honor of the lost men. This context guides our translation of these two long compound words, which we divide as follows:

HÄL-Á-DHIR: WEPAIN-BÄDHUM

HÄL-Á-DHIR was most likely a salute to the mourners of the court on the memorial occasion when the poem was recited. Therefore, the Old Icelandic spelling for "death" = HAEL (G 353) may not apply here. In Middle English, MS gives "Hailen" = "to greet, to say 'hail.'" Bosworth-Toller (BT 504) gives several forms for the greeting that in English usage is illustrated by "Hail to the Chief!" In the BT dictionary, the *Laym.* source gives: "hal, hael, haeil, hail, hol," all used as a greeting or salute. Therefore, HÄL = HAEL = HAIL = "Hail" as in the sense of a greeting or salute.

A = Á = "to," denoting a personal relation, as in meaning III (1) (Z 29). The greeting to the mourners would be a very personal thing.

DHIR. The greeting is "Hail to you, those, or them . . ." DHIR is the object of the preposition "Á" and is therefore in the dative case. It does not contain an "M" so DHIR is not "them" or "those" (Z 540). Consequently, DHIR should represent the second person "you," also in the plural dative. But the plural dative of "you" is "ythr," (Z 540, "th" = the edh), which would awkwardly result in two adjacent vowel sounds. It would not contribute well to the couplet rhythm, and there is no "Y" in DHIR. But here the author is addressing the nobles of the court who are in mourning, and he therefore used the nominative plural case "dér" = "you" ("d" = DH, the thorn rune) that was used when addressing a person or persons of importance (G 313). "dér" with the trilled "r" supplies the major and minor emphasis that forms the element of couplet rhythm, rhythm that would be lost with "ythr."

WEPAING. This word appears three times in the inscription. An examination of magnified images from two photos showed that in lines 2 and 16 the first "M" rune is probably dotted. This dot phonetically converts the "M" into a "W" or a phonetic "V," just as in the Kensington runestone inscription where the dotted "M" = "W" or "V" is used repeatedly. Interpreting the first "I" as an "E," the "B" as a "P," and the ligatured IN as ING, the first six runes become WEPAING, which would be the neut. pl. acc. participle adjective form of the Anglo Saxon verb "wépan" = "to weep" (BT 1204) meaning "to cry aloud, to lament loudly." A similar Norse word "oepa" (Z 526) means "to cry."

BÄDHUM (overbarred "A") = BAEDHUM. This word follows DHIR and is the indirect object of "Á." It is therefore the plural dative neut. (BT 67, meaning II) of the Old Norse BATH and the Anglo Saxon BAED, a baptismal font (Z 536). These two words would then be literally "weeping fonts" = "overflowing fonts" or poetically, as in this poem, "weeping fountains." See "font" in *Webster's New Twentieth Century Dictionary, Unabridged Second Edition* (New York: World Publishing Company, 1973), 713. "Weeping Fountains" is the poetic metaphor for the mourning families of the lost Norsemen. The final translation would be: "Hail to you, Weeping Fountains!" Poets composing in the fourteenth century Norse frequently used extravagant metaphors, called kennings. Examples include "branda elgr" = "elk of beaks" (G xli), which is the metaphor for a ship with pointed bow and stern, and "ná-saer" = "sea of the body" = "blood" (G 372).

Line 3:

AHR = "ÅR" = "year," Garde, *Danish Dictionary* (1991). We know the year numbers are not calendar years because the types of runes are not consistent with AD 1010. Instead, the year number is the age of Haakon, here the sum of two decades: runic 10 plus runic 10 = 20. The Old Norse word for ten is TÍU. The old word for a decade is TIGR (Z 435). We assume the author intended to use the old "decade" for ten to obtain the desired rhythm and rhyming using the trill of the end letter "R" in the three couplets of that poetic line.

FIGURE 41: The UI bindrune (U inverted) representing the royal "We." From a Malcolm Pearson high-resolution photo of Side #1 of the Spirit Pond inscription runestone. Used with permission. The runestone is now curated at the Maine State Museum, mainestatemuseum.org.

The joined VI bindrune is a puzzle because the expected form would be a separated V I, equivalent to V E = "vér" (G 293), which would translate as "we" but with the trilled "R" omitted. "Vér" was often used in Norse when a king was speaking. But the omission of the trilled "R" to maintain the couplet meter takes away the sound of the royal "we" in Norse and it conveys the wrong meaning of a mansion or sanctuary (Z 477). The author's remedy was to convert the voiced "V" sound to the unvoiced "W" of the Middle English "royal we." To accomplish this conversion the author used the bindrune form UI with the middle leg shared to form a second "U" to make it UUI, and carved it with a striking resemblance to an inverted "W," Figure 41, equivalent to the royal "we." The double UU was a visual reminder that the unvoiced sound of a "w" was to be spoken in the recitation.

The "royal we" was used in England as early as AD 1169 by King Henry II in the investiture controversy with his barons (Wikipedia source, June 2009). The double UU, the predecessor of the "W," Figure 42A and B, was occurring as early as AD 1058 in Old English. This example in Old English of the use of UU, in the first listed name of "Eaduueard" (Edward), the predecessor of the "W," is found in: *Charter of a gift of land at Northtun by Ealdred, Bishop of Worcester, Worcester, AD 1058.* Figure 27 in: *A History of Calligraphy* by A. Gaur (Cross River Press, 1994). The "W" also occurs in the name "Olaws" (Olavus) on the 1316 Gotlandic gravemarker,[94] Figure 42B.

There are two related possibilities for ULESA. In Old Icelandic (Z 268) LESA is "to grasp" or "to gather," and in Anglo Saxon "lesan" has been used in the sense of "gathering people together" (BT 635). The verb form is analogous to "risa" (Z 542). The preceding "U" represents the negative "un," and ULESA is thus translated as: "ungathered" or "ungrasped," meaning physically "lost" (drowned). In Old Icelandic the negative: "ú" = "un" is widely used. The usual verb form here would be "ulesum" = "(we) lost," or if in the subjunctive: "ulesim." But

---

94. The 1316 inscription is: "ADNO: DOMINI: M: CCC: XVI: RLV: APRILIS: OBITU: OLAWS: DE: HIRIBY: CUIVS: AIM: REQESCAT: IPACE +" In Latin: "Anno Domini M CCC XVI relevatus Aprilis obitus Olavus de Hiriby cujus animus requiescat inpace" In English: "year of the Lord 1316 'relieved of pain' in April 'passed away' Olavus (Olav or Olaf) of Hiriby whose spirit rests in peace." This gravestone image is from: Lettering in Ornament: An inquiry into the Decorative Use of Lettering, Past, Present and Possible, Lewis F. Day, Second Edition, revised, copyright 1914, B.T. Batsford Ltd. 94 High Holborn, London.

here Haakon, the King, is speaking with emotion using the "royal we," which is in effect "I." Therefore, because his meaning is "I lost . . ." he used the preterite singular subjunctive form "ULESA." Note that here the use of the "we" (royal we) with the singular form "ULESA" is quite different from the "we" with the plural form "várum" in line 6 of the Kensington inscription. There the "we" is in the East Norse dialect, used in the plural sense.

FIGURE 42: A: An AD 1058 example of the use of the "UU" prede-cessor of the "W" in Old English. From Figure 27 in: *A History of Calligraphy*, A. Gaur, Cross River Press, 1994. B: This gravestone slab from a church floor on the island of Gotland illustrates the use of shortened word forms to fit the inscription into a limited space. Note the two "U's" that form the inverted "W," and the two overbars.

SVEIT (Z 421) is a company or body of men. SVEIT is also a cognate of the modern "suite," a company of attendants, as for example, "the suite of a visiting prince." In the LK there is a small dot by the staff of the "K" to make it a "G." The overbar above the "L" denotes an absent "A." Thus, LAG (Z 258) implies "companionship" of the staff, as Carlson suggests. See S. Carlson, *The Spirit Pond inscription stone: Rhyme and Reason*, NEARA Journal Vol. 30, No. 3&4, 1996, 77. In Old Icelandic "felagi" is equivalent to "fellows" or "comrades" (Z 134). Hence, "we lost the company of companions twelve" ("tolf," G 292, as spoken in the poem) or in complete form: "In year twenty we lost the company of twelve companions." The twelve companions in the king's retinue were analogous to the twelve Disciples of Christ in the royal customs of those times. Next we are told where the companions twelve and their crew of five were lost. The context requires a unit of distance.

Line 4 and 5

RISE is the short form of "daghrise." This is a unit of distance equivalent to a twelve-hour day of sailing that covered about seventy-five statute miles, and was in common use by Norse sailors of those times. VEST = "vestr" = "westwards" (G 395) and NOR = "nordher" = "northwards" (G 373). The abbreviated forms were used to maintain the couplet rhythm. The coordinates, in RISE units relative to Spirit Pond, of the location where the ship sank were: "westwards twelve" (EIN TVEIR) = runic 12, "northwards ten" (TIGR, G 292) = runic 10. Strictly speaking, "ten" would be TIU (G 292), but TIGR with declining emphasis on the trilled "R" has a better rhythm. The men and their ship were therefore lost approximately 900 miles west and 750 miles north of Spirit Pond, at a location off the southern coast of Hudson Bay.

SAGAMJ begins a new sentence, and appears to be a compound word that is incomplete, as indicated by the absence of word separator dots after the overbarred "J."

If we naively continue onward to line 5, we could complete the word with "UNG." Thus, SAGA = "story, history" (Z 346), "M" is a short version of UM = "of, about" (Z 447 meaning 8), and JUNG = "young" with implication of nobility as in JUNG-HERRA = "young lord" or "young prince" (Z 234). That poetic line would then read SAG-AM-JUNG SKEGG-HIL-MAN. This rendition is unacceptable because the resulting rhyming is not good, and because we have ignored the overbar above the "J," Figure 37, and its implied missing letters. To resolve this problem we make a bold assumption that the missing letters are in fact UNG and that the inscribed UNG represents a different word. An examination of the historical background of the inscription tells us that the inscribed UNG is the short form of FOLKUNG, just as RISE is the short form for "DAGHRISE." This resolves the problem because now we have: SAG-AM JUNG FOL-KUN-G', which is an exact fit to the context and gives perfect couplet rhythm if the last "G" has a declining emphasis.

Line 5:

Completing line 5 we have: SKEGGHILMAN HAAKON FAN, with declining emphasis on the first and third "N," which also contributes nicely to the rhyming and rhythm of the poem. SKEGG, the first part of the compound word, is somewhat like a modern Danish word: "skikkelig," meaning "upright, decent." There is a possible double meaning here, because in Old Icelandic "skikkja" (Z 373) is a cloak or mantle, an article of clothing worn by those of the nobility, and SKEGG (Z 370) = "beard," which is our preferred interpretation.

HIL is the root of "hildingr" = "chief, hero" and "hilmir" = "chief, prince" (Z 198). A reasonable translation, using the root for the short form "HIL," would be "bearded chief man," a macho and flattering nickname for the king.

MAN = "man" (BT 666, MS 142), indefinite pronoun, active voice.

FAN = "found," 3d pers. pret. sing. of "finna" = "to find" or "to discover." The meaning here is "discovered" (G 344).

Line 6:

HRING or KRING m. sing. is the accusative form of "hringr" = "ring" or "circle" (G 356, Z 210, 249).

"Í" = "by means of" or "by" (Z 230). With the second ligatured

"IN," there is no "GING." Therefore,

KING = GENG = GENGR (Z 163), with the trilled "R" omitted to maintain the couplet rhythm in the recitation. This word is like GANGR (Z 160) = "walking" or "motion of any kind," but GENGR implies "being able." That is, "able to" or "fit to walk," or "able to leave home" (Z 163). In this context "able to go" or "able to sail" is appropriate. In Middle English, "genge" can have the meaning of an "expedition" (MS 99), and the combined meaning could be "by being able to make an expedition . . . "

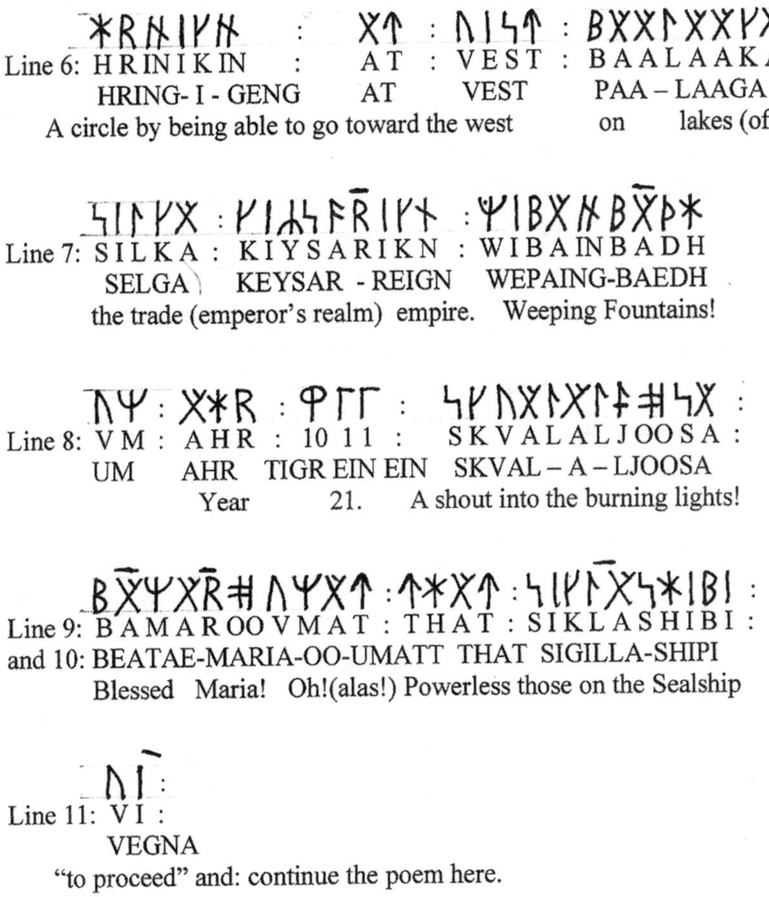

Line 6: HRINIKIN : AT : VEST : BAALAAKA :
HRING- I - GENG AT VEST PAA – LAAGA
A circle by being able to go toward the west on lakes (of)

Line 7: SILKA : KIYSARIKN : WIBAINBADH
SELGA KEYSAR - REIGN WEPAING-BAEDH
the trade (emperor's realm) empire. Weeping Fountains!

Line 8: VM : AHR : 10 11 : SKVALALJOOSA :
UM AHR TIGR EIN EIN SKVAL – A – LJOOSA
Year 21. A shout into the burning lights!

Line 9: BAMAROOVMAT : THAT : SIKLASHIBI :
and 10: BEATAE-MARIA-OO-UMATT THAT SIGILLA-SHIPI
Blessed Maria! Oh!(alas!) Powerless those on the Sealship

Line 11: VI :
VEGNA
"to proceed" and: continue the poem here.

FIGURE 43: The Spirit Pond inscription translated, lines 6–11.

AT = "towards" (Z 21).

VEST = VESTRI (Z 486) with the RI poetically omitted to maintain the couplet rhythm.

BAA = prep. "on" or "upon." This is an intermediate fourteenth-century form in the evolution from "upp á" in Old Norse to "på" in modern Norwegian (G 311).

LAAGA = "löga," the accusative plural case of "lögr" meaning "sea" or "water" (Z 283, G 368). LAAGA is close to the Latin root word for lake = "lacus." LAAGA therefore implies "lakes." Although "A" and "Å" are not identical, the last shared "A" in LAAGA apparently also serves as a preposition "Á" = "in" or "of" (Z 29).

Line 7:

SELGA, possibly from SELJA = "to sell" (Z 355, meaning 2), and SELGA might be the combination of two short forms equivalent to SEL for "selja" and GA for "ganga" = "go to sell" = "trade" after restoring the poetic word inversion. A documented path to the "trade" definition is found in Anglo Saxon under "sellan" (BT 861). Meaning IV is: "to give one thing for another." A cited usage is " . . . ge se de hi sylle ge se de hi bycge." Here "ge . . . ge . . . " is "both . . . and . . . " (BT 363). The citation translates as "both that of his sales and that of his purchases" or simply "his trade." The abbreviated form of the cited usage could be " . . . 'sylle ge' . . . ," which in the Norse equivalent becomes SELGA = "trade."

KEYSARI = KEISARI (a weak noun) = "emperor" (Z 238). The short form KEYSA would be the genitive case in Norse (Z 537), but this is not a Norse word and the "R" is overbarred on its right side, indicating the double RR. This combines with the Latin word REGN to form "emperor's realm" or "keisara-doemr" or "empire" (Z 238).

REGN = "regne" (MS 185) = "kingdom." The runic "A" in KEYSAR-REGN is the only rune in the inscription with a staff and two flags, a runic form used in Roman times when the title of "Caesar" = KEYSAR became synonymous with the ruler of the land. The flagged "A" was widely used in quite old futarks; for example: in Vadstena, Sweden;

Breza, a Jugoslavian church; and Charnay, a grave field in France.[95] The skald probably used it because it was a customary old form with the KEYSAR title. The sentence in lines 5, 6, and 7 reads: "Skegghilman Haakon discovered a circle by being able to sail toward the west on the lakes of the trade empire."

WEPAING BAEDHUM = "Weeping Fountains" as on line 2.

Line 8:

AHR = year + runic 10 11 = AHR' . . . TIGR' . . . EINN'EINN' maintains the couplet rhythm by trilling the "R." EINN'EINN is poetic license, which maintains the rhyming and rhythm in contrast to "ellifu" = "eleven" (G292), which does not. EINN'EINN recited rapidly distinguishes the positional number 11 from 1 + 1 (see Appendix G). It was year twenty when the retinue was lost. It is now year twenty-one, and the recitation of the saga continues and the tragedy is described.

SKVAL = "a shout" (Z 384).

Á = "to" or "into" (Z 29, acc. of place).

LJOOSA = "ljósa," acc. pl., = "burning lights" (Z 276). Its literal meaning is "a shout into the lightning of the storm" or figuratively "a shout into the heavens."

Lines 9 and 10:

The emotional "shout into the burning lights!" leads directly to the interpretation of BAMAR with its overbars as the shouted phrase: "Blessed Maria!" MAR is the abbreviation for MARIA, the Virgin Mary. Cappelli[96] gives three abbreviations with overbars for "blessed": BA and BAA = BEATA; and BAE = BEATAE, which is the feminine form. The "A" with overbar is a doubly abbreviated form: first, "A" = AE, and second, AE = EATAE. Both "bae" and "mar" are cited as used in thirteenth-century manuscripts; see Figure 59 in Appendix I. In the context of this tragic situation described in the inscription, BEATAE MARIA is a cry to the Virgin Mary. The translation reads

---

95.   R.I. Page. *Reading the Past: Runes* (University of California Press/British Museum, 1987), 18.

96.   Cappelli. *Dizionario di Abbreviature Latine ed Italiane*, 31, 213. U. Hoepli, ed., (Milano: 1961).

BAMAR = BEATAE MARIA = "Blessed Maria!" Our interpretation is supported in Figure 44, where we show a magnified image of the runic "A" with rays emanating from the cross point, indicating the sacred character of the name. See Appendix I for Latin abbreviations of "Beatae Maria." Note that in SK-VAL-Á-LJOO-SA BE-AT-AE-MA-RI-A the recitation becomes an excited rhythmic set of triplets with the despairing cry to the Virgin Mary, as might have been made during the storm when the ship sank, followed by: OO = "Oh!" or "alas!" an exclamation of distress. The dramatic nature of this line in a public recitation is obvious. An alternative is OO = "ever," or "always." In (G 400, 401) "ae" = "alas!" "ever," or "always," but "Oh!" or "Alas!" is a better fit to the mood of the poem.

FIGURE 44: The greatly abbreviated form of the runic "Blessed Maria," the "shout into the burning lights" when the men on the Sealship saw the stricken ship going down. The rays emanating from the second runic "A" show the sacred character of the name. From a Malcolm Pearson high-resolution photo of the Spirit Pond runestone inscription. Used with permission. The runestone is now curated at the Maine State Museum, mainestatemuseum.org.

"Ú" = "un," a negative prefix (Z 456, 459). MAT = MÁT, nom. of MÁTTR = "strength, might (power)" (Z 290) with the trilled "R" poetically omitted, hence: "powerless."

THAT can be considered as a compound word with shared "A." "those" = THÁ, m. pl. acc. (G 294, "DÁ" before AD 1225), plus "on" = AT (Z 20), although "Á" and "A" are not strictly identical. "Those" is the object of the understood "were" and TH plays the role of "D" (the thorn) in west Norse after about AD 1225 (G 268), indicating the unvoiced sound of "th" at the beginning of words.

At first sight SIGLA suggests a form of the verb "to sail" and the overbarred SIGLA would function as an adjective. "That sailing ship" would be an acceptable form, although redundant. However, "sailing" = "sigling" (G 380) is unacceptable because the remaining "A" in SIGLA would be unexplained. With the overbar, the missing letters can be supplied by the historical context, and we have:

SIGILLA, which is a feminine singular adjective translated from the Latin as "seal."[97] The complete word is "Sealship" = SIGILLASHIPI, dat. (Z 537), the indirect object of the omitted "were." That is, Haakon's ship was the "Ship of the Seal" (the royal seal.) An example, the seal of the City of Elbing, is shown in Figure 45. See Appendix I, Figure 59, for Latin versions of the abbreviation for "sigilla" and "sigillum."

Note the negative implication of "U" in UMAT = "unpowered, powerless," like ULISA in line 3. Thus: "Beatae Maria! Alas! Powerless those on the Sealship . . . "

Line 11:

VE stands alone with an overbar. It is an abbreviation for VEGNA (Z 478) meaning "to proceed" or "to continue," see Figure 59 in Appendix I for Latin versions, which mean the opposite side, "verso," as in "flip side" of a coin. That is, the poem is to be continued on this side of the stone. However, it has a double meaning. This abbreviation has also been made part of the narrative sentence, and cleverly fits into the meter. The sentence reads: "Powerless (were) those on the Sealship to proceed to obtain . . . " The incorporation of the VE into the poem and on the stone in this way is the mark of a clever and skillful poet.

---

97. Traupman, *New College Latin and English Dictionary*, (New York: Bantam Books, 1995).

FIGURE 45: A "Ship of the Seal" example: City of Elbing about 1350. Source: Dr. Gabriele Hoffman, Schiffahrts Museum, Bremerhaven. The Latin inscription around the perimeter is "SIGILLUM CIVITATIS ELBINGENSIS" (Seal of the City of Elbing).

Line 12:

NÁ = "to obtain" (Z 309), "to possess."

EGG is "edge" (Z 103). The genitive form is EGGJAR with the trilled "R" poetically omitted. EGGJA is used in the sense of getting an advantageous position. "Getting a winning edge" is an expression that is still frequently used in the world of sports.

AKTAR (Z 7, 541) = AKTA, 3d pers. sing. = "to devote attention," with trilled "R" again omitted.

BAA = PÅ = "of, with." PAA UMB is "in regard" (Z 447). The overbar above the "B" in line 13 indicates the missing "U" that is needed for the emphasis on the first syllable in the couplet. In the context of the men on the Ship of the Seal who would have wanted to aid the sinking ship, we have: "Powerless (were) those on the Ship of the Seal to proceed to get an edge to devote attention in regard . . . "

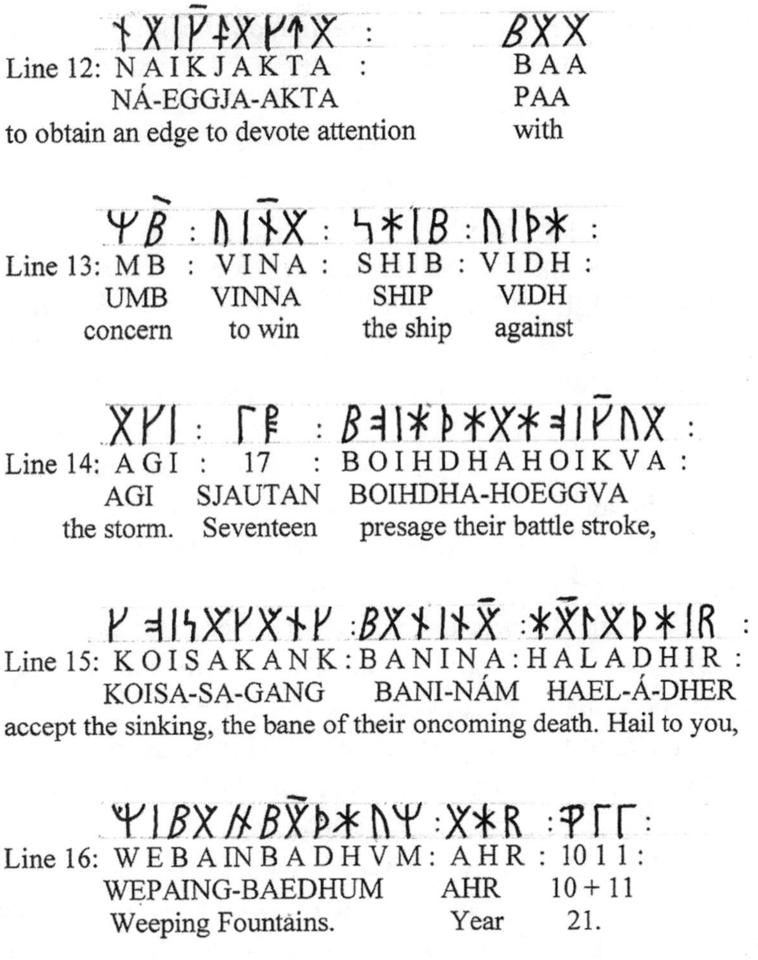

ᚾ᛭ᛁᚹᛂᚷᚹ᛭ᚷ :   ᛒᚷᚷ

Line 12: N A I K J A K T A   :   B A A

NÁ-EGGJA-AKTA   PAA

to obtain an edge to devote attention   with

ᛉᛒ̃ : ᚾᛁᛣᚷ : ᛋ᛭ᛁᛒ : ᚾᛁᚹ᛭ :

Line 13: M B   : V I N A   : S H I B : V I D H :

UMB   VINNA   SHIP   VIDH

concern   to win   the ship   against

ᚷᚹᛁ : ᚽᛂ : ᛒᛱᛁ᛭ᚦ᛭ᚷᛱ ᛱᛁᚹᚾᚷ :

Line 14: A G I   :   17   : B O I H D H A H O I K V A :

AGI   SJAUTAN   BOIHDHA-HOEGGVA

the storm.   Seventeen   presage their battle stroke,

ᚹ ᛱᛁᛋᚷᚹᚷᚾᚹ :ᛒᚷᚾᛁᚾ�X̄ :᛭ᚽ̄ᛁᚷᚦ᛭ᛁᚱ :

Line 15: K O I S A K A N K : B A N I N A : H A L A D H I R :

KOISA-SA-GANG   BANI-NÁM   HAEL-Á-DHER

accept the sinking, the bane of their oncoming death. Hail to you,

ᛉᛁᛒᚷᚼᛒᚷ̃ᚦ᛭ᚾᛉ :ᚷ᛭ᚱ : ᛂᚽᚽ :

Line 16: W E B A I N B A D H V M : A H R : 10 1 1 :

WEPAING-BAEDHUM   AHR   10 + 11

Weeping Fountains.   Year   21.

FIGURE 46: The Spirit Pond inscription translated, lines 12–16.

Line 13:

VINNA = "to win" as in a contest (Z 493).

SHIB = "ship," acc.

VIDH = "against" as in a contest (Z 487).

AGI (line 14) has the meaning of "turbulence, uproar, terror" (Z 6), which in this context would translate as "terrible storm." The most consistent interpretation of lines 8, 9, 10, 12, and 13 is: "A shout into the burning lights! Blessed Maria! Alas! Powerless those on the

Sealship to proceed to get an edge to devote attention in regard to win the ship from the terrible storm." The men on the Ship of the Seal had their own troubles in the storm and were unable to get into a position to assist the doomed ship.

Line 14:

"runic 17" = "SJAUTAN."

BOIHDHA is the fourteenth-century form of the older word BJOHDHA = "bjódha," (Z 56, 542) pl. pres. 3d. pers. = "to have presentiment of," akin to the modern English "bode" and the Old English "bëodan" = "foretell" or "to indicate by signs: presage." Probably the doomed men could foretell their fate as the storm worsened. The OI inversion and the "I–J" exchange are apparently changes in the language that evolved in the twelfth or thirteenth centuries. This is an equivalent of "the Great Vowel Shift" that occurred in the English language.[98] The reason for inserting the "H" before the "DH" is not obvious, although the word would then be pronounced as a triplet BOI-H-DHA to match the HOEG-G-VA. The author may have borrowed the HDH from the Anglo Saxon (BT 883) to imply a strong sense of inevitability, as in "Mann slihdh thinne oxan . . . " = "thine ox shall be slain . . . " (Deut. 28, 31). A translation would be: "Seventeen presage their inevitable battle stroke."

HOEGGVA = HÔGGVA, genitive pl. (G 235) of the noun "högg" (Z 225) = a "stroke, blow," as in a battle, closely related to the verb "höggva" = "to strike" or "to cut down," a phrasing often used in Norse memorial inscriptions as shown in Terje Spurkland's *Norwegian Runes and Runic Inscriptions*. The genitive form implies the possessive "their."

---

98. "kjósa" in Old Icelandic is "to choose" with variant forms "kaaus, køri, kosinn, kørinn," in which the last word may be the equivalent of the Danish "kaaren.'" In Anglo Saxon "c(k)iosan" (BT 155) or "ceosan" with imperative "ceós" (BT 152) and "kjós" (Z 241) is "to choose" or "to accept." Although the "JO" sequence was retained in Old Icelandic for some time, in Scandinavian dialects the "JO" became "OI" before the fourteenth century. This inversion may have occurred near the beginning of the Middle English period about AD 1150 when the "e" was dropped in the Old English word "ceósan" and it became "chosen."

Line 15:

KOISAGANG is a compound of three words with a shared "SA." KOISA, pl. 3d. pers. (Z 241) "kjosa," is used here in the Anglo Saxon sense of "accept by choice what is offered" (BT 152, 155, "kiosan" in Old Saxon). Here is another example of a vowel shift, JO to OI.

SA is a short form of "sja" or "sae" = "sea," (Z 365) and is shared with KOISA.

GANG, an Anglo Saxon word (BT 361) = "going." SA GANG = "sea-going" = "sinking."

"BANI" = "bane" (Z 42). "Bane" is "a source of harm or ruin," meaning 2, page 89 in *Merriam Webster's Collegiate Dictionary*, 10th edition, 1997.

NÁM (Z 310) is the dative case of "nár" = "corpse, death." In the dative case the word is "the indirect object of a verb, or the object of some prepositions, or a possessor," *Webster's* . . . p. 294. Also: "the case of a noun which expresses . . . in many languages an approach to something," page 463 in *Webster's New Twentieth Century Dictionary*, unabridged second edition, 1973. Thus, Lines 14 and 15 translate as: "Seventeen presage their inevitable battle stroke, accept the sinking, the bane of their approaching death. Hail to you, Weeping Fountains." A side note: the "narwhale" is so named because of its deathly white corpse-like color.

Lines 15–16:

HÄLADHIR: WEPAINBÄDHUM = Hail to you Weeping Fountains, as on line 2.

AHR 10 +11 = Year 21, as on line 8.

Even today we have the custom of dating legal documents at the end instead of the beginning as we do in correspondence. The words for twenty-one "10 + 11" = TIGR EIN-N'-EIN-N' also complete the poem by end rhyming with BA-NI-NÁ-M'. In the recitation, to distinguish the number eleven from the sum of two ones, the speaker would have made a very deliberate separation before and after the ten, and would have spoken the two ones with no separation somewhat like this: AHR' . . . TIGR' . . . EINN'EINN'.

APPENDIX G:

THE PENTADIC NUMBER SYSTEM AND RUNIC DATING

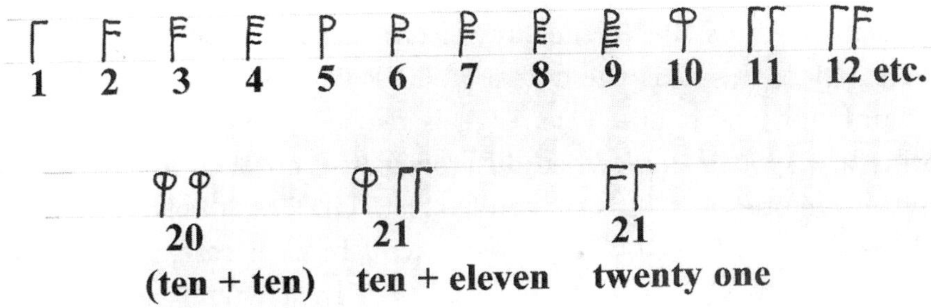

FIGURE 47: The pentadic number system. In this system, the year date twenty-one can be written in two ways. By using the positional notation for eleven in the sum of ten plus eleven, and by pronouncing the eleven as separated ones, the poet achieved the desired meter and rhyming of the chivalric poem on the Spirit Pond stone.

A current opinion on the usage of runic numbers like those shown in Figure 46 is found in the January 2010 posting on the Wikipedia site (http://en.wikipedia.org/wiki/Pentimal_system).

It is stated there that the earliest known common use of the so-called pentadic system is found in Early Modern age calendar sticks.

With Einar Haugen's (incorrect) identification of the Spirit Pond year numbers as AD 1010 and 1011 in mind, Wikipedia states that "the rune for 10 is used interchangeably for 0, 10, and <1,0> with little consistency." However, we see no evidence that zero was used in the Spirit Pond numbers. Nils Lithberg depicts a calendar of AD 1399 in which the numerical values are shown as single pentadic runes with the highest number of 23 shown as the sum of two tens plus three, all on one staff.[99]

Apparently in the fourteenth-century Scandinavian calendar numerals had not yet taken on the forms of the Arabic base 10 positional system. Nevertheless, we find that both the Kensington runestone and the Spirit Pond inscription confirm some use of the Arabic positional system with runes in the mid-fourteenth century. On the Spirit Pond stone the author used the positional system twice each for eleven (11), twelve (12), and seventeen (17), but for 20 and 21 he used the sums 10+10, the sum of two decades, and 10+11 respectively, where the 10 is the decade = TIGR (Z 435), not a date, and is certainly not a zero. Likewise, + (11) is also an interval of years. These forms are spoken somewhat differently to conform to the poetic rhythm. In one case, 12 is spoken first as TOL-F' = "twelve" and then subsequently as EIN' TVEIR = "one two." In each case, 11 would be spoken as EIN-N' EIN-N'. In both cases of 17, it would be spoken as SJAU-TAN. In line 6 of the inscription, we have rendered "north ten" as NOR TIG-R' because of its superior rhythm and declining emphasis with the trilled "R," although strictly speaking this is a coordinate number and, but for poetic license, it would be NOR TI-U.

---

99. N. Lithberg, AD 1399 calendar in Figure 79 in "Comptus med Särskild bänsyn till Runstaven och den Borgerliga Kalendern," 326 pp. including a summary in German (Stockholm: Norstedt & Sons, for the Nordiska Museets Handlingar, 1953).

FIGURE 48: The Kingigtorssuaq runestone, retrieved from a cairn off the western Greenland coast in 1823. The author of this inscription used an ingenious method of abbreviating the word forms of the runic numerals that give the date of 1336, according to our interpretation. Listed as GR 1 in the Rundata catalog, National Museum of Denmark, Copenhagen.

The Kingigtorssauq inscription is an example of an imaginative use of abbreviations to represent numbers. This runestone was found in 1823 in the vicinity of Upernavik off the western coast of Greenland at latitude 73°N. The translation, as given by Arild Hauge on the website http://en.wikipedia.org/wiki/File:Gron-rune-kingigtorssuaq.jpg (accessed April 2011) is: "Erling Sigvatsson, Bjarne Thordarson, and Enride Oddson Saturday before gangdag (Rogation Day, April 25) made these stone cairns ??????"

The year date at the end of the inscription was not known but was presumed to be in the range of 1250–1333. It is likely that the six runes at the end are numerals, the sum of which gives the date of the inscription. This date can be derived by using simple assumptions regarding the abbreviations used for the word forms of the six runic numbers. The abbreviated word forms are located between the "M" and "Y" runes at the top and bottom of each of these runes. The purpose of the "M" and "Y" runes is to designate them as numerals instead of letters. The third, fourth, and fifth runes are each a pentadic staff with a circular arcs near the top to represent a "10," as repeatedly found on the Spirit Pond inscription. The sixth rune is "s," or could be read as two "s's" if rotated 180°, thus representing the double "s" sound of "sex," the Old Norse number "6" (G 292). The second rune can be viewed as a bindrune consisting of two "t's," one upright and one inverted. They share the short angular bar, and each resembles the other "t's" in the inscription that have only one angular bar. The abbreviated word form is "tíu tigir" = "ten decades" = "100" (Z435, G 293). The first rune is a bindrune combining "s" below and "t" inverted above with the horizontal bar and the angular bar inscribed together. This would be the abbreviation for "thú sund," which is the modern Icelandic word for "1000," as reported in a 7 November 2010 communication with Valdimar Samuelsson of Reykjavik. However, "thú sund" in medieval times was based on the "long hundred" = 120,[100] and meant "ten long hundreds" = 1200 (G 293). The year date would therefore be 1200+100+30+6 = AD 1336.

---

100. J. L. Byock. *Viking Age Iceland* (London: Penguin Books, 2001), 55.

APPENDIX H:
ABBREVIATED WORDS IN AN ICELANDIC TEXT: PALEOGRAPHY

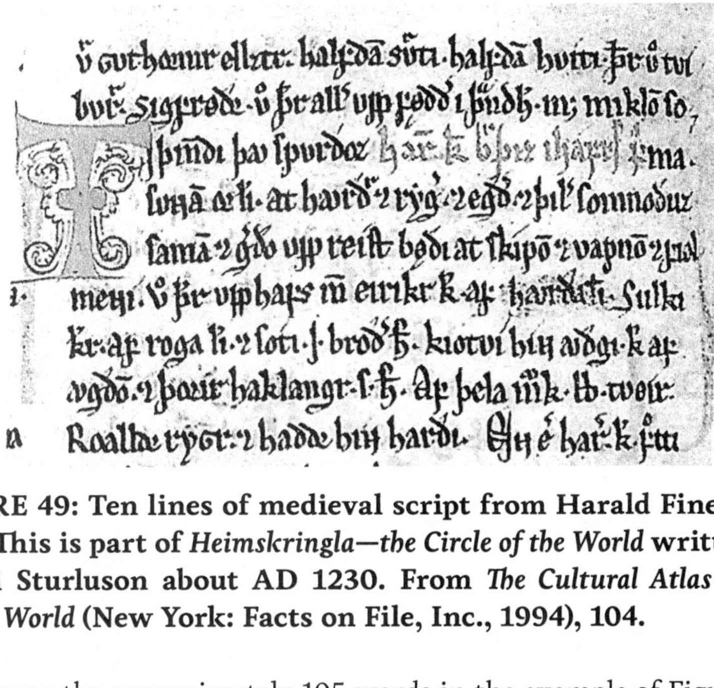

FIGURE 49: Ten lines of medieval script from Harald Finehair's Saga. This is part of *Heimskringla—the Circle of the World* written by Snorri Sturluson about AD 1230. From *The Cultural Atlas of the Viking World* (New York: Facts on File, Inc., 1994), 104.

Among the approximately 105 words in the example of Figure 49, 19 have overbars and about 34 have superscripts of "r," "v," "o," "u," or "s" to indicate longer words. Several examples of unadorned single letters representing words also occur. Note that a single "k" with an attached large comma at the top of the staff represents the "King," as in line 6 where "eirikr k" = King Eirik in the nominative case. Of course, in runic carvings, the small superscripts are not practical, and only dots and overbars were used.

Appendix I:
MEDIEVAL ABBREVIATION PRACTICES:

As Applied to the Spirit Pond and the Kensington inscriptions

> "Take a foreign language, write it in unfamiliar script, abbreviating every third word, and you have the compound puzzle that is the medieval Latin manuscript."
>
> —D. Heimann and R. Kay

The Spirit Pond inscription stone as well as the Kensington rune stone, both of the medieval fourteenth century and carved in runes, use devices of abbreviation borrowed from those used in Latin of the same era. The step from abbreviated Icelandic Norse written in the Roman alphabet to abbreviated Norse written in the runic alphabet is a small step indeed. In medieval Europe, Latin was the language of the Christian Church as well as that of the formally educated nobility, continental traders, and university students. By the year 1300, universities had been founded at Cambridge, Oxford, Paris, Toulousse, Seville, Padua, Bologna, and Naples, among others.[101] The step from Latin, used by the Church, to Norse was a natural one in response to the needs of Icelandic commerce and daily needs of ordinary Norsemen. The use of abbreviations was passed along to runic writings because the same technical limitations on writing still applied. The printing

---

101. R. Kitterick. *Atlas of the Medieval World* (New York: Oxford University Press, 2004).

press did not exist in Europe (introduced about 1450), no dictionaries giving standard spellings existed yet, and all text was copied by hand. Paper had not yet caught on in Europe, especially Scandinavia. Vellum and parchment, the writing media of the age, was expensive and time consuming to produce. Keep in mind that a cow, sheep, or goat had to be slaughtered for the skin. The skin then had to be soaked in lye, stretched, scraped, dried, and cut before an experienced scribe could even consider putting a quill pen to the surface, after he ground and prepared his own ink.

An inscription in stone had its limitations, too—quarrying and transporting it, shaping it, preparing the surface, making and sharpening the chisels to carve it, and planning out what was to be inscribed (this wasn't always done, however, giving less than ideal results). Great skill was required to carve it. There were always the issues of weight, limited space that could be inscribed, and the technical difficulties of carving that are unique to each type of stone. Abbreviation went hand in hand with all the difficulties associated with getting the words put into a written form. It saved space and time (hence, saved money) and saved the scribe or letter carver's hand from tiring quite so quickly.

As Latin of the Church spread farther north into Scandinavia, the accompanying abbreviation with its devices of overbars, dots, signs, marks, and superscripted letters went with it. The practice was adapted as needed into other languages: French, Spanish, English, and the Norse of Scandinavia. By the 1200s, if not before, Icelandic manuscripts were being penned on vellum, written for the most part in the Roman alphabet and liberally borrowing abbreviation devices from Latin usage. In Scandinavia, prior to the introduction of Christianity and Latin written in the Roman alphabet (officially around year 1000 with some earlier influences), the letterforms of choice were runes. They were easier to carve on a stick of wood, and less complicated to execute in stone. Runes were all the same height—no capital letters and small letters. If you didn't know how to spell a word, sounding it out worked just fine and it was still understandable to a reader. Runes were easier to learn for everyone who used them. Runes did not die out quickly with the introduction of the Roman alphabet and they coexisted for many centuries, even into the 1500s and beyond in some areas, such as the Island of Gotland in the Baltic.

Archaeological excavation work at Bryggen (Bergen, Norway) has revealed numerous runic inscriptions—most on wood, some on animal bones, a few on metal or stone, with the greatest concentration of them dating from 1250–1330. They vary from religious and secular writings in Latin (but using runic letters) to Old Norse poetry, everyday messages, business correspondence, love notes, etc.[102] Two examples of earlier use of runes to write Latin are as follows: 1) a leather shoe, also found at Bryggen, from the later 1100s, with the phrase "...Amor vincit Omnia...," using sounded-out spelling, meaning "Love conquers all," which was stitched around the ankle and down to the toe; and 2) a rib bone from the 1100s, found at Sigtuna Uppland, Sweden; inscribed with "manas kruks maria matra tomina" on one side, while on the other, "kruks markus kruks lukus kruks ma...," meaning "hand (of the) cross Mary Mother (of) God," and "cross (of) Mark, cross (of) Luke, cross (of) Ma[tthew]...."[103]

It is interesting to note that some of the same fluidity of letter usage in Latin was also occurring in Norse runic writing. For many centuries, in Latin, the letter "u" represented both the "v" and "u" sounds, as well as the "v" representing both sounds. A late thirteenth-century northern French or English gothic style (the term "gothic" lettering style has no direct association with the place name of Gotland) manuscript page that is hanging on author Westin's wall reads, letter for letter, "...qui uenturus est iudicare uiuos et mortuos..." Using letters that make more sense in the twenty-first century, it says, "...qui venturus est judicare vivos et mortuos..." ("...who comes in is judged life and death..."). It was common to see this interchangeability within the same sentence on a manuscript page.

On the dedicatory page of Gospels from Lund Cathedral, Sweden,

---

102. T. Spurkland. Norwegian Runes and Runic Inscriptions, Betsy van der Hoek, translator (Rochester, NY: Bboydell Press, 2005), 174.

103. E. Rosedahl and D. M. Wilson, eds., From Viking to Crusader—Scandinavia and Europe 800–1200, (New York: Rizzoli International Publications, 1992).

c. 1140, St. Lawrence, the patron saint of the cathedral, looks down over other people in the illustration. Written over his head, he is identified with "BEATVS LAVRENTIVS," "Beatus Laurentius" (Blessed Lawrence). In runic writing, the inverted "U" represented both the "u" as well as the "v." The runic letter "B" represented both the "b" and the "p." In the Latin manuscript "the Gospels of Maelbrigte," written not long after 1138 and now in the British Library, London, we see the letters "b" and "p" used interchangeably on the same page in the words "baptismum" and "babtizo" (baptism and baptize).[104] In Roman alphabet Latin, the letter "i" represented both the "i" and "j" within context. (See above Latin quote.) The rune letter "i" also represented both "i" and "j" in context. The word "cuivs" in Fig. 42, transcribed as "cujus" (meaning "whose") also illustrates both the u–v and i–j fluidity in Latin.

We give two examples of how abbreviation was used with the Roman alphabet in Scandinavia. The first is a carved Latin language stone grave-slab from Gotland, Sweden, dated 1316, Figure 42. The second example, Figure 49, is a section of the Heimskringla, copied by hand on vellum in the early 1300s, using the Roman alphabet. It is, however, not written in Latin, but in Old Icelandic Norse. It was originally written by Snorri Sturluson in about 1230. Each example uses abbreviation in ways that were typical of the time. The Icelandic Heimskringla adapted the Latin abbreviation devices that work for it, and is riddled with them. It would make sense that the cost of a decent piece of writing vellum on Iceland versus continental Europe would be at a premium cost, due to limited grazing land and fodder production. This would explain why so much abbreviation was applied, using the space on each skin as economically as possible.

An excellent source of information is *Elements of Abbreviation in Medieval Latin Paleography*[105], which is an English translation by D.

104. R. Aris. *Explicatio formarum litterarum: The unfolding of letterforms* (St. Paul, MN: The Calligraphy Connection, 1990). www.vanstockum.nl (accessed April 2011).

105. A. Cappelli. *The Elements of Abbreviation in Medieval Latin Paleography*, translated by D. Heimann and R. Kay (KS: University of Kansas Libraries, 1982). This is the preface to *Dizionario di Abbreviature, Latine ed Italiane*/Dictionary of Latin and Italian Abbreviations, by A. Cappelli, U. Hoepli, ed. (Milano: 1961).

Heimann and R. Kay. It is the preface to the original Italian language
Dizionario di Abbreviature, Latine ed Italiane, Dictionary of Latin and Italian Abbreviations by Adriano Cappelli. Heimann and Kay, the translating authors, hash out for us in English the basics of how Latin abbreviation was used. Using these authoritative sources and *The Unfolding of Letterforms* by Rutherford Aris, as well as some of the author's personal observations, we explain some of the uses of Latin abbreviation in the following examples. Many of these apply to the inscriptions on the Spirit Pond and Kensington runestones, but not all parts of Latin and the corresponding forms of abbreviation transfer to runic Norse.

Selected Forms of Latin Abbreviation:

1) Cappelli states that "Even in inscriptions (stone), the horizontal bar often serves simply to indicate an abbreviation," which means that the bar can indicate one or more missing letters. Renowned paleographer, Rutherford Aris, used the term "overbar." The wavy line indicated "r" or a syllable containing an "r," such as "ra, re, ar," but also "a" or a syllable containing an "a." In manuscripts of the 1300–1400s, especially those written in Gothic script (a heavier weight, more dense lettering style), the wavy line developed further into a broken overbar, or two dots closely spaced. Overbars, as well as dots, were probably the most common form of abbreviation because bars or dots were easy to execute, whether in stone or on vellum. Examples:

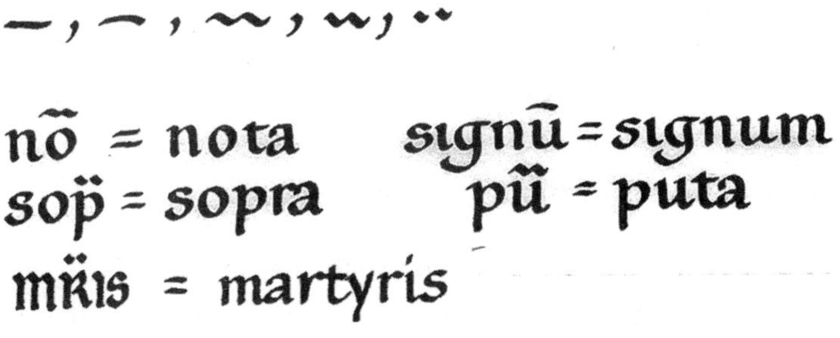

— , ⌐ , ∿ , ∾ , ··

nõ = nota   signū = signum
sop̈ = sopra   pũ = puta
m̈ris = martyris

FIGURE 50: Bars and dots.

2) This sign represents "r" as contained in a syllable, when written above the line of writing. It is actually one of two versions of the letter "r" that evolved from a capital "R" during the medieval period, into what we would now describe as a "lowercase" letter. We show the evolution below of both "r" forms:

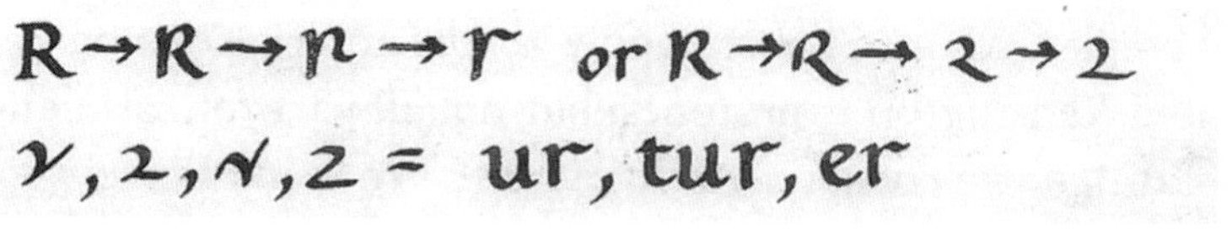

$$R \rightarrow R \rightarrow \textit{n} \rightarrow r \quad \textit{or} \quad R \rightarrow R \rightarrow 2 \rightarrow 2$$
$$\textit{r}, 2, \textit{n}, 2 = ur, tur, er$$

FIGURE 51: Evolution of the "r" from uppercase "R."

3) This medieval variation of "r," when written at the end of a word, and having a slash or variation of a slash through it, means "-rum." Sometimes, a capital "R" was used in a lowercase sense, with an abbreviating slash through its leg, also meaning "-rum." We give an example here of the word "ecclesiarum" from a manuscript written at Canterbury, England, sometime between 1272–1278. Examples:

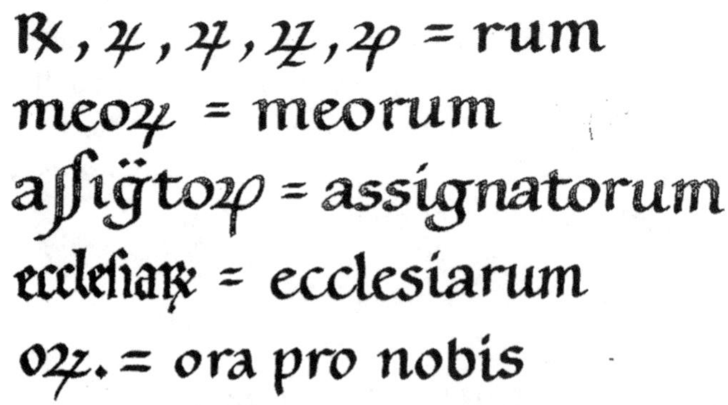

$$R, 4, 4, 4, 4 = rum$$

meo4 = meorum

aſſigto4 = assignatorum

ecclefia4 = ecclesiarum

o4. = ora pro nobis

FIGURE 52: Examples of the use of the slash.

We have a commonly used expression, both medieval and current day, especially in the Catholic Church, that uses this abbreviation device along with a period/dot. The dot entirely changes the meaning to signify the full phrase of "Ora pro nobis," or "Pray for us," as shown above.

4) The following sign, looking somewhat like an arabic numeral 7, means "et" or "e" in Latin; usually with the English meaning of "and." It is used in the same way as an ampersand, "&." Examples:

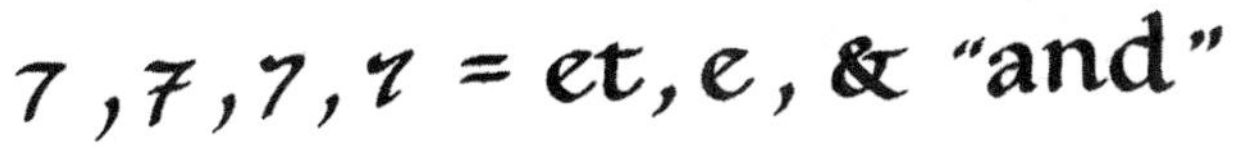

$$7 , 7 , 7 , 7 = et, e, \& \text{ "and"}$$

FIGURE 53: The ampersand.

5) The following are some fairly standard uses of under and overbars:

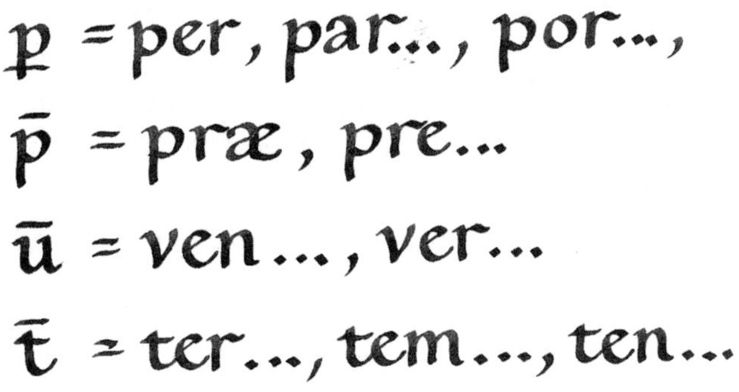

$$\underline{p} = per, par..., por...,$$
$$\bar{p} = prae, pre...$$
$$\bar{u} = ven..., ver...$$
$$\bar{t} = ter..., tem..., ten...$$

FIGURE 54: Overbars and underbars.

6) These are examples of Latin abbreviations that could also apply to Norse. They are a diagonal slash, a somewhat backwards question mark, a vertical wiggle, a somewhat backwards "c," and a horizontal slash that is often through the ascender of a letter. These signs stand for a vowel, often with an "r" attached to it, before or after the vowel:

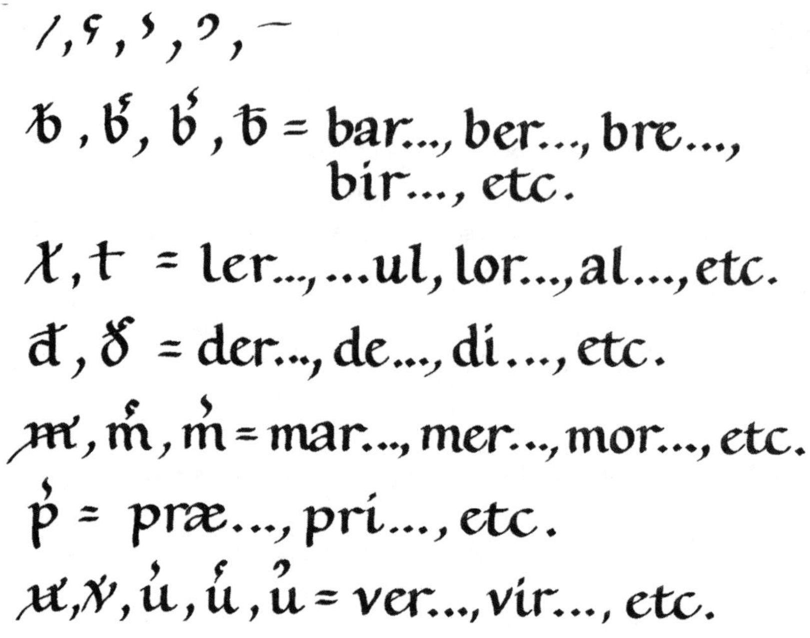

/, ꜱ , ꜱ , ꜱ , ⁓

Ƀ , Ƀ́ , Ƀ́ , Ƀ̄ = bar..., ber..., bre...,
bir..., etc.

Ӿ, ꞇ = ler...,...ul, lor...,al...,etc.

đ, ẟ = der..., de..., di..., etc.

ⅿ, ḿ, ḿ = mar..., mer..., mor..., etc.

ṕ = præ..., pri..., etc.

ꝩ,ꝩ, ú, ú́, ú̂ = ver..., vir..., etc.

FIGURE 55: Slashes, wiggles, etc.

7) A dot/period on the line of writing, colon, semi-colon stood
for missing letters in more commonly used words,
understood by knowledge of Latin and the context. A sign
resembling a "3" stood for "-et" and "-ent." Examples:

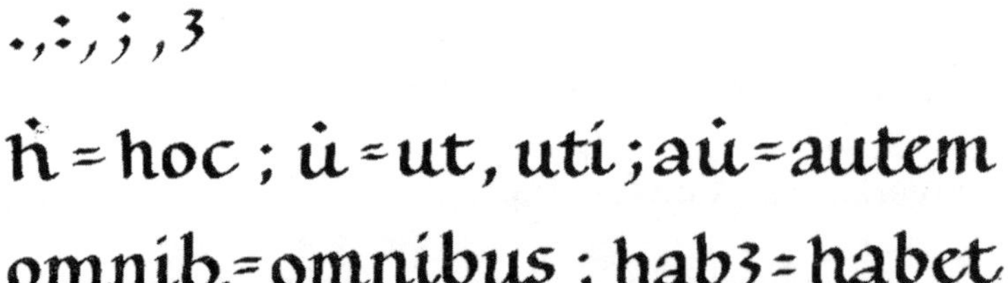

•,∴, ; , 3

ħ = hoc ; ú = ut, uti ; aú = autem

omnib. = omnibus ; hab3 = habet

FIGURE 56: Dots, colons, and semicolons.

8) A tiny vowel superscript above a consonant generally stands
for that vowel with an "r" before or after it. For instance: "ar,
er, ir, or, ur"; or "ra, re, ri, ro, ru." Caution: There are
numerous exceptions to this.

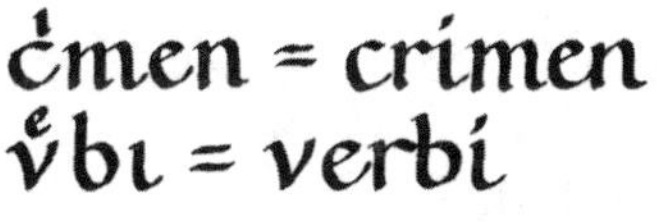

c̓men = crimen
v̓bı = verbi

FIGURE 57: Vowel superscripts.

9) In Latin, "Q" or "q" has no "u" following it if the vowel is
   written above it:

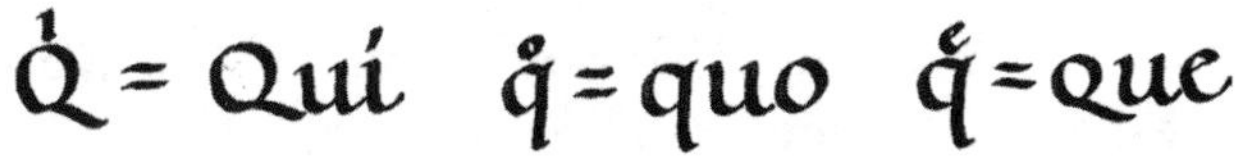

Q̓ = Qui   q̓ = quo   q̓ = que

FIGURE 58: The absent "u" in "qu."

10) The following abbreviations in runic form are found at
    important places in the Kensington and Spirit Pond
    inscriptions:

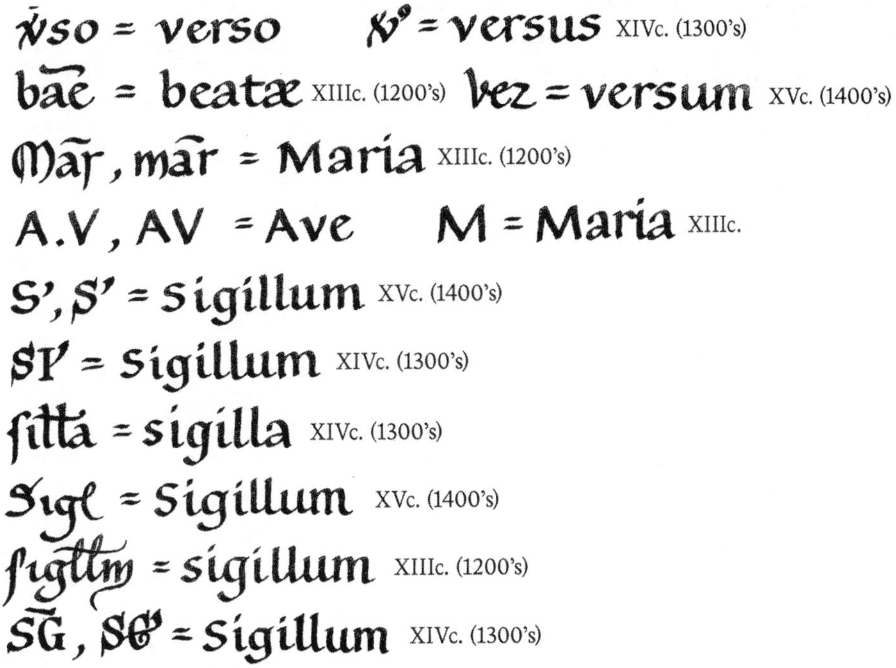

v̄so = verso   v̓ = versus XIVc. (1300's)

bae = beatæ XIIIc. (1200's) vez = versum XVc. (1400's)

Mãr̄, mãr = Maria XIIIc. (1200's)

A.V, AV = Ave   M = Maria XIIIc.

S', S' = Sigillum XVc. (1400's)

SV = Sigillum XIVc. (1300's)

fitta = sigilla XIVc. (1300's)

Sigl = Sigillum XVc. (1400's)

fıgtllm = sigillum XIIIc. (1200's)

SG, SG' = Sigillum XIVc. (1300's)

**FIGURE 59: There were multiple ways of abbreviating the same
word or root word.**

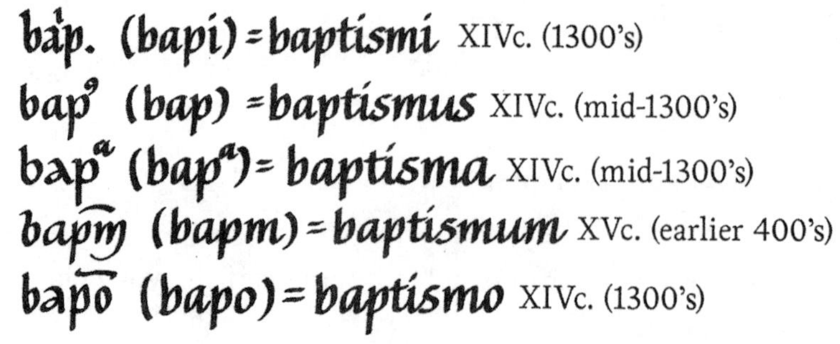

bàp. (bapi) = baptismi XIVc. (1300's)

bapᵍ (bap) = baptismus XIVc. (mid-1300's)

bapᵃ (bapᵃ) = baptisma XIVc. (mid-1300's)

bapm̄ (bapm) = baptismum XVc. (earlier 400's)

bapō (bapo) = baptismo XIVc. (1300's)

FIGURE 60: This shows how many different forms of the word "baptism" were expressed in abbreviated Latin form.

The abbreviations in Figures 59 and 60 are found in thirteenth-, fourteenth-, or fifteenth-century manuscripts and stone inscriptions. Understanding the above examples of abbreviation devices, among others, is a key to reading medieval writings and inscriptions. Such puzzles can be unfolded further if the context of history and place is understood. Cappelli's dictionary is a good place to start, but it is a tip of the linguistic iceberg of the North.

APPENDIX J:

EPISTEMOLOGICAL CONSIDERATIONS AND A CASE OF DÉJÀ VU

Epistemology: "The study or theory of the nature and grounds of knowledge, especially with reference to its limits and validity."

We find that the high consistency of the facts relevant to the Spirit Pond inscription argues convincingly for its authenticity. However, we find no compelling reason in logic that says the inscription *must* be authentic.

One of the most contentious arguments by the opponents of the authenticity of the Kensington runestone from the time of its discovery also applies to the Spirit Pond inscription: "The runestone is not authentic because some of its runes are not found in the fourteenth century literature"—with the implication that if they were found the runestone would be authentic. This combination of argument and implication is logically flawed because (a) if not found in the literature the possibility still exists that a legitimate runesmith could have used runes that were not part of the known set in the literature, and (b) if they were found, the possibility still exists that a forger knew of them and used them in his forged inscription.

The Spirit Pond inscription's authenticity has been questioned on linguistic grounds because some Anglo Saxon words were used among the Norse words—with the responsibility of the stone's proponents to show a parallel example where a Scandinavian mixes in Anglo Saxon and middle English words (in the literature) in the same fashion. This contention has the same logical flaws as the "missing runes" argument: (a) if not found in the literature this does not logically eliminate the possibility that a fourteenth-century skald made the inscription with a mixture of words, and (b) if found this does not eliminate the possibility that the forger knew of this practice and used it in his forged inscription.

The same dual argument could be applied to any unusual element in the Spirit Pond inscription. There is no strictly logical reason, *improbable though it may be*, why a forger could not have done all the historical research that we have done to reveal the context of the Spirit Pond inscription, even including the analysis and reinterpretation of the 1354 proclamation in the face of all the contrary opinions of historians who have examined the proclamation. Therefore our authenticity arguments can never be logically complete, and, in addition to our highly consistent facts, we must rely on probability arguments to make our case. In doing so we can safely assume that a forger's goal would be to use mostly elements in his inscription that would not throw suspicion on the authenticity of the inscription, which is "The saga of a young Folkung." A collection of examples that are contrary to the forger's goal therefore raises the probability of authenticity to a convincing level. Here is a list of five examples:

The above-mentioned use of Middle English and Anglo Saxon words in the inscription had earlier led linguistics professor Einar Haugen to label the inscription as a forgery. A forger would not have used such words, but a skald with diverse literary tastes could have done so.

A forger would not have used Haakon's age for the year numbers in the inscription because it was customary to use either the year of our lord, AD, or the year of the king's reign, and this departure from custom together with Anglo Saxon and Middle English words did in fact confuse Einar Haugen and caused him to label the inscription a forgery. But in the context of the kings, father and son, the use of Haakon's age is both tactful and appropriate.

The choice of such a small stone is not appropriate for a memorial inscription and a forger would have selected a larger stone for his work, a stone that would not raise the doubts that have been raised by such a small stone.

The customary purpose of a runestone is to commemorate an event and the purpose of the inscription is to inform the reader of the stone of that event. But instead of constructing the text for the reader of the inscription, the text is instead a memorial poem to be read to the kinsmen of the lost men who were in the king's court in Norway. This objective is not consistent with a forger's goal of a story told to achieve authenticity in the minds of present-day readers of the inscription on the coast of Maine.

No forger striving for apparent authenticity would have chosen this chivalric poem as his literary format instead of simple prose. In the poem, every abbreviated word form, every compound word, every unusual choice of words to achieve rhyme and meter is an invitation to the authoritative skeptic to reject the authenticity of the inscription because it does not match preconceived ideas of how such a document ought to have been written. Therefore the medieval poetic complexity of the inscription is itself a strong indication of authenticity. In that regard, Benedict Carey's test for honesty in a story applies. In a 12 May 2009 article in the *New York Times*: "Judging honesty by words, not fidgets," he makes the contrast between false stories that are tightly concocted and lacking in detail, and true accounts that are often replete with more details than needed to describe the event. By this measure the Spirit Pond inscription is a true story. It is not likely that a forger, making a plausible fictitious account of Haakon's explorations in the Western Lands, would have made only the short mention of Haakon's accomplishments while writing all of these other dramatic details:

1: Seventeen "kinsmen" were lost in a storm on Hudson Bay.

2: Twelve of the men are characterized both as "kinsmen" and "a company of companions."

3: The author used the royal "we."

4: The tragic event occurred in "year 20," the age of King Haakon.

5: "A shout into the burning lights! Beatae Maria! Alas!"—an appeal to St. Mary in abbreviated Latin.

6: The men on the commander's ship could not "get an edge" to save the doomed ship from the storm.

7: The doomed men "presage" their fate and "accept" it.

8: Two salutes to the "weeping fountains," the mourning families of the lost men.

Quite aside from the epistemological argument, the widespread variability of dialects and cultural levels of different authors in medieval times makes it unwise to judge authenticity based on consistency of a runic document with known literature forms.

A CASE OF DÉJÀ VU

The rejection of our study and its supporting evidence by authorities of history and archeology (reviewers for the *Hakluyt Society Journal*, 2009) parallels a similar initial rejection of the now famous cave paintings of Altamira. These paleographic works of art were discovered in 1879 by Marcelino Sanz de Sautuola and his daughter, Maria, near his estate in the Cantabrian Hills of northern Spain. Sautuola examined the paintings and in 1880 he announced the discovery in a published booklet in which he described the cave images of bison, horses, and other animals of Paleolithic time.[106] The authorities contemptuously rejected his discovery as not being authentic because the paintings did not fit their preconceived ideas of prehistoric human culture. Likewise with the Spirit Pond runestone, the authoritative wisdom has been that the Spirit Pond runestone is a hoax, and its poetic inscription violates preconceived ideas of the format and

---

106. M. de S Sautuola. *Breves apuntes sobres objetos prehistoricos de la Provincia de Santander, Santander,* 1880. Sautuola's discovery and its eventual acceptance are described in *The Cave of Altamira,* Antonio Beltrán ed. (New York: Harry N. Abrams Inc., 1998).

linguistics of memorial runestones.

In the prevailing opinions of 1880, stone-age men were viewed as unintelligent and lacking in any artistic talent. One critic proposed that the paintings were done for money in a fraudulent effort to discredit the new concepts of evolution proposed by the science of paleontology. But other cave paintings were soon discovered, and gradually the skeptical opinions began to change. More than twenty years after the Altamira discovery, one scholar, Emilé Cartailhac, who had initially opposed the discovery, published an apology in *L'Anthropologie* titled "Mea culpa d'une sceptique" or "I am guilty of being a skeptic." The psychology of the skeptical scholars in 1880 is described by Antonio Beltràn. He writes:

> The skepticism with which it (Sautuola's work) was
> originally received is a lesson in the lack of humility in
> scholars. As it often happens, many of the established
> authorities, without taking into account the
> limitations of existing knowledge, believed they were
> in possession of absolute truth. In the case of the
> Altamira paintings, "truth" took the form of theories
> that were undoubtedly legitimate as hypotheses, but
> were fallacious and misleading as articles of faith (*The
> Cave of Altamira*, page 8).

These words would apply equally well to current authorities' denials of the authenticity of the Spirit Pond inscription. The development of new knowledge in the minds of skeptics, based on evidence that conflicts with the conventional wisdom, requires that the skeptics become sufficiently familiar with the evidence to enable the replacement of the old idea by the new in their minds. If the skeptics do not consider the new evidence, the replacement will never occur. Even if it does, familiarization takes time, and many years may likewise pass before we see a "mea culpa" in regard to the Spirit Pond and Kensington runestones.

GLOSSARY

Abdication. The act of giving up a high office, authority, or function, especially that of a king.

Althing. The annual national meeting of Icelanders where disputes were adjudicated. Smaller local gatherings were called "Things."

Ambulatory. A low, roofed structure that surrounds the central stone tower in a medieval church.

Ballast. Stones placed in the bottom of the ship to stabilize it, especially when the cargo was light.

Baltic Region. The lands surrounding the Baltic Sea, which connects to the North Sea and the world ocean by a narrow strait between Denmark and Sweden.

Barry Hanson. A chemist who initiated a modern investigation of the surface characteristics of the Kensington runestone.

Bergen. The modern name for Norway's principal port on the southwest coast of Norway. The Medieval spelling was "Bryggen."

Betrothal. A formal arrangement for a future marriage.

Big Cormorant Lake. The lake in western Minnesota where ten of Commander Knutson's men were massacred.

Bindrune. Two runic letters combined into one by using shared parts.

Bishop Eirik Gnupsson. An official emissary of the pope to Greenland. He visited Vinland, and in 1117–1118 he wintered over somewhere on Vinland or Whitemansland, and subsequently circumnavigated Greenland, as inferred from names that he applied to Baffin and Ellesmere Islands. His original map has not been found, but these names appear on a subsequent probable copy of his map.

Carbon 14 Dating. Carbon 14 is a radioactive isotope component of the carbon that is taken up from the atmosphere or water by plants or animals. Carbon 14 is created in the atmosphere by nuclear reactions with nitrogen caused by cosmic rays from distant parts of the universe. Half of a given number of carbon 14 atoms will disappear radioactively in about 5,000 years. A measurement of the radioactivity of the carbon 14 in a standardized and uncontaminated sample of wood or other organic matter can often give a reliable age measurement.

Carpon Cove. The probable site of Leif Eriksson's houses on northern Newfoundland.

Charlie Hughes. Authors' husband who assisted in the excavations in South Dakota and who first recognized the mixture of present and future sense in Magnus's 1354 proclamation.

Chivalric Poem. A poem that displays or advocates knightly qualities of nobility, courage, respect, fairness, etc.

Cogship. A larger merchant ship with enclosed deck, developed to meet the needs of the medieval Baltic trade of the late thirteenth century. The cogship's rudder was at the center of the stern in contrast to the earlier Viking ships that had the rudder mounted on the side.

Couplet Meter. In medieval poetry, a rhythm in which emphasis is placed on every other syllable.

Curator. A person in charge of a museum, a library, etc.

Daghrise. Or "dagrise." A twelve-hour journey of about seventy-five miles.

Dead Reckoning. Ship navigation or other travel using estimates of direction and distance traveled without the aid of celestial observations.

Duke Erik. He was a Swede and father of Magnus, and was murdered by his brother, King Birger.

Dynasty. A series of rulers from the same family.

Einar Haugen. A Harvard linguistics professor who examined the Spirit Pond inscription in 1971 and described it as "a few Norse words in a sea of gibberish." He was apparently unaware of the extensive use of abbreviations in this runic document.

Epic. A long narrative poem or story, typically about a hero or heroes of high station. As an adjective: dealing with majestic events of historical or legendary importance.

Erik XII. The first son of King Magnus. Erik rebelled and was named king of Sweden, but died with all his family shortly thereafter when struck by the "children's plague." After a delay of three years because he was in the Western Lands, Haakon was acclaimed as Sweden's king to succeed Erik.

Estuary. An arm of the sea at the lower end of a river.

Excommunication. To be cut off from membership or the privileges of the Church.

Firesteel. A small horseshoe-shaped piece of hard steel used to start a fire by striking sparks from small stones.

Folkung. The clan name of a high-ranking medieval family group in Sweden.

Före. A voyage with trading implications. The modern term "foray" has the implication of an attack or invasion.

Glacial Till. The mixture of sand, clay, soil, stones, and other debris that forms by glacial action and is left behind when the ice is finally melted.

Graenaveldi. The name of a large area on the plains of the Dakotas and western Minnesota occupied by Norse farmer-traders in medieval times and characterized by numerous holestones, located mostly close to streams. This name appears in writings of Jon Duason, a modern Icelandic historian, in a quote from Sturla Thordarson, a medieval Icelandic historian.

Gragas Konungsbok. Old Icelandic law book.

Graywacke. A hard sedimentary rock that has been altered by heat and pressure, and which consists of quite small crystal grains, mostly silica sand.

Great Lakes. The chain of lakes on the border between Canada and the United States. The lakes include: Superior, Michigan, Huron, Erie, and Ontario.

Haakon Magnusson VI. He was the second son of Magnus and was empowered as king of Norway in 1355. In 1354 his father assigned him to the upcoming expedition, probably to get Haakon out of the country for a few years. With Knutson, he explored extensively, but was forced to return in 1362 to honor his betrothal to Princess Margrethe of Denmark with marriage in the spring of 1363.

Hanseatic. Pertaining to the German city-states on the south coast of the Baltic Sea. The Hanseatic League was a powerful trading group that dominated trade in the Baltic.

Hjalmar Holand. A modern student of history who argued the authenticity of the Kensington runestone over the latter half of his lifetime. More than anyone else, he is credited with keeping the authenticity issue alive during the twentieth century.

Hoax. A trick or fraud, sometimes intended as a practical joke.

Holestone. A stone or boulder containing a chiseled hole hammered out with a broad blade chisel, and used by the Norse as a property boundary marker or as a mooring stone, or rarely, to hold a stake for tethering an animal or flying a banner.

Hop. The Norse word for a small lake connected to the sea. The lake could be sailed into only at high tide.

Hornrock. A granite boulder in eastern South Dakota, containing a deeply incised and weathered image of a Norse drinking horn.

Hoyerweg. The main travel route. The ancestral word for "highway."

Humic Acid. Any of various organic acids obtained from decaying vegetable matter.

Ingebjorg. Princess of Norway and mother of King Magnus.

Ivar Bardson. A strong priest/ administrator who was assigned to Greenland to strengthen the Church system there. Ivar took over the responsibility for tax and tithe collection until his return to Norway in 1364.

Jorvik. A Norse word for a trading village on a stream not far from the sea. It is the ancestral word for "york" in English.

Judi Rudebusch. She has done much research into Norse culture and history as related to Norse artifacts on the central plains. She and Valdimar Samuelsson identified the holestones as legal property boundary markers in medieval times.

Lake Agassiz. A giant lake formed in Canada, the Dakotas, and northwestern Minnesota when the great ice sheet melted but the drainage to the Hudson Bay was still blocked by the glacial ice. Instead, the melt water flowed southward by way of the great River Warren in the path of the present Minnesota River.

Landnámabók. The Icelandic book of settlements with the people's lineages up to the twelfth century.

L'Anse aux Meadoows. The first Norse dwelling site in North

America to have been validated by years of archeological work. It is located on the tip of the northern promontory of Newfoundland.

Lawrence Mills. Professor emeritus who assisted in the South Dakota holestone investigations.

Leif Eriksson. A Greenlander. He was the first Norseman known from the sagas to have lived for a time in the Western Lands, that is: on Newfoundland. He is thus credited with the discovery of America, although his voyage followed as a result of Bjarni Herjulfsson's sighting of Newfoundland and the Labrador coast a few years earlier.

Magnus Eriksson. A king of both Norway and Sweden who had a strong ego. He was forced into a delayed abdication in 1343. After starting a war against Russia that was cut short by the onset of the plague in 1349, he launched an expedition to the Western Lands to restore the lost fur trade in 1356.

Mandans. A tribe of Indians living in North Dakota and having both blond Norse and darker Indian attributes.

Massacre. In human conflict, an act of complete destruction, e.g., "The outnumbered men were massacred."

Metaphor. A word or phrase denoting one kind of object or idea that is used in place of another to suggest a likeness or analogy between them, e.g., "weeping fountains" for the mourning parents of the young men lost at sea.

Minions. Servile followers.

Mooring Stone. A holestone used to moor boats to the shoreline. In the typical usage, the boat's line was attached to a pin, which was dropped into the hole in the stone.

Narragansett Bay. The long inlet in Rhode Island where many Norsemen settled after they emigrated from Greenland to join their friends in the Western Lands.

Nelson River. A major river from Lake Winnipeg to Hudson Bay, and an important route for the fur trade both in medieval and early modern times.

New England. The group of states that includes Connecticut, Rhode Island, Massachusetts, New Hampshire, and Vermont. In a loose sense, Maine may at times also be included.

Newport Tower. A medieval stone structure in Newport, Rhode Island, having the architectural characteristics of Scandinavian churches of the fourteenth century.

Norombega. A well-populated medieval Norse settlement in Rhode Island on Narragansett Bay.

Nykoping Banquet. The Christmas celebration in 1317 at which King Birger of Sweden betrayed his brothers, Duke Erik and Duke Valdimar, by capturing them and imprisoning them and allowing them to subsequently starve to death.

Olof Ohman. A Swedish immigrant farmer who discovered the Kensington runestone when grubbing out tree stumps on a hill in 1898. His son, Edward, was the first to recognize the runes on the stone while it was still clasped in the roots of a poplar tree stump.

Ombudsman. In a dispute, a person designated to act as an advocate, often for the weaker party, in an effort to resolve the dispute and come to an agreement.

Orm Østenson. King Magnus's "regent," who recorded the 1354 proclamation. He took care of royal affairs in Norway when Magnus was absent. This man was a Swede. He was an example of the favoritism that Magnus showed for the Swedes and which so irritated the Norwegians.

Overbars. Short lines inscribed or written above abbreviated words to indicate missing letters.

Oxbow. A U-shaped bend in a river, typically occurring on terrain that is nearly flat.

Paul Knutson. A law speaker at the Gulathing of Bergen, Norway. He was named to be the commandant of Magnus's expedition to the Western Lands to restore the fur trade. He constructed the medieval church now known as the Newport Tower, explored extensively, and led a thirty-man expedition into the central plains area of South Dakota and Minnesota, where he set up a runestone near Kensington to commemorate the loss of ten of his men who were massacred by Indians. He attempted to return to his base in New England by way of the Great Lakes, but his fate is unknown.

Peat. Slightly carbonized vegetable matter formed by partial decomposition in a wet environment.

Plague. A medieval epidemic of a rapidly communicated disease that was usually fatal. The disease is now known to have been spread by fleas on rats, and may at times have been transmitted by personal contact or airborne particulates due to coughing.

Poison Ivy. A three-leaf ground plant containing a poisonous sap. Contact with leaves or roots that transfer minute amounts of sap to the skin usually causes an allergic reaction with unbearable itching.

Rebar. A steel rod commonly used for reinforcing concrete in building construction.

Red River. Sometimes called the Red River of the North. It runs from Browns Valley on the western boundary of Minnesota to Lake Winnipeg in Canada. Like the Nelson River, it was an important fur trade route.

Richard Card. He acted as an ombudsman for Walter Elliott in the dispute over the ownership of the Spirit Pond runestones.

River Warren. The giant river that carried great volumes of water from the melting ice sheet lying to the northwest of Minnesota twelve thousand years ago. The Minnesota River now occupies part of the wide bed of the ancient river.

Rogation Day. A day of prayer on or about April 25. It was also the day for walking to revalidate the neighborhood land boundaries.

Root Lines. The traces of the roots that had enclosed the Kensington runestone. Organic

acids from the roots in contact with the stone's surface bleached the dark patina of the surface giving a grayish trail where the roots had grown. This evidence implies many years of root growth prior to the time that Olof Ohman dug up the stone.

Runes. Any of the letters of an alphabet used by ancient Scandinavians or other Germanic peoples.

Saddle. An area of land with the surface configured like a horse saddle.

Scablands. Deeply eroded channels through eastern Washington State. These chasms were the result of a series of more than thirty successive giant floods caused by the repeated failure and restoration of a glacial ice dam in northern Idaho that formed ice age Lake Missoula.

Sealship. The flag ship of the nation or city-state as depicted on the official seal used on important documents.

Settje Stone. A holestone found near Bullhead Lake in eastern South Dakota. When found, the hole was nearly full of iron rust, probably the remnant of an iron rod that had stood in the hole for centuries since the Norse had lived in the area.

Skaane. The disputed southernmost province of Sweden, claimed by Denmark.

Skald. A poet, often a poet in his official capacity in a king's court.

Skraelinges. The Norse term for the native peoples of North America.

Solutreans. Ice age people of France and Spain who made beautiful symmetrical spear points with a distinctive style. The same style was used for making the Clovis points that are found widely in North America, thus implying ice age migration of Europeans to North America.

Thorfinn Karlsefni. A wealthy Icelander who sailed to Greenland to investigate the possibility of settling in the new lands that Leif Eriksson had explored. He spent one winter at the site of Leif's houses, and a second winter at a location to the south, probably at the mouth of the Merrimack River in Newburyport, Massachusetts, which matches the description in the sagas. Although hostilities with the Indians forced him to return to Greenland and Iceland, his successful bargaining with the Indians for furs introduced the Norse to the lucrative fur trade that strongly influenced Greenland's history in the following 300 years.

Valdimar Samuelsson. An Icelandic engineer with a strong interest in Norse history. He identified holestones as property boundary markers that were used in Iceland from the time of settlement.

Vinland. Part of the Western Lands to the southwest of the island of Greenland. Vinland extended from Newfoundland to the Hudson River. In medieval times the Western Lands were sometimes viewed as part of the country of Greenland.

Vinland Map. A map of Vinland, on a controversial document prepared for the Church Council of Basle, Switzerland, about 1440.

Vinland Voyages. Voyages of exploration and settlement in the Western Lands made by Greenlanders and Icelanders during the period from about 1003 to 1017. The descriptions of these voyages were retained orally in the sagas until written down in the 1200s.

Walter Elliott. A carpenter and amateur arrowhead and pot hunter. He discovered the Spirit Pond runestone while looking for arrowheads in 1971.

Weathering. The process by which the slightly acidic rainwater dissolves different kinds of small mineral grains in a rock at different rates over time, and consequently slowly increases the microscopic roughness of the surface.

Whetstone River. A small stream in eastern South Dakota that empties into the head of the Minnesota River. The many holestones along the river and its tributaries suggest a substantial population of medieval Norse farmer-traders.

Whitemansland. The coastal regions of Labrador and Quebec.

Winch. A powerful machine with one or more drums on which to coil a rope, cable, or chain. The machine was used for hoisting heavy weights or, in Olof Ohman's case, for pulling up stumps.

Winchell, Newton Horace. A geologist and University of Minnesota professor who headed the committee that investigated the Kensington runestone discovery and its authenticity in the 1910–1912 period. The committee's verdict was that all the physical evidence pointed to the authenticity of the runestone inscription.

York. A medieval name for a trading village on a stream somewhat inland from the sea.

York Factory. The name of the trading post and store at the mouth of the Nelson and Hays Rivers at the southwest corner of Hudson Bay. It was the headquarters of the Hudson Bay Company, which was chartered in 1670 to trade for furs in Ruperts Land, the old name in the charter for a large area surrounding Hudson Bay.

BIBLIOGRAPHY

Aris, Rutherford. *Explicatio formarum litterarum: The unfolding of letterforms*. St. Paul, MN: The Calligraphy Connection, 1990.

Batey, Colleen, Helen Clarke, R.I. Page, and Neil S. Price. *Cultural Atlas of the Viking World*. Oxfordshire, England: Andromeda Oxford Limited, 1994.

Beltrán, Antonio. *The Cave of Altamira*. New York: Harry N. Abrams, Inc., 1999.

Blegen, Theodore C. *The Kensington Rune-Stone: New Light on an Old Riddle*. St. Paul, MN: Minnesota Historical Society, 1968.

Bosworth, Joseph. *An Anglo Saxon Dictionary*. T. Northcote Toller, ed. Oxford: Clarendon Press, 1989.

Brymner, Douglas. *Report on Canadian Archives*, Ottawa 1889, 1890. Pierre la Verendrye's *Journal (1738)*, in *South Dakota Historical Collections, VII*, 340 ff.

Byock, Jesse L. *Viking Age Iceland*. London, Penguin Books, 2001.

_____, "Grágás: *The 'Grey Goose' Law*" in *Viking Age Iceland*. London: Penguin Books, 2001. The Gragas was first written down and published at Haflidi Másson's farm on Iceland in 1118.

Cappelli, Adriano. *Dizionario di Abbreviature Latine ed Italiane*. Milano, U. Hoepli, ed., 1961. 31, 213.

_____. *The Elements of Abbreviation in Medieval Latin Paleography*, translated by D. Heimann and R. Kay, University of Kansas Libraries, 1982. Preface to *Dizionario di Abbreviature, Latine ed Italiane* (Dictionary of Latin and Italian Abbreviations,) A. Cappelli, U. Hoepli, ed. Milano, 1961.

Carey, Benedict. "Judging honesty by words, not fidgets." *New York Times*, 12 May 2009.

Carlson, Suzanne. "The Spirit Pond inscription stone: Rhyme and Reason." *NEARA Journal*, 30, No. 3&4, 1996.

_____. "Stumbles and Pitfalls: Indeed!" *New England Antiquities Research Association (NEARA) Journal*, Vol. 34, No. 1. 2000, 15–32.

_____. compiler. *The Newport Tower: Arnold to Zeno*. John Dranchak, ed., Edgecomb, ME: New England Antiquities Research Association monograph, 2006.

Carter, Rob. "Radiocarbon Dating of the Newport Tower." Edgecomb, ME: NEARA Journal, vol. 41 Number 2, winter 2007, 35–41.

Catlin, George. *North American Indians*. P. Matthiessen, ed, New York: Penguin Books, 1989.

Day, Lewis F. *Lettering in Ornament: An Inquiry into the Decorative Use of Lettering, Past, Present and Possible*, Second Edition, revised. London: B.T. Batsford Ltd., 1914.

Drilen, Erik. "Maybe the Vikings made it Norse America." Minneapolis *Star Tribune*, 24 May 1992, 21A.

Duason, Jon. *Landkonnun og Landbam Islendinga I vestur Heimi* (Exploring and settling of Iceland in the western world), Reykjavik: 1941.

Ellis, George, and John Morris. *King Philip's War*. NY: Grafton Press, 1906.

Finsen, Vilhjalmur, ed. *Gragas: Konungsbok*. 2 vols. Copenhagen: 1852.

Gaur, Albertine. *A History of Calligraphy*. New York, London and Paris: Cross River Press, 1994.

Gordon, Eric. V., *An Introduction to Old Norse*. A. R. Taylor, ed., second edition. New York: Oxford University Press, 1957.

Gould, Stephan J. "When the Unorthodox Prevails," *New Scientist*, 28 September 1978.

Greenhill, Basil. *The Evolution of the Wooden Ship*. New York: Facts on File, Inc., 1988.

Grønlands Historiske Mindesmaerker, III, 120–122, Copenhagen, 1838–45.

Gullov, Hans C. "Natives and Norse in Greenland," *Vikings, the North Atlantic Saga*, Fitzhugh and Ward, eds. Washington: Smithsonian Institution Press, 2000.

Hale, John, Jan Heinemeier, et al. "Dating ancient mortar," *American Scientist 91*, 2003, 130–137.

Hall, Robert A. *The Kensington Rune-Stone: Authentic and*

Important, Lake Bluff, IL: Jupiter Press, 1994.

Hanson, Barry. *A Defense of Olof Ohman: the Accused Forger*, Maple, WI: Archaeology ITM, 2002.

Hardwick, Paula. *Discovering Horn*. Guilford: Lutterworth Press, 1981.

Harper, Douglas. *Online Etymology Dictionary*, 2001–2010. www.etymonline.com.

Hauge, Arild. http://en.wikipedia.org/wiki/File:Gron-rune-kingigtorssuaq.jpg (accessed April 2011).

Haugen, Einar. "The Runestones of Spirit Pond, Maine," *Man in the northeast*. Vol. 4, 1972, 62–79.

Haywood, John. *Historical Atlas of the Vikings*. New York: Penguin Books, 1995.

History of Hâkon VI Magnusson's coinage (www.dokpro.io.no/umk_eng/myntherr/hvi.html), 2011.

Holand, Hjalmar. R. *America: 1355–1364*. New York: Duell, Sloan and Pearce, 1946.

_____, *Westward from Vinland*. New York: Duell, Sloan and Pearce, 1940.

Ingstad, Helge. *Westward to Vinland, The discovery of pre-Columbian house-sites in North America*. New York: St. Martin's Press, 1969.

_____, and A.S. Ingstad. *The Viking Discovery of America*. New York: Checkmark Books, 2001.

Kehoe, Alice. *The Kensington Rune Stone, approaching a research question holistically*. Long Grove, IL: Waveland Press, 2005.

Kunz, Keneva. Translator, *The Sagas of Icelanders*. New York: Penguin Books, 2001.

Landnámabók, Sturlubók version, Eiriki Rognvaldssyni, ed., Wikipedia 2011.

Larsen, Karen. *A History of Norway*. Princeton and New York: Princeton University Press, 1948.

Lithberg, Nils. AD 1399 calendar in Figure 79, "*Comptus med Särskild hänsyn till Runstaven och den Borgerliga Kalendern.*" Stockholm: Norstedt & Sons, for the Nordiska Museets Handlingar, 1953.

Magnussen, Johannes, Otto Madsen, and Hermann Vinterberg. *Englsk-Dansk Ordbog*, Golden Valley Bookseller: Nordisk, 5th edition, Copenhagen, 1937, Oxford: Clarendon Press, 1888.

Mallery, Arlington, and Mary R. Harrison. *The rediscovery of Lost America*. New York: E.P. Dutton, 1979.

Maps of the National topographic system of Canada, Natural Resources Canada, Ottawa,

Canada, K1A OE9. Coastal maps in Index #1.

Mayhew, Anthony L., and Walter W. Skeat. *A concise dictionary of Middle English from AD 1150 to 1580.* Oxford: Clarendon Press, 1888.

McKitterick, Rosamund. *Atlas of the Medieval World.* New York: Oxford University Press, 2004.

Minnesota Atlas and Gazetteer, fourth edition. Yarmouth, ME: DeLorme Mapping Company, 2003.

Moberg, Vilhelm. *A History of the Swedish People, Vol 1.* Minneapolis: University of Minnesota Press, 2005.

Morrison, Samuel E. *The European Discovery of America.* New York: Oxford University Press, 1971.

Mowat, Farley. *West Viking, The ancient Norse in Greenland and North America.* Toronto: McClelland and Stewart Ltd., 1965.

Nielsen, Richard. "About the West: Early Scandinavian Incursions into the Western States," *Journal of the West,* January 2000, Vol. 39, No. 1, 72–86.

Nielsen, Richard, and Scott Wolter. *The Kensington Rune Stone, Compelling New Evidence.* Duluth, MN: Lake Superior Agate Publishing, 2006.Nilsestuen, R. M. "Evidence shows Kensington Runestone is no fake," Minneapolis *Star Tribune.* 12 July 1992, 23A.

Nydal, Reidar. *Radiocarbon Vol. 31.*Tucson, AZ: 1989. 976–985.

Online Etymology Dictionary. www. etymonline.com. (2011) Douglas Harper. 2001.

Oxenstierna, Eric. *The Norsemen.* Translated and edited by C. Hutter. New York: New York Graphic Society, 1965.

Page, Raymond I. *Reading the Past: Runes.* Berkeley, CA: University of California Press, 1993.

Projekt Runeberg. 2011. http:// runeberg.org/gronland/3/0145. html.

Reykholar 1572: Stofnum Arna Magnussonar. Reykjavik. Personal communication.

Rider, Sidney S. *The Lands of Rhode Island,* 1904. La Vergne, TN: General Books, 2009.

Rosedahl, Else, and David M. Wilson, eds. *From Viking to Crusader: Scandinavia and Europe 800–1200.* New York: Rizzoli International Publications, 1992.

Satava, David. "Columbus's First Voyage: Profit or Loss from a Historical Accountant's Perspective." *Journal of Applied Business Research.* Vol. 23, Fourth Quarter, 2007.

Sautuola, Marcelino de S. *Breves apuntes sobres objetos prehistoricos* de la Provincia de Santander, Santander, 1880. Sautuola's discovery and its eventual acceptance are described in *The Cave of Altamira*, Antonio Beltrán ed. New York: Harry N. Abrams Inc., 1998.

Sawyer, Birgit, and Peter Sawyer. *Medieval Scandinavia: from Conversion to Reformation, circa 800–1500*. Minneapolis: University of Minnesota Press, 1993.

Schledermann, P. "Ellesmere: Vikings in the Far North." William F. Fitzhugh and Elisabeth Ward, eds., *Vikings: The North Atlantic Saga*. Washington and London: Smithsonian Institution Press, 2000. 248–256.

Seaver, Kirsten A. *The Frozen Echo, Greenland and the exploration of North America ca A.S. 1000–1500*. Stanford, CA: Stanford University Press, 1996.

Skelton, Raleigh A. Thomas. E. Marston, and George D. Painter. *The Tartar Relation and the Vinland Map, The Vinland Map and the Tartar Relation*. New Haven, CT: Yale University Press, 1965.

Spurkland, Terje. *Norwegian Runes and Runic Inscriptions*. Betsy van der Hoek, translator, Rochester, NY: Boydell Press, 2005.

Stanford, Dennis. Smithsonian National Museum of Natural History lecture, "The Ice-age Discovery of the Americas: Constructing an Iberian Solution." 44th Annual Nobel Conference at Gustavus Adolphus College, St. Peter, Minnesota: 8 October 2008.

_____, and Bruce A. Bradley. *Across Atlantic Ice, The Origin of America's Clovis Culture*. Berkeley CA: University of California Press, 2012.

Stuiver, Minz, et al. *Radiocarbon 40*. 1998. 1041–1083.

Sturluson, Snorri. *Heimskringla: the Circle of the World*, written about AD 1230. *The Cultural Atlas of the Viking World*. New York: Facts on File, Inc., 1994.

Thompson, Claiborne W. *Studies in Upplandic Runography*. Austin, TX: University of Texas Press, 1975.

Traupman, John. *New College Latin and English Dictionary*. New York: Bantam Books, 1995.

Verrazzano, Giovanni. *Cellere Codex*, A. Bachiani, ed., translated by E. H. Hall. *Fifteenth Annual Report of American Scenic and Historical Preservation Society*. Albany: 1910.

Wahlgren, Eric. *The Kensington stone: a mystery solved*. Madison, WI: University of Wisconsin Press, 1958.

Waidmann, Curt. F. "Who Built the Newport Tower? The cartographic evidence." *The Newport Tower, Arnold to Zeno.* Edgecomb, Maine: New England Antiquities Research Association Monograph, 2006. Wallace, Birgitta. L. "The Viking Settlement at L'anse aux Meadows." *Vikings, the North Atlantic Saga.* Washington: Smithsonian Institution Press, 2000. 208–231.

_____, and W. Fitzhugh. "Stumbles and pitfalls in the search for Viking America" in *Vikings: The North Atlantic Saga.* Washington: Smithsonian Institution Press, 2000. 374–384.

Warme, Lars G., *A History of Swedish Literature.* Vol 3. Lincoln and London: University of Nebraska Press, 1996.

Webster's New Twentieth Century Dictionary, unabridged second edition, 1973, 463.

Whittall, James P. Jr. *"The Spirit Pond Runestones."* Edgecomb, ME, New England Antiquities Research Association Publications, 1972.

Wikipedia. http://en.wikipedia.org/wiki/Pentimal_system (accessed 2011).

Winchell, Newton H. *The Aborigines of Minnesota.* 1911, Internet: Gustav's Library, 2011.

Wrenn, Charles L., ed. *Beowulf, with the Finnesburg Fragment.* London: Revised edition by Bolton Harap Limited, Pub. 829 3 B45, 1973.

Zoëga, Geir T. *A Concise Dictionary of Old Icelandic.* Toronto: University of Toronto Press, 2004.

ABOUT THE AUTHORS

Robert G. Johnson received his Ph.D. from Iowa State University. After a puzzle-solving career in industrial research, he joined the Department of Geology and Geophysics at the University of Minnesota to work on the mystery of past climate variations. The American runestone controversy was just another perplexing problem with a solution that resulted from a joint ten-year effort with co-author L. J. (Janey) Westin. Johnson has published many research papers and one book: *Secrets of the Ice Ages: the Role of the Mediterranean Sea in Climate Change* (Glenjay Publishing, 2002).

Initially a professional calligrapher, **Janey Westin** pursued paleographic studies of medieval manuscripts, stone inscriptions, the structure of letterforms, and the tools and materials of the trade. This work expanded into stone letter carving and sculpting. She has carved letters smaller than an inch and up to two feet high in limestone, marble, granite, quartzite, bluestone, sandstone, slate, and more. Westin is a longstanding Portfolio member of The Colleagues of Calligraphy, her regional guild. She has taught calligraphy, letter carving, and sculpting at international calligraphy conferences, at stone sculpting symposiums in Colorado and Indiana, and at local venues in Minnesota. Westin attended the Minneapolis College of Art and Design and has a B.A. in Japanese from the University of Minnesota. Her studio, Paper & Stone, is located in Edina, Minnesota.